THE GENIUS FREQUENCY

THE
GENIUS
FREQUENCY

AN OWNER'S MANUAL
FOR
THE COSMIC MIND

by John J. Falone

Library of Congress Cataloging-in-Publication Data

Falone, John, 1947
    The Genius Frequency / John J. Falone
    Includes indexes.
    p. cm.
    ISBN 1-893157-13-X
    ISBN 13 digit 978-1-893157-13-2
    Falone, John, J. I. Title
    1. Body/Mind/Spirit   2. Philosophy   3. Science   4. Self-Help
    Library of Congress Card Number: 00-107908
    CIP

First Edition Published by Global Light Network, 2000

Design: John J. Falone
Editing: Donna R. Stewart

Published by
Bridger House Publishers
P.O. Box 2208, Carson City, NV 89702, USA
1-800-729-4131

Printed in the United States of America
10 9 8 7 6 5 4 3 2

THIS WORK IS HUMBLY DEDICATED TO

THE ONE,

IN WHOM AND BY WHOM

EVERY LIVING ATOM

HAS ITS BEING;

AND TO

THAT COLOSSAL BEING,

HUSBAND TO MOTHER EARTH

AND ALL HER CHILDREN,

MANKIND

Acknowledgments:

To DONNA ROSE:
a living work of art
whose depth of love, compassion,
support and understanding provided the Light
for me to see through the dark days.

TO MY PARENTS:
John & Irma, & my sister, Jo Ann:
the most loving and supportive family
a man could hope to have in this world.

TO RUSS MICHAEL:
world reknowned author,
friend, soul brother & confidant,
who put his own plans on hold in order to
publish this work.

TO BEA & STEVE THOMPSON,
for their friendship, vision, generosity
and unflagging support for this work.

TO THE 12 SPONSORS,
of this publication who
helped open the doors to prosperity
in times of need. To supporters of this work
known & unknown.

AND TO NOT LEAST OF THESE,
the children of man and my animal friends,
especially to Nykoh, whose unconditional love
buoyed my heart upon waters of hope,
taught me the power of friendship,
and how God works through nature.

CONTENTS

HOW TO USE THIS BOOK

To think, study, or read is to contemplate. Any subject one focuses upon creates certain frequencies and harmonics commensurate with the frequency of that which is contemplated. The reader will always benefit from any manner of study when contemplating high frequency concepts.

However, for those who strive to maximize the results of this work, it is recommended that the reader become familiar with the terms used and the context in which they are framed.

To facilitate this goal, the reader will find a glossary, an index, and a list of the questions used in this work in the back of the book. Even skimming through the glossary first will significantly enhance the comfort level and comprehension of the main body of this work.

Also, reading the list of questions will provide an excellent primer for the mind to accept new information and an indication as to areas of life treated within the study.

The index may also be used in advance to locate topics of immediate interest and, of course, as a reference after the book is read.

The concepts used in this work operate on many levels of understanding. *Therefore, it is not necessary to completely comprehend any single concept before moving to another section.* The most important concepts will be repeated from many different angles so that what is not clear at one point in the study will become clear in another. The mind will make the necessary connections automatically as the conscious and subconscious states begin to blend and interact in the Divine Process of creation.

Remember, the genius of mind operates as a holograph, not as a train.

jjf

PROLOGUE

A quick browse through a local book store will reveal increasing numbers of works that breach not only traditional academic stricture, but even science fiction. No longer is it a simple matter of finding the conveniently marked book shelf from which one may select a well defined genre and know absolutely that a similar book is not on another shelf. Specialists are storming out of their predefined territories: doctors on psychology; psychologists on physics; physicists on healing; science fiction writers on ethics; and the most amazing of all, the layman on just about everything.

Although this may prove disconcerting to the academic world, to others it is the dawn of something new, exciting, refreshing – an increasingly brilliant light at the end of a maze of tunnels created by centuries of intellectual conglomerates. In a most undefined way, things are beginning to make sense. The sharp lines of demarcation establishing the domains of institutional castles and forts are dissolving – their contents of knowledge gushing through the cracks in the dams that once formed the reservoirs of information exclusive to the dam builders of government, industry, science, and religion. It seems as though chaos is replacing order, a prospect thoroughly frightening and contrary to the promised increasing order by mainstream western mind.

Ironically, chaos has become a subject of study and is quite in vogue in today's scientific literature. Imagine, "chaos" as a subject for scientific study! Yet upon examining this most fascinating "scientific" frontier, one is faced with a remarkable, if not glaring, contradiction. Studies indicate that chaos is actually a systemic process of creation.

In short, formulas for chaos produce fractal geometries, graphically represented by those most beautiful perpetual sea horse tails and various geometric forms, symmetrical or asymmetrical, nested infinitely within a scaleable matrix of truly stunning textures of familiar forms. A scientific subject called chaos – what a novel and exciting idea. Sea Horse tails, endless patterns from chaotic numbers somehow producing order – Nautilus shells spiraling into and out of eternity through the mathematical proportion of 1.618, otherwise known as the Golden Mean. Thus, one key to chaos is the Golden Mean value. Unfortunately, it is not stressed in scientific journals because the Golden Mean is not "news." But then, neither are Sea Horse tails and Nautilus shells.

What does chaos and the Golden Mean have to do with breaching tradition? It has to do with the inescapable and recurrent reminders that true knowledge, as wisdom, is not a lifeless collection of per ipso statistics from de facto objective criteria. When viewing the beautiful graphic representations of chaos and fractal geometries, one is struck with the process of creation and how the resultant form of that process is the process itself.

In the same way, physicists have been struck with shocking evidence of a process known as the particle/wave phenomenon. It seems that everywhere in research, a certain fundamental pattern of light, a process of creation, appears to remind all seekers of truth that **all** is interrelated – all is process. The simple yet cryptic axiom, "as above, so below," echoes in the subconscious canyons of antiquity.

The ancient Hermetic axiom, "as above, so below," tolls its universal harmonic in the bell-towers of the heart, calling all congregations of science, religion, and government into the common dome of understanding. Chaos, the Golden Mean and the ancient Hermetic axiom – all are woven together in a tapestry of creative process that reigns supreme in the seemingly separate and diverse manifestations that we witness in this third dimensional reality.

Yes, the boundaries are dissolving, the dams are breaking, and the bookshelves are confused as they collect works that seem to defy categories. Perhaps there will someday be a section labeled "WISDOM." At any rate, there are many who are discovering that the answers to all questions are locked somewhere deep within each individual and that these answers are phase locked in a type of universal matrix of thought resonating within every atom.

In search of this elusive and mysterious unified field theory of individuality; the author, tired, confused, and battered from the warring factions of private industry, government, science, religion, and philosophy, opted for the only remaining reference: self. A trip within was required as the final frontier of a personal quest that resulted in a greater understanding of the universal processes of life and the purpose of existence. What else could ever be discovered?

In the many years that the author searched through the outer archives of earthly references, only confusion, anguish, and apathy resulted. However, when the process was turned inward, deep into the heart of life, a significant moment catalyzed a series of changes. These changes were not merely attitudinal. They seemed almost chemical in nature, physical as well as mental.

This "significant moment" resulted in a new optimism, a peaceful restlessness, if you will, that urged, in no uncertain terms, to begin this work. Perhaps this urging was the "still, small voice within." For the record, the author is not a witness to any "voice." No trances, no personality substitutions, no sensational psychic phenomenon were experienced. It can only be described as a powerful feeling-that-spoke. Although it is far too elusive to accurately describe, the fact remains that the feeling was powerful, wonderful and inspiring enough to fuel such a monumental effort.

The elusive feeling of power and peace was somehow personal, yet not personal. The urge was to write. The growth of the question, "Write what?," seemed to keep pace with the relentless urge. This pendulum of conflict eventually gave way to genuine humor. It was laughable that a person who had not even dreamed of writing a book could suddenly be in the height of turmoil over what to write. It was then, in the spirit of laughter and with child-like abandon, that an attempt was made to satisfy this impossible longing.

The feeling beckoned: Just write. Write anything. A blank canvas. No ideas. This strange feeling, urging, gently, lovingly. First came the word "canvas" – "Divine Canvas." Yes, that's it. Every creation is authored by an artist. Then, pictures flood the mind. They swarm chaotically, like leaves in the crystal winds of autumn. Words began to tumble through fingertips. Each leaf was a thought-form that seemingly blew, randomly, aimlessly across the landscape of mind.

All of those thoughts seemed so important and yet so pointless. It was then that something began to emerge from the chaos – something that rendered those autumnal leaves, those thought-forms, as secondary to a process that guided them and gave them life. Even more, they not only seemed to be following some pattern, some process, they were being driven and animated by that very process. Flashes of lucidity, like summer lightening, revealed the tree to which those leaves still clung. The tree would breathe the leaves to it and from it. The idea of the tree did not move, but the process of "tree" could indeed travel: through time. The words began to flow.

Each thought-form, each idea, as a fractal of the process, flowed into and out of pulsating patterns that were freely inter-changeable: in one moment, bird; in the next moment, tree. It was becoming clear. Thought-forms were fractal geometries that nested within a process of life. One was a part of another. One explained the other. One affected the other. One created the other. Like a choir, the ancient, Hermetic axiom sang its song of genius in the hearts of men.

The work joyfully continued and developed into a dialogue with self. The process was the instructor. The lessons were meditations to charge the mind with light and intense contemplation to focus awareness upon the process. The challenge was to "freeze-frame" the process – to apprehend a cross section of reality long enough to attempt to describe it, yet knowing that its motion was ceaseless. Neither chaos nor order by themselves could render a whole thought-form, a complete equation. Chaos and order seemed to be inherent within the process. Yet the process was neither of the two.

Each realization was a fractal, a part and yet the whole. Chaos and order did not represent evil and good when viewed from *process*. The three became a Trinity creating reality even as we have come to know it. Each was represented as an archetypal personification. Thus, "MA," represents the female, expansive, radiative forces appearing as chaos in material order, dispersing elements into random, gaseous states. "RA," represents the order, the gravitational frequency in material solidity that pulls the radiative forces of the female, expansive frequencies into itself: into seed. And "YA," represents the process itself, appearing only as a mysterious force that somehow binds the other two.

This triumvirate of mind yielded the name, "MAYARA," as used throughout this document. In the earliest efforts of this work, the author experimented with means by which focusing upon the process would yield results in the medium of the written word. A list of questions were compiled and contemplated. This method proved to be most beneficial and productive. Somehow, posing a question to the process of self formed a template into which the process of mind flowed. As the work progressed, questions and answers fulfilled a cyclic process. The results were quite astonishing.

The author makes no claims to know of any disincarnate entity, supernatural being, or alien contact of any kind. The use of the name, "MAYARA," is a tool used to disconnect the limitations of the personality and the altered-ego from the potential of mind as a process of life rather than a function of an individual brain.

Admittedly the syllabic Trinity of "YA," "RA," and "MA," has profound roots in the subconscious syntax of archetypal mind. The reader may even regard the use of this "tool" as a psychological metaphor or vehicle used by the author. Regardless, after months of deliberation concerning the inclusion of this archetypal tool or vehicle, the decision was made to present the present work to the reader in the original format that became, for the author, the very creative process of mind that made the work possible. It is hoped that the decision to include it will, in itself, help bring to light the process of mind.

Thus, even in the mechanical act of reading this material, an understanding should be forthcoming that may lend some insight into how the mind functions and of what it is composed. The author confesses that this is quite an ambitious statement. Yet at some point, for all of us, a step must be taken into the unknown of self. The final decision as to the veracity of what the author has discovered is, of course, in the mind's eye of the beholder.

From this perspective, then, whether some or all of the statements within this document are believed or not believed is of little consequence. Conveying the process, the "YA" of our existence, is far more important. For the Process yields the truth on a personal level. All relativism aside, the "truth" is revealed by degrees, and by degrees it encompasses the universality of the creative process of mind. In the final analysis, the truth seems to be a process rather than an object or reaction.

Is it truth or is it fiction? Is it fact or is it speculation? Is it order, chaos, or a process of mind that reveals the secrets of existence – the answers to the "big" questions? It is the sincere hope and desire of the author that after contemplating this document, truth will be revealed as process of mind, not as content, thereby opening up the reader's creative keys to higher processing.

Since we all are sustained by the same creative process, it is not unreasonable to assume that if truth is process, then the truth, indeed the very mysteries of life, can be known to all, and that in all, *genius* is inherent.

There is nothing to believe or not to believe in this work. Although reality may be unique to each individual, the truth is a process of mind in a universal scale of proportions. What you are about to read is the result of the author daring to explore the unknown self. What emerged is for you to contemplate. Most importantly, it is to encourage the reader to trust in self and to reap the rewards of personal revelation – not to begin yet another institution of religion, science, or government, nor to attract blind followers, nor even to argue with established norm, but to overcome the limitations that shroud, in secrecy, our ultimate freedom. This work exemplifies the results of seeking within. It is a message to all those who dare to explore the depths of wisdom within self.

May the Light of Peace fill your hearts with desire for a new world of peace and prosperity for ourselves and the children.

John J. Falone

THE GENIUS FREQUENCY

THE DIVINE CANVAS

"RECREATING YOUR LIFE"

> "You have waited so long for this moment."

MaYaRa: Entertain a grand thought: Freedom. The word freedom, in its objective meaning, can be analyzed as polarized opposites. Simply, this means that you can look at it two ways: Freedom from and freedom towards; freedom from limited thinking and freedom towards creative genius. Perhaps it is difficult for you to imagine yourself as a genius (something you were taught is reserved for the "gifted few"). But, for a moment, release your pre-judgments and let us help you examine this thought. First, we should like to have you think in terms of unlimited thinking by examining the parameters of limited thought. We should like to have you erase, as it were, what you think you know about yourself and begin again.

Think of your life as a blank canvas, a Divine Canvas upon which you fashion an ideal life, a new beginning, with room to experiment with new or old ideas which can redefine the you that you have thought you were into a you that has a power to change! You need only ask for it, desire it. A blank canvas cannot be judged, for it possesses only potential. As we proceed, compare your blank canvas to the cluttered one that you have painted throughout your life – think of it belonging to someone else. Walk through the gallery of your mind and witness the paintings. Now come before the Divine Canvas once again. When you are ready, refreshed and open to new ideas, we will guide you through other galleries as well as your own.

Unlimited thinking. What does that mean? How is it achieved? By not thinking in the sense you usually ascribe to it. As you wander through the gallery of your collective souls – not stopping to judge each work – realize that you are an awareness that feels. Your feelings change as you witness each new or old painting. Now stop at one of the paintings and think/feel about it. This is the stage where you begin to describe it. You begin to realize that every description is a limitation – for you cannot describe the painting without identifying with it in some way. In addition, this process of description will pull or push you toward a positive or negative value or polarity. As you begin to think or ascribe reasons as to why you are repelled or attracted to the painting, you create yet another painting containing your personality and all at the cost of your awareness. A great confusion thus begins as you add clashing colors and attach increasing amounts of your awareness to each painting. You may also see that an equal amount of this awareness is attached to the paintings from which you are repelled, as well as those to which you are attracted.

The Divine Canvas is your magic screen upon which you may recreate any picture you desire and when you install it in your gallery it will be more refined. Each of you has the power to continue this recreation until a perfected creation is manifest. That is a law of the universe. If you use primarily the intellect to describe your painting, it becomes difficult to recreate, due to its analytical nature. This is compounded by the fact that you attach increasing amounts of your awareness energy to it. Use your Divine Canvas to experiment with the paintings, or concepts, that we present to you now. The paintings are actually thought-forms and you are free to picture the unlimited potential of your creative nature. You are free to re-create your life.

As we guide you through the gallery of human potential, we shall use other thought-forms to exercise different levels of awareness. We shall guide you in spirals rather than straight lines. This necessarily exerts stress on the intellectual functions, preventing it from isolating a portion of your painting at the expense of the completed masterpiece. However, in the initial stages of this work, we shall use intellectual thought-form paintings, to which you are accustomed. For even limited thought-forms, when applied to a new order of power or frequencies, can release the tenacious beast of the intellect from the gallery of your soul and permit you to explore every room and wall which contains a wealth of information for your inspiration. We design these thought-forms so that the intellect will be overwhelmed, requiring you to reach deeper into a wellspring of genius within you.

Questioner: How can the intellect block our creativity?

MaYaRa: It is essential to differentiate and redefine terms when attempting to comprehend the true nature and function of mind. We realize that it is disconcerting, at the very least, to regard the intellect in terms other than with awe and reverence. However, if you are persistent in your studies, you shall see that the intellect is only a subset of the true mind of genius; and this shall be a recurring theme throughout this book, as our purpose is not only to supply you with exciting revelations, but also to remove the inherent blocks to your understanding.

It is for these reasons that we have posed the Divine Canvas as a starting point. Clear the slate, if you will, and begin this adventure with us with the opened eyes of a child. Perhaps, you shall reassess the nature of mind, as well as your true potential as genius. Let us begin anew, then.

For all of the so-called progress attributed to the intellect, it can also be a very limiting factor in your higher education. The intellect is an ornery little child, skipping merrily, as it were, decorating the space of your awareness with the balls and chains of descriptions and possibly a few anchors or two known as "degrees." Ironically, education, as you have come to know it, is the main obstacle in the attainment of unlimited thought. Unlimited thought springs from the space in your consciousness-awareness aura. Even more ironically, this is a state of not-knowing. For the intellect would claim that if it cannot be described, it cannot be known. Thus, we shall let the intellect have its way, for now, as we state that there may be more intelligence in not-knowing than in knowing – a strange premise, indeed.

All genius – not a personality type, but a universal quality of mind – is found in this space of not-knowing. For if the universe is infinite, it must also be ever-changing; and if is ever-changing, one cannot "know" something for any time at all before it changes again. One could also postulate this in the negative: If the universe were changeless, not dynamic, then it could neither expand nor contract, nor move in any way. Then, and only then, could the intellect apprehend an absolute, changeless truth. But alas, there could be no life in such a universe, no awareness, no consciousness. In fact, no creation could be sustained in a non-dynamic universe.

Thus the intellect, regardless of how many times its knowledge is proven wrong or obsolete, continues to declare and defend "the facts" of what it knows. How can this be? It becomes evident now, that mind, by its very nature, must possess something other than intellect as a quality of awareness. It would seem rather absurd to suppose that only those on earth with what you term "high IQ's" can contribute profound ideas to humanity. Indeed, could you honestly look at your history and state that genius is only produced through your educational systems?

Questioner: Isn't that proven by our great scientists and inventors, who were highly educated individuals?

MaYaRa: Quite true. However, there are far more exceptions to your statement than confirmations. Did not the ignorant apostles of the Great Master exhibit great genius, speaking in hundreds of different languages on thousands of subjects? Perhaps you regard this as myth. Consider then, how your genius Einstein failed in his scholastic training; branded by his teachers, not only as a slow learner, but as a hopeless case. Once again we must define our terms and be precise with the words. You are only considering geniuses of "fame." However, genius is not reserved for the famous. Genius is a frequency of mind made available to everyone. Indeed, it is found everywhere, in all walks of life.

There are, indeed, many unknown men and women who tap into this "Genius Frequency" who are not exalted by society at large: healers, seers, channels, mediums, therapists on all levels of body, mind and soul; dishwashers, bums, priests, teachers, mothers, fathers, and most probably any number of children. Anyone can tap into the Genius Frequency of unlimited thought. You shall see that genius may serve the intellect but it is not, in and of itself, the intellect.

Questioner: I guess that a better question might be: What is genius?

MaYaRa: Yes, this is an excellent query.

To begin, look for the genius within yourself. By knowing that you are all great artists in your own right. Realize that your intent is your brush; your frequency, the color of thought-vibration; and your mind, a four-dimensional holographic canvas where a vision is created. And that vision, if held long enough and amplified with the booster of feeling, will result in a phenomenon known as reality.

Sound complicated? It is indeed complicated to describe in terms that the intellect can grapple with in its vain attempt to satisfy an insatiable urge to analyze the unspeakable. Yet your very life-processes operate on a Genius Frequency which, for the most part, remains a subconscious activity.

Overload

It has been proven time and again in your history that a peculiar phenomenon occurs when the so-called "conscious" mind is overwhelmed with conflicting data. That is, a connection is suddenly made on another level of thought process, yielding a clear, concise solution to a hitherto incomprehensible problem. Some of your research has suggested that the discovered solution resides in the nebulous nether lands of thought between waking and sleeping. Millions of research hours have resulted in much argument and inconclusive evidence, because the frequencies of mind used while the research was carried out was of a different frequency than that which they sought to understand. Every intuitive flash, hunch, premonition or answer to a prayer is received and sent by a special frequency. It is a frequency that is universal.

It is also the area or frequency of thought, that the intellect passionately guards against for the purpose of blocking the channel to this frequency. Why? Because the intellect is a function of the altered-ego and is set within the limited parameters of sensory input.

Earth education, then, based only upon the sensory frequencies of the environmental impact plane, forms a collective consciousness base, which is interpreted by the altered-ego as the "common sense" of survival, or "survival of the fittest." It might be said that the so-called "fall" of man occurred when his pure, spiritual soul-ego was tempted into the grand illusion of control by seizing the instinctive/cellular memory of the life cycle and using it to control and manipulate the root-races of earth; with the attached promise, that whomever possessed the control of this elemental force would forever be the predator and never the prey. Later, in this book we shall delve far more deeply into these issues.

Questioner: Then what is the difference between the intellect and the altered-ego?

MaYaRa: The intellect is a gift acquired by the individualization of the pure soul-ego. You might say that it is a reflective by-product of a process of mind which was meant to be a faithful servant of man in his practical, day-to-day living within the earth dimension. It becomes altered-ego by fostering the subtle thought that some people, indeed the whole of creation, must be the faithful servant unto others (gods) who possess the greater portion of this illusory control over elemental forces. Simply, the altered-ego is a mechanism of self-service, rather than service to that which is created by the ONE CREATOR.

Questioner: I am beginning to understand from what we must be free. Towards what must we be free?

MaYaRa: Inherent in the LAW-OF-ONE is the Law of Confusion, which states that the true reality of God-Mind alignment can only manifest through absolute free choice in the face of contrasting illusion. For this reason, beings who choose, possess the awesome power to transform darkness into Light or light into darkness.

There is nothing that you "must" do. There is only choosing to align with THE ONE SOURCE of your being, the breath of your existence.

THE BRAIN: AS RECEIVER/TRANSMITTER

Let us examine, then, freedom towards the Genius Frequency by turning the intellect upon itself as we contemplate the functions of thought and mind. It is hardly a new concept that the brain is a receiver/transmitter. Although this concept is gaining acceptance in your social understanding, the true power of its implications is overlooked.

Radios, frequencies, channels, etc. are easy enough to understand. However, there is much inherent confusion in this. For the receiver/transmitter is inundated by thousands of "stations" in a simultaneous bombardment of thoughts, which bring no peace of mind. Therefore, to the intellect, it is only a useless allegory that gives confusion another viewpoint. One leaves the receiver on; and an entire lifetime is spent scanning or switching channels until one is dizzy and finally falls asleep.

When the intellect is cut off from the Divine Source, it is easily bored. Hence, it becomes quite fickle, perpetually seeking ever new "fashions" of thought and resultant actions to appease its voracious appetite for diversions of superfluous knowledge which it claims to possess, however briefly. We endeavor to entice the intellect with a fashionably new, yet ancient, truth – one that is forever.

If the brain is a receiver, then it can be turned off. If it can be turned off, then it may rest in a state of clear potential. If we add to this clear potential, the functions of a receiver/transmitter, then the polarities of the same entity are interactive and interchangeable regarding the Genius Frequency. Let us now work with the concept of Divine Receiver upon our blank canvas.

DIVINE RECEIVER

Since very few will argue that it is possible, with varying degrees of difficulty, to shut down the receiver, it is a good place to start. It is humorous to note the extra resistance exhibited by the same group-mind toward the transmitter side of this concept.

When the receiver is at rest, it exists in a state of unlimited potential. Although this aspect of meditation has been extensively expounded upon, let us examine this perspective from a slightly different angle. The state of unlimited potential is the state of pure thought or pure mind. So, one might wonder: What is this state of seeming thoughtlessness or mindlessness? It simply cannot exist. One cannot surrender to the function of pure mind and be mindless. Rather, one becomes mind itself, potentia et al. You see, this becomes as you might term, a "sticky" subject open to much skepticism. Perhaps, we should find a more substantive study if we approach the transmitter concept instead.

It would not be too speculative to liken the transmitter/ mind to the intellect on at least the base levels of understanding. After all, your waking moments are filled with declarations of "I know this" and "I don't know that" etc., that fits nicely with our examination of a transmitting mind. For without the ability to transmit its desires and feelings, the intellect would have little to do. What reason would there be to know anything if there were no way to transmit that information to the outside world? Now it appears that we are uncovering something of importance.

Don't forget that we are painting pictures upon the Divine Canvas of space/time. As we proceed, it might help if you were a true sportsman, for the altered-ego does not take a kindly attitude toward tinkering with its foundations, even though these are built upon sand.

So, if you shut down the transmitter you have no intellect, as you term it. Correct? Now if you have no intellect, then precisely what are you? Dead? A vegetable? Or perhaps some type of receiver. It seems that we have traveled into, what may be termed, two "dead ends." On closer reflection, perhaps we have traveled in a circle, which is much in keeping with creative thought; and much to the dismay of the intellect that would much rather enjoy a "train" moving from point "a" to point "b". Let us compromise the two by delving deeper and creating a spiral of thought upon our Divine Canvas, the perfect blending of circles and cubes. So, back to the transmitter/mind.

Thus, the transmitter/mind is shut down and you are unobstructed potentia. What is that? It is the polarity of nothing/everything acting as ONE. Could that be infinity? Let us find out. But first consider this: Though the transmitter is shut down it is still plugged in, as it were. To what? To the Source. What Source is that? Perhaps at this juncture, as in any great creative act, a good digression is in order. So, for the moment let our mental construction float out there in the space of your Divine Canvas; and create another one and study that for a time in space.

Create a grand blue and white jewel and call it earth. Create poles that can handle current of awesome proportions to keep it in motion, electrified and "attractive." Now create a universal power source to continue this awesome feat for aeons upon aeons of space/time. Notice that as it spins upon its own axis, as well as around a parent star, the entire affair spins around a galaxy and you have created a rather beautiful spiral which not only avoids redundancy, but solves the dilemma of a "kamikaze" planet of no return. It is a splendid creation that runs perfectly as long as it is powered continually by a source.

THE DIVINE CANVAS - A PROCESS

If you are asked to explain your creation, you might describe it as a perfect combination of an electric motor and a battery. It takes a charge and holds it for a period of time like a capacitor, and it transforms the energies like a transducer. It is a capacitor of universal energies transducing them, in part, into elemental forces. You would explain that it is a thinking embodiment of elemental forces, charged and propelled by a universal source and organized or guided by mind energies. You notice that this creation, this manifested collection of mind energies in material form, generates a unique set of life force equations. These equations become your tools of creation.

There are universal equations built into the atomic fabric of material worlds that are designed to retain any combination of charges. These charges hold equations within the magnetic structure of its polarities and eventually manifest these combinations in forms ranging from variations on trees and flowers to war and famine. So, great care must be used when introducing new thought-forms for these tend to perpetuate for long periods of time. By creating this planet, you begin to realize functions of your own consciousness which you had not noticed before; such as the force of momentum. Let us look at these as a creation within your Divine Canvas.

Like your planet Earth creation, you notice that when your consciousness body resides within it, it is subject to the laws inherent to its processes. You begin to realize that when your receiver/mind of consciousness is on, you tune into the frequencies of collective earth-thoughts trapped in the electromagnetic fields of space/time, thus limiting their frequencies to that dimension of creation. Whatever thoughts you transmit, regarding what you may think about its condition, also is trapped in the electromagnetic frequency. It is all contained within your polarized realm of "reality."

For these reasons, life upon earth is as ugly, revolting and painful as it is beautiful, attractive and pleasurable.

Now, take your two creations, the planet and your functions of consciousness/mind and merge these into one giant consciousness composed of many smaller units. Of course, you are still creating in the time/space of your Divine Canvas. As an observer, try to understand the interactions between thought-forms and laws of nature, as these influence each other to create circumstances.

Imagine, in your Divine Canvas, that you volunteer to merge your consciousness with earth consciousness and all thought-forms trapped within its electromagnetic lines of force. Of course, if you enter that creation, you need a physical body. A physical or consciousness body is composed of a collection of laws pertaining to that creation. You use your consciousness to fabricate a body, using the elemental powers and laws of earth for purposes of directly interacting with it. Imagine yourself manifesting for the first time in the present time of earth evolution and see what happens. Ready?

First, you sense your awareness being pulled in many directions at once. You realize that you have the ability to tune into different frequencies of thought. You notice, also, that if you do not focus upon a given frequency, unlike a radio, your mind drifts aimlessly, picking up frequencies at random. You notice that every object, event and thought-form has its own particular frequency or combinations thereof; and you seem to have a natural tendency to regard some of these as pleasant and beautiful, while others you try to avoid. You become aware that other entities have tendencies toward other frequencies, which are not the same as yours. You separate them from your consciousness and tune them out, as it were – you have fallen into the first trap. That is, you have created an altered-ego which is part and parcel of the magnetic polarities of your electrodynamic earth field, which in turn develops an intellect for the purpose of defining what it judges as attractive or revolting. A struggle ensues as the natural opposing frequencies are identified and sides are chosen which must be defended. Soon you are lost and confused, and you begin scanning through the available frequencies with your receiver, only to discover a never-ending conflict of polarities.

Now, we can symbolize this quandary as an intersection, a crossroad. Although there are four directions in this dimension, there are seemingly only two choices. Four is the numeric representation of light manifesting as material reality. It is also the cross. However, it takes only two lines intersecting to form four directions for a total of six, the number of the cube which signifies material containment of light.

Since most lower frequency thought-forms are trapped in the earth's gravitational field, the most immediate or the loudest are received from the horizontal plane of earth: Right/left, good/ evil, cold/hot, communist/capitalist; countless issues, each with its pros and cons, all pounding upon your awareness aura, all demanding a decision to transmit your choice, to transmit your side, to transmit your identity.

Let us stop the action for a moment, for this is a most crucial moment in our examination. In addition to the physical laws of electromagnetism there is a second mechanism that can magnetize a thought-form. We shall define a thought-form as the holographic matrix of energy fields that manifests reality as you know it. This second mechanism of consciousness is I-dentification. Without I-dentification, thought-forms could not bind themselves to the auric field of the earth/mind/body complex of the entity.

Questioner: What is the opposite of I-dentification?

MaYaRa: There is no opposite to I-dentification, for it is a function of the primordial ego, a fundamental resonance with the Creator, just as one upon the earth is fundamentally I-dentified with one's parents and siblings.

The pure, original ego of every being I-dentifies with the divine impulse of LOVE-LIGHT/GOD-MIND, a colossal thought-form manifested by the UNIVERSAL, INFINITE POINT OF INTELLIGENCE of the GOD-ALL-THAT-IS, which is the sovereign Principle of Unification of all life/light/matter, everywhere, eternally, that allows everything to BE, to find its way back to the source as a Co-Creator. It has no polarity. It has no opposite. ALL is contained within its GOD-MIND. IT is the LAW OF ONE. That is why I-dentification is such a powerful force.

Understand that what we term "altered-ego" is a system of knowledge organized around a system of dialectic thought-forms which embody the illusion of an opposite of each and every thought-form and being. The altered-ego creates the illusion of the crossroad which compels the human power of I-dentification to continually choose between itself and something else which must be the opposite of it.

With that as a foundation of understanding, you may now understand how such perverse thought-forms such as dehumanization are the military software of the machines of destruction. For if you are caught in the polarities of the altered-ego, even though you may strive to be and I-dentify with qualities of righteousness, your altered-ego will construct an opposite image of a subhuman who is intent upon destroying all that you hold true. This process is entirely electromagnetic. It is an attribute and function of earth processes and in no way is this to be considered consciousness. It only appears to be so through I-dentification. So you see that the altered-ego compels you to I-dentify with one phase of a polarity.

Questioner: I understand what you say about dehumanization, but don't we make choices in deciding whether or nor to act that way?

MaYaRa: Of course, you are free to choose by Divine Decree. The question here is: Choose what? If you introduce a thought-form into the magnet of earth-mind and it automatically presents its twin, the opposite of that thought-form and you choose one or the other, what you have actually chosen is the opposite of that which you created.

From our perspective, which is quite different from yours, any thought-form created on the frequency of the altered-ego does not constitute a valid choice, as it lies strictly within the realm of the physics of earth-plane illusion.

DEHUMANIZATION

Use your Divine Canvas and view your earth from the perspective of a visitor who studies the actions of its inhabitants with a keen eye and a clear mind. We shall continue examining this thought-form of dehumanization, since it has evoked such confused emotions within you. Move into the fourth dimension of mind with us and study this most perilous condition of the human dilemma. You will be amazed at what you will see.

The illusion of dehumanization is the ungodly offspring of the altered-ego which forces the natural ego of I-dentification into an illusion of separatism and protectionism against an opposite force, or enemy, who must be rendered as subhuman. For it is impossible to kill or injure another life-form without the motivating force of fear generated from this illusion.

Questioner: What can we do to free ourselves from this trap?

MaYaRa: Through meditation and contemplation you can create a Divine Canvas to begin to recreate thought-forms that are free from the electromagnetic generation of polarities. In other words, by disconnecting attention from the dense material realms, it is free to move and to be aware of other dimensions.

When you are operating on this frequency, you begin to sense the presence of other energy domains. There are other frequencies of Light (capitol L) that create vehicles of consciousness that can tunnel through all dimensions of universal domains. Later we will discuss this SuperLight.

Meditation is the first step in controlling the receiver/ transmitter mechanism. What happens when you open the receiver to a random channel or one with which you "normally" I-dentify? You suddenly return to your mundane world. Your feelings of peace are short-lived, for soon enough the whirling thought-forms of mass-consciousness locked in the earth's auric field will impose upon you and you I-dentify with these again.

Understand that there is much wisdom and truth magnetized within the earth's and your auric fields. There are also many destructive and painful thought-forms. Thus, you have a rendering of chaos reenacted as human scenarios.

Questioner: It seems that we need a filter to screen this information.

MaYaRa: This is a partial truth. Why engage in a war of thought-forms armed with shields and "filters," as you term them, when you can tap into the Genius Frequency? Just by raising the frequency of thought, the power of GOD-MIND will stream into your auric field, transforming and perfecting even the faulty thought-forms of partial equations. Since the world is also a thought-form, your world also changes. When enough of your other-selves accomplish this, the world moves again toward perfection. That is true evolution.

Questioner: Can you define the process that can lead us toward the Genius Frequency?

MaYaRa: The answer is LOVE-LIGHT/GOD-MIND. We perceive that you struggle with so simple a truth. Notice how tenacious the intellect is! If you were to write a book that contained the absolute answers for every entity in any dimension it would take virtually no time to read. For there would only be those four words.

You see, in your terms, we can only examine with your language – which is the intellect – what is not the truth in order to arrive at that which is! It is a sad day for the intellect to surrender to the TRUTH that LOVE-LIGHT/GOD-MIND is a process that cannot be captured and manipulated by the will of the intellect, thus it cannot be explained by linear speech patterns.

If, for example, you possess a finely-crafted, handmade timepiece, and the object evokes much wonder and you are compelled to take it apart for purposes of further understanding, you no longer have the timepiece but a collection of parts, minus the process.

In the same way, you may have words to describe the composition of a tree, in a linear sense, but the description will not grow one. Only the open-ended channel of the Genius Frequency – the unlimited, abundant, creative impulse of ALL-THAT-IS, divided and subdivided into infinite energy harmonics of thought-forms, organized and unified by the Grand Desire of LOVE-LIGHT/ GOD-MIND – can create a tree.

You see, the Divine Process is the missing link in the intellect. The process is the Divine Overview that reveals the entrapment of light particum organized into the matrix of thought-forms, so that the atoms and molecules of light geometry race into the harmonic lines of PRE-THOUGHT or archetypal forms. So it is for every life/thought-form that manifests – for the purpose of manifesting in every conceivable form the glory of THE ONE for us to behold and emulate.

Questioner: Although the process of I-dentification can be mis-used; it can, if used wisely, magnetically attract us to the Genius Frequency.

MaYaRa: A most intelligent and noble observation.

Each and every one of you is a seed crystal of the Divine Mind, which supports ALL CREATION. Thus you are a living hologram, or micro-replica of that creation. In other words, your true I-dentity is synonymous with GOD-MIND. What other I-den-tity could you have?! It is for this reason that we have stated that dehumanization is an illusion.

Questioner: Then how should we deal with the evil deeds and thought-forms that certainly exist within our plane of existence?

MaYaRa: You may perceive these as partial-life equations. Alter one geometric harmonic and a mutation is produced which must suffer a half-life function of entropy. To elucidate this seeming pa-radox inherent in your thinking process, let us return to the "cros-sroads" where we stood before our splendid digression.

The intellect will describe "crossroads" as two lines inter-secting at right angles, extending in opposite directions. That is three dimensional thinking. Let us examine this concept through the Genius Frequency. Thus, we shall visualize in the fourth di-mension and in doing so, we shall use the holographic powers of holistic mind to unravel the illusion of polarized perception. It is really very simple. Even a child can do it. Indeed most children *do* do it.

So you stand perplexed at the crossroads of life. Thought-forms entrapped in the magnetic field of the earth-body inundate the transceiver (mind, body, soul, etc.), seemingly forcing it to choose left or right, good or evil, this country or that, this food or that, this religion or that. It promises that if you decide one way or another, your problems will be solved for you and you will now be on the side that is righteously upholding that which you have I-dentified with, surrounding you with the comfort and safety of numbers. But without fail, once you have decided, you discover that the side you have chosen also has two sides, and on it goes. Where does it go? It goes back to you. You see, when you become tired, disgusted, and fairly dizzy from the wild pendulum of life, you begin to multiply the divisions back to ONE, regardless of how many life cycles you need to accomplish this.

Three dimensional thinking reasons that the road ahead is obviously the future, and road behind obviously the past. The left and right is usually a political-moralistic view held at any given moment. However, since matter is in continual motion, the crossroads is, in reality, spinning. You can see what a messy affair three dimensional thinking can be. Perhaps some gentle mental gymnastics will clarify this seeming dilemma.

Square off at the crossroads. Now, concentrate upon the road that symbolizes your so-called past/future direction. Still your mind for a moment. Still the receiver portion of your mind until the past/future road begins to tilt. Stop it when it becomes perfectly vertical. Now you have a cross. Now you are beginning to perceive from a fourth dimensional perspective. For the ancient symbol of the cross was the primary teaching tool which demonstrated the law of four of material reality, or in modern perception, the marriage of space and time. Yes, space/time is the crucifix of the material body upon which your consciousness-awareness is crucified until you take the appropriate steps to transcend into the higher dimensions from which you came.

But to be a true holograph, you should see the image or concept as you walk around it. We have not yet achieved this in our example. For if you let your mind walk around the cross, until you are on the same plane as the intersecting lines, there will be a point where the cross will vanish. Your world suddenly ceases to exist. So add one more line intersecting the others, on a perpendicular plane, and you have the needed six directions. Notice that it only takes one line to create two directions when introducing it into the parameters of space/time. You drew three lines and came up with six directions! The point of perception indicates the point within space/time awareness. Now you may float around it, never losing sight of the cross, yet remain unattached from it. Practice viewing it from different angles.

You may suppose that there are many other dimensions and this is a correct supposition. Although the scope of this work does not permit an in-depth examination of all dimensions; we will, nevertheless, use aspects of these in our next exercise.

Now, place yourself in the epicenter of the four dimensional cross. Choose a distance that equally limits the length of the lines radiating from your center. Begin to add lines by radiating them from the center in a straight line to the given distance, remembering that each new line will travel in opposite directions from the center. Continue to add as many lines of light as you can imagine. You have just created a sphere of light! Step out of it and you view it as three dimensional object. Centered within it you perceive it as fourth dimensional.

Questioner: Can you elaborate upon that last statement?

MaYaRa: Indeed. Your consciousness is presently in a state that views all objects of reality, including its own nature and mind, from the outside as a surface reflection. This is three dimensional perception. When you are one with the center of any object, you are ONE with its totality. Becoming that thought-form sustains its form and life functions by acting as process, rather than the description. Thus the ancient teachings have taught that you become what you contemplate, whether in hatred or in love. When you become one with any object, its secrets are readily available to the inquiring mind.

What we have described above is fourth dimensional perception. All telepathy, clairvoyance, "seeing," psychic healing, problem-solving, inventing, communing with nature spirits, channeling guides, intuition, hunches, inspiration and astral travel are manifested in this dimension. With the Genius Frequency as your point of departure, all this and much more is open to those whose hearts are pure enough to resonate in this frequency.

It is all a matter of changing viewpoints by changing frequency; moving your point of present awareness to the center of your life, rather than the reflection of it, opens doors to the other side of Life/Light. The Genius Frequency is a type of high frequency light which can transcend dimensions, a vehicle to transport your consciousness into different aspects of GOD-MIND.

Questioner: In speaking about the symbolism of the cross, you mentioned being crucified to space and time. Is this a fourth dimensional understanding of the crucifixion and should this perspective be used in understanding the event instead of what is traditionally taught?

MaYaRa: Indeed, it is a fourth dimensional understanding and by no means is it to be understood "instead" of anything! It is not our mission to debate the veracity of that momentous event.

The perspective of opposing viewpoints is an obstacle of the intellectual process, which we shall contend with continually in this work. As reflected in your query, the tendency for the altered-ego to reject one premise in order to accept another is the crux of misunderstanding and limitations in the thinking process and the very root of misunderstanding. Understand that we endeavor only to add too, not oppose, preconceived perceptions. It is critical in a true teach/learn method of expanded awareness, through the intellectual functions that you use at present, to approach all knowledge, all information from the standpoint of inter-dimensional and extra-dimensional perspectives. Knowledge can become wisdom only by increasing the window area of the mind in perceiving various angles of perception simultaneously.

With this in mind, understand that when viewed multi-dimensionally, all historical "facts," contemporary or mytho-logical, exist on at least seven levels of understanding. Thus, the event of the "crucifixion" exists also on as many levels or dimensions of understanding.

The fact that Joshua (Jesus the Christ) elected to manifest as a physical embodiment is in itself a subject of vast scope, demanding answers to the question: Why should a direct emanation of The One Creator need or desire to "descend" or manifest in a severely restricted form, within the laws of earth density, when such an entity had no need to do so? You see, when the question is properly framed, there is no need to replace one doctrine or concept with another; there is only the need to experience the seven levels of understanding. Only then can one ascertain a Truth and not merely a partial equation of entropy.

Thus, the "crucifixion" is an event which incorporates the physics of space/time as well as other dimensions of reality. It is a foregone conclusion, then, that the teachings of The Christ were given on seven levels, which explains the need to teach in parables. Perhaps you may now understand that in addition to being crucified to a wooden cross, the cross representing the human body born of space/time is the cross that consciousness is crucified upon when born into your realm or dimension of density.

Questioner: Yes, thank you. Now I am reminded of many passages in the Bible which mention the "end of time." This suddenly takes on new meaning in light of what you have just communicated. Could you elaborate on this cryptic statement?

MaYaRa: Indeed, when you begin to open your mind to the Genius Frequency, the many levels of awareness will converge upon a Grand Truth that will give new depth of meaning to the otherwise incomprehensible statements used by Masters throughout millennium.

When contemplating the statement, "I will be with you, even unto the end of time," or in other translations, "...even unto the consummation of the world," – which is a space/time manifestation – one is immediately faced with an enigma when approached from a third dimensional perspective. We shall use the power of the Genius Frequency to illuminate this "cryptic" statement by removing it from the cultural contexts of history and religion, and place it upon the Divine Canvas of your mind, so that it may expand and reveal its secrets by penetrating to the center of its meaning. The question surfaces as: If the teaching is centered around eternal life, then in what context is Omega, or end of time used?

The statement, "end of time," even in contemporary terms, is validated by the disciplines of physics and geophysics, which have documented the various cycles of the atom in fission and fusion states; and your earth in terms of cataclysmic geology, plate tectonics, etc. Thus it is not so difficult to understand that an entity, such as a Master, possessing the power to consciously govern the very cellular integrity of the body on an ultra/intra-dimensional level, would not be ignorant of such far reaching concepts. The fact is that the earth, as all physical bodies, has a life cycle as structured by factors of entropy, diminishing proportionately to its harmonics and sub-harmonics. The earth's clock is set in multiples of 12,000 years. At the elapsing of such a time cycle, the earth is given a new face, a new orientation. Consciousness that has sufficiently evolved, at that point, is removed into higher dimensions of frequency and the lower ones recycled. This moment or phase of the cycle is referred to in your ancient teachings as the "harvest." The statement is not so cryptic after all and is actually quite straightforward.

Questioner: Then where do we stand in relation to this cosmic clock?

MaYaRa: You stand on the brink of eternity, beloved. The earth is a nest, as it were, on the edge of a precipice; and humanity is beating its fledgling wings in preparation for the moment when they are lovingly nudged into the abyss, to either take flight into true freedom or plunge into the depths as life is recycled.

Realize that "time," as you know it, is a function of the frequency harmonics with which your solar system resonates. Change the frequency, and the time base or qualitative and quantitative relativity of your space/time experience creates a new reality. The Masters knew of this and taught it as an individual revelation. The message of Jesus The Christ was the same personal revelation, with one tremendous addition: that there would be an end of time beyond which you may continue to live under a new fifth dimensional harmonic, if you so choose!

It is not so mysterious as it might seem. The adjustments of the harmonics of which we speak are simply the promised assistance by the Masters of Light in the natural cyclic degeneration of any isolated mind or solar system, of which yours is no exception. These adjustments are designed first to awaken the earth-body consciousness, of which each of you is a reflection in the downward spiral of entropy, so that life may continue in other dimensions. It is all around and within you, manifesting itself in a great restless turmoil within the sudden surge of unprecedented masses of embodied entities upon the shifting crust of the earth, at a time of communication explosions, resulting in an instantaneous image transfer between all parts of your globe.

Think of the signs that you take for granted, such as the pictures of earth from the moon. The higher beings of Light made those breakthroughs a reality by imparting the knowledge for the skills in question to humanity, though few altered-egos will admit to such an humbling reality. This assistance was not administered for the purpose of worshipping technology, nor for any illusions claiming that man's arrogance will gain control of the earth and eventually save him from himself. There is an incredible irony here that each entity upon the earth has endured lifetimes within aeons, for the purpose of reaching this glorious moment of liberation, only to be overwhelmed by the illusion of confusion and fear. The travesty of the human drama is that you are reaching this point of ultimate liberation, while denying the glorious victory with self-hatred.

You have waited so long for this moment. You are free to choose, since choice is the only freedom there is. Although this has always been a grand truth, never has it been more critical to your ultimate liberation than it is now. Why? Because you are receiving direct assistance from higher beings made of Light on a planetary scale. You have the added bonus of the Universal Energy and all of its unlimited abundance at your beckoned call through the Genius Frequency.

Your earth-body has moved from a space/time frequency to a time/space frequency. Your thoughts have more power upon the Divine Canvas of creation than ever before in the history of the earth. Your thought-forms are manifesting quicker than ever before. Why manifest thought-forms of fear, when you can shift your viewpoint to a fourth dimensional understanding of the cross of time, plus the vertical ascension into victory over death? NOW is the time to contemplate the thought-forms of abundance and joy for the entire family of man, regardless of what the superficial picture represents to your altered-egos.

Realize that you are presently being liberated by real Masters (not the false space gods), with helping hands of love extended. The Divine Canvas of the NEW ORDER of life is unfolding (not the political new world order). Realize that you are not trapped. Realize that the ancient thought-forms of pain, suffering and eternal want are not part of your original programming as entities of GOD-MIND. The former limitations are the false programming locked within the solar mind of your planetary system and trapped within the cubic function of space. Thus, you shall overcome the seeming insurmountable odds of solar intelligence, which must devour itself. That intelligence has isolated itself and its dependent planetary bodies from the replenishing Light of God-Mind for its own self-glorification.

The Divine Canvas of your life is awaiting your masterful brush stroke. At any moment of your lives (plural), you may begin with a new canvas upon which you may create a new destiny. What this requires is unlimited thought through the Genius Frequency.

Questioner: It does not seem so simple to grasp unlimited thinking. How can one explain unlimited thought with limited thoughts?

MaYaRa: The reason that one does not graduate from your educational system of life with a degree in unlimited thinking is, first, that no such degree is recognized as even a remote possibility; and second, because you worship the intellect, which is a product of a most limited form of awareness mechanisms, and which is a function of, what we refer to as, the altered-ego.

Questioner: Great intellects have led humanity into golden ages and have inspired us to heights of achievement. How, then, are we to regard the intellect as so limited?

MaYaRa: Forgive what might appear as a condescending attitude toward the intellect. You might also bear in mind that most of these entities were laughed at and mocked for decades and centuries in your counting when, suddenly, the idea was accepted by those who eventually re-wrote history and celebrated the achievement as their own.

The fact remains, however, to any probing mind that great civilizations have been, and are now being, decimated by the self-gratification and edification indulged in through the worship of their accomplishments. Indeed, they even fight over who shall be in control of the gifts left behind by a Master or by one assisted by a Master.

Your most intelligent scientists concur on the notion that even the "brightest" of humans use only 1/10 of their mental capacities. Inherent within this dim thought is the greatest news of all. With 90% of the receiver/transmitter (mind) yet to be awakened: there is an unlimited thought with which to begin to paint your Divine Canvas. You may also see from this simple reasoning how the intellect, dim though it may be, can instantly transcend itself, opening vast new horizons of co-creation with higher beings of Light, *who work only through the ONE CREATOR. Then, you can re-create your life, your earth.*

As it stands, you are dominated by the intellect because you I-dentify with its descriptions of your world. We perceive a question forthcoming.

Questioner: Yes, I was wondering if the altered-ego is the same as the intellect?

MaYaRa: Yes. Your assertion is correct, but the thought-forms of your associations are scrambled. Permit us to now embark upon a beautiful digression from which you may glean a clearer understanding of why your statement is true, yet is very misleading when pursued in depth.

Pure intelligence is a direct function of pure ego. Pure ego is a direct function of the first stage of individualized soul-group consciousness. An example of this is the animal, plant and mineral kingdoms. These represent the function of pure ego in that they are highly organized and that they impeccably express their being according the laws of nature, or original projected energy reflections of the intelligent matrices which maintain their perfected purpose. Understand that these so-called laws are living entities. They are not laws carved into stone tablets or written upon parchment.

All of this appears to the intellect as the backdrop of the human drama; when, in reality, these and more kingdoms are in you, as well as you in them.

It is even more important to understand that mankind did not evolve from these kingdoms. Rather, mankind evolved simultaneously with them as a total projection of creation onto the backdrop of the Divine Canvas of Mind.

Up to this point in creation of your local universe, there was perfect cooperation between ALL life forms. In the human realm, the Genius Frequency was open to all Masters in realms of the Creative Life Processes, that manifested their thought-form energies by organizing the elements of earth.

In this state of freedom, the highest possible frequency of LOVE-LIGHT/GOD-MIND could touch and operate intimately with all life-forms for the purpose of accelerating the evolution of individualized consciousness beyond the factors of entropy and decay inherent in a singular sun system. In that original state of pure Genius Frequency, there was no difference between objective, abstract, mathematical reality and subjective, mythological, archetypal reality. Therefore man's powers were indeed awesome. He was the orchestrator, the conductor of the Life-Force and all manifest subdivisions of powers under the LAW OF ONE.

Working within the LIVING LETTER of the law, man was capable of genetic alterations within himself as well as the root-races of earth. In other words, because he is also a replica of all life-forms in toto, he was able to genetically alter other life forms for the advancement of all. This he did without test tubes, laboratories, or instruments of any kind – only through the powers of his

Heart-Mind. Unfortunately, he opted for creating various grotesque hybrid beings, which he used as his slaves.

He possessed the powers of ascension, whereby he could increase the light frequency of his cellular mass, disappearing and reappearing in different locations and dimensions by the intent of his will. To live beyond 900 earth cycles was simply a decision to regenerate a duplicate body. The transformation of entropy and death was no more a consideration than it is to leave one's auto vehicle and board an air ship. Nothing was impossible for him, as he was one with THE ONE. The channel of his receiver/transmitter operated at 100% capacity and tuned only to the Genius Frequency.

Realize that this frequency is ever-present, streaming from the Infinite Point of Intelligence/Consciousness, and LOVES all life into existence. Without IT there could be no life anywhere, ever, not for a moment, not even by accident.

What we have described, in this most limited language, is the origins of the pure intellect, which is a totally experiential reality. The "modern" tendency to objectify reality, based upon sensory feedback of three dimensional physicality, laid the foundation for the dangerous downward spiral into the polarized vortex of good/evil that you now struggle with unto each death cycle, and which claims you for a repetition of the preconditioned pattern. In other words, when the pure ego-intellect contemplated the thought-form of dominance over the root-races for the purpose of self worship and self-service, the altered-ego was born and the exalted consciousness of mankind was plunged into the dark awareness of confusion and fear.

The newborn terror of death and annihilation, processed through the now limited altered-ego, producing a system of death-producing thought-forms consistent with the ongoing dogma of "survival-of-the-fittest," "kill-or-be-killed," "sin-and-punishment," and the like. The atrocities performed in the name of God are even more absurd, as well as tragic. The result of this thought-form manifested a life-form that fed, not from the LIGHT of THE ONE, but from the only other available source of energy, another life-form.

For those of you who don't understand, may we remind you that when a holistic thought-form, created by THE ONE, is polarized in the dual opposing energy patterns such as the earth's electromagnetic field (a material realm), the result is what you now see about you: shortened life spans, diseases, dehumanization of kindred spirits, and an endless list of atrocities.

We perceive that you reflect upon the teaching of the Adam and Eve story and we may assure you that although this myth contains a great deal of truth, it has become a mere ploy in religious dogma to further remove you, personally, from the requirement of responsibility in an ongoing travesty, which each of you are challenged to correct in the NOW moment. The fact is, life has not changed. You have changed. And you may change once again. It has always been your decision.

Tune into the Genius Frequency once again. Realize that the positive and negative polarities of your earth life are but a subdivision of the ONE RAY of LOVE-LIGHT/GOD-MIND. Eternal life is your heritage. You walk, live, and breath within the Genius Frequency. You are not unworthy or helpless to co-create life on a global scale. Tune IT in. You are part of The One. You are part of us. We encourage you. We wait for you. We love you, each and every one.

LIVING THOUGHT-FORMS
"CO-CREATORS IN THE ONE"

> "If you entertain the notion that there is nothing
> that you can do to improve your life and the
> condition of the world, think again!"

Questioner: Please explain your statement in the preceding material: "Every thought-form since the beginning of time is trapped in the magnetic aura of the earth." If this is true, how can we possibly begin to control it?

MaYaRa: The query reflects three dimensional thinking. "Control" is a great illusion upon your plane of existence. You may choose among preconditioned thought-forms. You may create thought-forms upon the Divine Canvas. But you may not control thought-forms. If that were possible, your entire universe would be in a hopeless state of enslavement by unscrupulous entities. Since the framing of your question necessitates a better foundation of understanding, we shall digress as usual to discuss the processes of creation before we directly answer your query. Free your mind now to explore the processes of creation, then you may fully grasp the intricate reality of thought-forms.

There is only ONE PROCESS of creation because there is only ONE CREATOR. All creation is a thought-form. However, to create the material realms, which is a crystallized reflection of the facets of THE ONE, a dual ray of energy is created and passed through itself, forming a pulse which appears to oppose itself. One glance at what you term a sine wave and you may instantly conceptualize this most simple yet profound of all understandings – the Yin Yang symbol is a sine wave!

You may create any truth you desire, but you cannot create the process; you are THE PROCESS and it is eternal. You may think any thought, but the Process of Thinking is not yours to create. The Process of Creation and Thought was built into you – indeed, IS you. You may draw an apt analogy using the example of the very technology you use to write this document. That is, you use a program which processes words. It does not write the words for you. It provides the structure or system whereby you may organize the words that symbolize thought-forms into a communicable form.

In the same manner, built into you is the Original Program sustained by what we term the Genius Frequency, with which you may create a life or life situation within the Process. There are partial equations of life which create a subversion of the program, much like your genetic and computer viruses. Since you are the program and the program is you, it is rather obvious that the only program which will be damaged is your own. Let us approach this from a slightly different angle.

The Divine Structure of this Process first creates thought which is light, crystallizes it through standing wave patterns, and organizes it to directly reflect the TRUTH of ITS existence. This Organized Truth is consciousness. Your scientists have reluctantly admitted for quite some time that matter is energy. Thus, it takes energy to think – energy is a form of mass – and the result is a matter-energy bundle we term a thought-form. When you think, you create thought-forms or energy/mass particles. You use the same Process as THE ONE. How could it be otherwise?

Again: You did not create the Process of thought. The Divine Process created the universe. You cannot process differently than dose the universe. You can only add new thought-forms to the universe with that portion of "Process" that you em-body. Perhaps now, you may better grasp the truth that you are what you create, because you are what you think.

The thought-forms created by the altered-ego are faulty and damaging because they support partial-equations to prove that you are not connected to the universe. It preaches a dogma: that at worst, you are a freak accident, isolated and alone upon a planet also produced by this freak accident; and at best, you are a faulty program that cannot save itself. All these thought-forms produce yet more thought-forms of despair, loneliness, and annihilation. These thought-forms are trapped in the magnetic aura of the earth, along with the Original Program. That is why there are so many thought-forms that refer to an evil somewhere below and a good somewhere above.

The altered-ego is a fragment of the Divine Process, encommpasing only your immediate solar thought-forms. That is, the self-consuming nature of your sun is what you see reflected upon the earth. Limited sensory inputs of a low frequency body can only interpret that to mean self annihilation. Since the altered-ego is blinded by the light of a lower order, this fragmented process of self consuming life becomes a terrible law of survival, only to, ultimately, succumb to that annihilation. Therefore, a faulty or artificial program can only generate and attract faulty and destructive thought-forms.

Questioner: Then can we say that the altered-ego is man-made?

MaYaRa: From the perspective of Universal Process, it is not man made, for it is a fragment of that process already created. The interpretation of your sensory life cycle is man-made. Limited thought-forms drawn only from three dimensional sensory observation of earth/solar processes give birth to thought-forms that coalesce to form the altered-ego. In other words, the Original Program provides 360 degree vision; and man, through limiting his focus or frequency, develops blinders. Only the blinders are man-made.

Take the analogy of the prism. Imagine the prism to be the size of earth. Three dimensional thought-forms reside on the refractive side. From that perspective, everyone who is not color-blind would readily agree that rays of color exist. If one among them claimed that there exists only One Ray, he would be the subject of ridicule; for it would be obvious to the altered-ego's sensory input that there is more than one ray. If one could grow larger or reduce the size of the prism, one would be immediately cognizant of the One Ray of light. One would deduce that the form of the prism was in some way responsible for the illusion that the One Ray appears to be many rays of color. Further, if one could BE the prism (which you are), one could study directly the process of creation by self-study (which you can).

What is man-made are the thought-forms or blinders created from his desire. A matrix of these human thought-forms creates an artificial subdivision of the Divine Process, becoming the altered-ego. This artificial sub-process and all the thought-forms that it produces or amplifies are magnetic entities. In other words, electromagnetism is the medium through which thought-forms of like frequency coalesce to form entities.

Each of you contributes to the creation of these energy-entities by what you think and contemplate, even in your so-called secret thoughts. In the fourth dimension there are no secrets. Therefore, every man, woman and child is contributing to a vast matrix or network of living thought-forms. You may justifiably speculate that the implications of this statement, on an individual and global scale, are quite perilous, indeed. We shall return to this staggering reality later in this segment. Let us first examine the primary frequency of creation.

Since electronic and electromagnetic forces must operate as pulsating dualities of plus and minus interchanges, there must be a third force that provides the medium for harmonic re-balancing in a universe of electronic flux that would otherwise cancel itself in an instant after its creation. This third force or medium is the frequency of LOVE from THE ONE and to be precise, this frequency is not the third force it is the First Force. Again, an electronic universe cannot exist save within the all encompassing sea of extremely high frequencies of Light.

The frequency of LOVE is the primary function in the Divine Process of Creation that manifests the binding force, organizing ALL matter from The Original Thought-Form to its manifestation as realms of the universe (and many universes). Thus even the most distorted thought-forms or partial life-equations, termed "evil," are LOVED into being by the Divine Process, with which all of you are endowed. Without this frequency-field, the universe would cancel itself. Also, it is not possible for anything manifested through this Divine Creative Process to exist without possessing the same attributes of that process. All worlds are created from it and exist within it.

Questioner: What constitutes a thought-form? How much thought does it take to cause it to become a thought-form?

MaYaRa: We interpret your query as hopeful that a certain degree, intensity, and/or size of a thought must be reached before it becomes an entity. This false hope is a result of your hesitation to accept the responsibilities of being a co-creator.

We must inform you that the most insignificant and fleeting of thoughts is in fact a thought-form, a living entity added to the growing pool of mass thought-forms trapped in the electromagnetic fields of consciousness of your earth dimension. Further, the entrapment of inconceivable numbers of bellicose and perverted thought-forms, since the beginning of time, collect into a massive pollution, of not only your planet, but also of your local universe. For they are released periodically during each millennia and must be dealt with and balanced with all other life forms, lest the entire galaxy be destroyed.

Every thought you generate or contemplate is activated by your personal life-force, inexorably connecting you to it regardless of its scale. In other words, even so-called "small thoughts" can act as small bacilli or viruses. Thought-forms exist by degree, in size and complexity, producing the community and global conditions on a macro-level, and personal human condition on the micro-level.

Your query expressed a hopefulness that most thought-forms are minuscule and therefore harmless and ineffectual. This is hardly the case. For in the above analogy, you can readily perceive that the microscopic virus can wreak havoc within an unbalanced body/complex even unto its physical death. The atomic particles, as another analogy, can pass through "solid" metals, demonstrating the ability to vaporize and poison physical systems at great distances and for long periods of time. Small is not necessarily insignificant.

Just as you no longer can argue that certain particles, due to their invisibility, do not exist; you cannot deny the existence of thought-forms. Thought-forms exist as living entities because they are created by the Divine Process which is inherent in you. Every moment of your life, you are creating or giving new life-force to living thought-forms in all shapes, sizes, functions, and colors. Now, this staggering realization is not intended to destroy your hopes for changing your world. In fact, by understanding this truth, the profound possibility of an "insignificant you" changing the world becomes not only an obvious possibility, but your duty as a co-creator.

Regardless of how bleak this scenario may appear at first glance, there is also a most hopeful view from another perspective. That is, the number of thought-forms in resonant harmony with LOVE-LIGHT/GOD-MIND created by humankind is also beyond counting. When you contemplate your world situation, you realize that monumental work must be accomplished. This task seems, at first, overwhelming, but further examination will reveal that significant work can be done BY YOU!

We are establishing here that thought-forms (whether generated by the human mind, the solar mind or the galactic mind) can and do influence the effects of life's scenarios. You not only create thought-forms, but you also amplify preconditioned and preexisting thought-forms just as you can build from a blueprint or remodel an existing structure. Thus, creating and contemplating harmonious thought-forms can be accomplished on a continual basis through your daily lives, as well as your sleep cycles. Contemplate: During the course of your day and night, what do you think? What type of thought-forms do you create or contemplate? What type of material in your newspapers and television to you I-dentify with?

As you sit complacently, watching your news programs or reading your newspapers, know that the thought-forms you contemplate, the ones that you tune into with your mental and physical receiver/transmitters, adds untold power to any given thought-form, regardless of its origin. You may not have created the original thought-form, but even in the most casual of agreements or by the most benign or vehement gossip, passive and active I-dentification take their tolls, for better or worse.

The responsibilities of a creator cannot be escaped nor minimized by rationalizing that you did not have a "hand" in any given manifest reality. The fact is that you are, indeed all, responsible for every action upon your earth plane regardless of the degree to which you are "active" in any given issue or situation. We cannot emphasize enough the potency of your thought-forms in the scheme of life. We cannot emphasize enough the power that each of you possesses to change your lives and the world as a whole. The time is now to wash the sand from mind's eye and gaze into the sun and star-filled sky, the splendor of the elemental kingdoms of earth, and into the hearts of your global family, realizing that you have and do participate in the creation of all.

Although you may accept this premise intellectually, you may not totally embrace the fundamental truth that you can change the world. Many philosophies, which are also thought-forms, prevail upon your planet, preaching dogma designed to divest individual consciousness of its true glory, withholding the unified reality of religion and science. The surest test of faulty scientific and religious dogma is the mutual exclusivity of the two. As more ancient documents are revealed in a timely pattern governed by the evolutionary program as set forth by the hierarchy of the ONE CREATOR, the true religious-scientific patterns of the One teaching will present themselves. The ancient documents of Light will agree with and enlighten areas of science and religion so that there is no difference between the two. There never was.

However, until that unified consciousness is a reality, the majority of mankind, individually and collectively, will serve only as an incubator for either the self-effacing dehumanization of their global family, or the unified nurturing life force of LOVE-LIGHT/ GOD-MIND. You see, it is up to each of you to pour in the thought-forms of Light, for the Love of THE ONE is so powerful that everyone is given a chance to experiment, to improve and correct their faulty, self-created programming.

Questioner: Is I-dentification a thought-form?

MaYaRa: I-dentification is a process. You may regard it as a passive incubation chamber. When I-dentification is directed by the altered-ego, a most subtle and dangerous atmosphere is produced. It may be likened to a petri dish, which exerts no power of its own until it harbors an atmosphere that stabilizes the conditions for the growth of various life-forms introduced by the experimenter.

We utilize the analogy of the petri dish, for there is little difference between a culture that spreads upon a continent and one that grows within a dish. What grows in this dish is up to you – individually and collectively, as co-creators in the original blueprint of creation. Let us delve deeper into the reality of thought-forms as living entities.

Each of your receiver/transmitter consciousness-systems (bodies, minds and souls) is like a womb and birthing canal which apprehends a thought-form in the fertile soil of the Divine Process and incubates it, adding more thought-forms and power to it, passing it along to another person/incubator, who in turn does the same until the thought-form manifests itself somewhere in the worldbody. Thus, it is electromagnetically attracted to other entities of like frequency who I-dentify with it through the altered-ego, boosting their power to spring into action. This is evidenced by an individual, with no previous predilection, who suddenly exhibits an act of Love or violence beyond their normal range of responses.

You are easily deceived into worshipping your heroes and persecuting your enemies. How long will you deny your responsibility to Life? To what ends are you diminishing your personal power and dignity to create a world of death rather than life for the children and families of the earth? Take a stand in the outcome of the final chapter of the world cycle that is upon you.

I-dentify with the Genius Frequency, which is your heritage. You are not greater than your criminals, nor are you less than your heroes. You have created them all. Take at least a few minutes of your day to incubate the thought-forms of a Christ or a Buddha, rather than that of corrupt public figures or mass murderers. Oh, you, righteous ones, abhor the corrupted as you contemplate in judgment. However, YOU I-DENTIFY WITH WHATEVER YOU CONTEMPLATE! That is a law of consciousness.

Your preoccupation, with whatever thought-form you choose to contemplate, amplifies its power. Take the time to develop the compassion of your hearts to embrace THE GOOD OF ALL. For you are responsible for incubating the thought-forms that resonate with destructive violence, as well as disease, war and plagues of the world. The more you oppose and abhor parts of humanity, the more you oppose and abhor parts of yourselves. Incubate the thought-form of LOVE-LIGHT/GOD-MIND that embraces the whole of life and you will give birth to a reality of joy, prosperity and health beyond your most hopeful dreams, individually and globally – you may take credit for that.

Now that you have a better understanding of the awesome power and responsibility of the passive receiver which incubates thought-forms, let us examine the transmitter side of your electromagnetic field of consciousness. It is useful to realize that at any given moment, your transmitter is tuned to the exact frequency as your receiver. Therefore, it is impossible to entertain and be entertained by lower frequency thought-forms of fear and hatred, for instance, without transmitting with increased power the same thought-forms into the world-pool of consciousness. Further, there is a time-delay in the incubation period of a given thought-form. Herein lies a great deal of confusion that we shall endeavor to expose to the Light of pure consciousness.

Since third dimensional mind apprehends thought-forms from the circumference of the wheel of life, rather than from the center; it finds itself perpetually trapped in either the past or the future and rarely, if ever, in the now. Past/future, good/evil, etc., spin their webs of confusion around your life. So you may spend moments or years or lifetimes receiving and incubating certain thought-forms that are transmitted at a later time, which is the future, relative to the past, when they were first empowered. This explains, in part, the laws of Karma.

This also explains why at some point in your life-cycle, you attempt to I-dentify with higher frequency thought-forms and succeed only in increasing your world view of the old, lower order thought-forms. Mankind appears more intelligent, only because it has more sophisticated reasons to support the old, lower frequency thought-forms, giving the illusion of evolution. While mankind may lay some claim to progressive thought, it is by no means indicative of evolution.

In the fourth dimension, your mind apprehends the center of any given thought-form or life-form. This is much different than your "normal" three-dimensional perception of surface reflections of objects. When an object is perceived in the fourth dimension, your mind apprehends it from the center or still point of its essence, resulting in an experiential moment of contact, a moment far more revealing than the mere reflection of that object. In that moment, you actually create space (which is consciousness) within space, suspending the illusion of time. Please bear with us in these digressions for they are important in the fuller understanding of the mechanism of thought-forms.

Now, remembering the analogy (Chapter 1) of the spinning wheel, we shall go deeper into the understanding of illusion, and find there the essence of thought-forms; with the added benefit of understanding in more depth the nature of the ancient term of karma, or in your modern syntax, the action-reaction principle.

As the planets spin in consciousness-space, forming a space/time continuum, illusions become layered in time, compounding three-dimensional confusion. Thus if you are not at the center of a thing, you can only be on the spinning surface, perpetually in the illusion of a past racing to a future, which never really comes. Perhaps this clarifies the propensity for adults to continually manifest adolescent and even infantile thought-forms throughout their lives, causing true evolution of consciousness to be a time consuming endeavor with painfully small steps toward true illumination in other dimensions.

Thus, karma, within your immediate lifetime, is easier to comprehend when you realize that old thought-forms can be transmitted in the "now" moment of your lives. You appear to be compensating for actions and thought-forms that occurred yesterday or long ago. This is only a result of the old thought-forms with which you presently I-dentify, causing them to attach themselves to your auric field through electromagnetic induction and resonance, producing a reality in the NOW moment.

This electromagnetic resonance of a thought-form appears as a matrix of geometries that glow in your auric field, attracting other entities who have similar geometric energy configurations within their auric fields. You are a living billboard, so to speak. The thought-forms of your beliefs and desires are not locked in some convolution of brain tissue. If the thought-forms were locked in brain tissue, there would be no communication on any level of consciousness.

Entities whom you attract and to whom you are attracted are resonating with similar geometric patterns in their auric fields. Thus, those so-called chance encounters are actually auric field resonances that are magnetizing and attracting an event. Together or in groups, the attractions are based upon double and multiple I-dentification. If you can actually abhor some of the thought-forms that you I-dentify with, you will abhor that part of yourself or the other entity or the group that you are attracted to because others may abhor the same things you abhor. So, too, what you love about yourselves, you love in others.

Questioner: Can the mind transmit and receive in different time frames?

MaYaRa: No. In reality, the receiver/transmitter operates simultaneously in the NOW moment. It is the space/time continuum of the thought-forms that create the illusion of a past/ future. The illusions of neurosis, psychosis and schizophrenia, for example, are a few of the conditions that result from I-dentification with living thought-forms that exist in the illusion of different time frames within the collective earth mind.

Questioner: Can you explain more about the "billboard" effect of thought-forms that reside in the auric field?

MaYaRa: The auric field which "displays" the thought-forms of each entity may first be grasped in the observations of what your psychologists understand as body language and the concomitant psychological descriptions associated with them. The day is fast approaching, however, when many will witness this energy field directly. At that point, there will be no need for the complicated and often misleading descriptions and categories as described by the altered-ego.

The resonant frequency of your earth has increased a great deal in the last decade and will continue to do so in geometric leaps of perception. Many of you have already glimpsed the auric field of other entities and objects.

ANIMAL AND HUMAN THOUGHT

Questioner: Since animals have smaller brains, is there a relationship between the size of the brain and the type of thought-forms, and do they also have auric fields?

MaYaRa: In our fourth dimensional exercises, described in Chapter 1, you radiated lines of light, infinitely, in 180 degree angles at a fixed distance from a center point in all directions, forming a sphere. This is more than mere mental gymnastics, however. It is the essential shape of all thought-form energies. The receiver function of mind apprehends thought-forms, thus perceiving objects. Animal awareness functions in the same manner. You shall soon discover that it is frequency and not volume that determines consciousness-awareness. The present infantile logic supporting the false axiom that larger brains equate to higher I.Q's shall be soon put to rest. Common sense will reveal that many animals with smaller brain capacity possess qualities of perception far superior to human counterparts. For example, the tiny bee brain makes inconceivable astronomical and environmental calculations, even under a clouded sky, while humans are easily lost on a freeway.

How does human thought differ from animal thought? Human thought is reflective and animal thought is refractive. In the animal kingdom, preconditioned thought-forms in a pure state are refracted through the auric field to give conditions for survival based upon the earth mind through electromagnetic fields of intelligence data, with little internal memory to confuse and interfere with the original transmissions.

The concept of the unique nature of human consciousness as being reflective is not new. However, as long as one regards thought as residing in the brain, the concept of reflection is fairly useless. Common sense once again interferes with a tidy explanation in terms of the altered-ego. All one can prove by conventional methods is that the human can remember more information – so can an elephant or even a spider. The concept of reflective thought is a good starting point for our examination because it evokes some key factors inherent in the meaning of the word "reflective."

The human mind differs in two ways. The overall resonating frequency of the auric field is higher, giving it the capacity to communicate with higher orders of intelligence and the brain has a larger capacity to retain memory as codified thought-form which can be accessed internally, rather than externally, as accomplished very adeptly by animal awareness.

Please take note of this crucial difference in the process of thought. While the increased size of the human brain results in greater storage of codified memory, this is not to be confused with thought processes. In other words, only blueprints of thought-forms are stored which can be stimulated in various ways to project during synaptic firings upon the auric field where the consciousness of the entire body resides. When codified thought-forms are thus projected against the auric shell, the body can relive in varying degrees a past event. If memory storage was synonymous with thought, all computers upon your earth would spontaneously develop DNA and out-multiply the lot of you.

The word "reflective" is appropriate for the obvious reason that in order to have a reflection, one must have a surface or dimension to reflect from. In the dimension of thought-forms, this surface is an electromagnetic shell of tension known as the auric field. This is produced by the sum of all energies, cosmic, planetary, and solar, which stream in and out of your personal point of existence, forming a field of equilibrium in the same way that a bubble forms a reflective membrane to equalize two opposing pressures.

Everything is alive and all material creation is a product of the electromagnetic polarities of active thought. Thus, every object of creation is a thought-form and has to some degree an auric field. Just as the skin of the bubble is composed of the soapy, raw material that seems to magically form a sphere, so too, does the auric field of every created object contain the same substance in rarefied form, seeking to form a sphere. All material objects are thought-forms crystallized in time. Even rocks are thought-forms and have an auric field. In summation then, we may state that auric fields are a collective body of radiating emanations that contain the totality of its composition in thought form.

Now we have established enough foundation to add another answer to your query pertaining to animal thought. Human thought differs from animal thought primarily in its capacity to see his own reflection in the auric field. The receiver portion of human mind receives trillions of thought-forms each moment from which certain preconditioned or magnetized thoughts, as codified memory, are ignited through resonance and added to the overall impulse. All of this is projected against the auric field which resonates with every harmonic of that conglomerate thought-form, striking it like a finger plucking a stringed instrument. The result is that a section of the auric field begins to glow brighter than the surrounding area. This may, in a limited sense, be likened to the electrons radiating against the phosphorescent material in your television tubes. The continuity of your daily lives is based on your receiver/transmitter functions of mind tuning into a specific area of the auric field which you define as reality.

The continuous focusing or tuning into that same area of your auric field, day after day, gives the illusion of space/time continuity. Every molecule, every mountain, pulsates as a wave, as does every thought-form that creates them. Thus, every auric field shares information with every other one, forming the cosmic tapestry of consciousness.

But to you personally, beloved entities, this truth is a most powerful revelation. For in each of your auric fields is the mirror image of the universe, although at present you choose to tune into one pinpoint of that universe which you call reality. However, the rest of the universe is there for the taking and creating. It is that close to you. You are that close to liberation at any given moment, if only you would begin to explore the treasures that you are.

You are preoccupied with the brain because you sense it as the major source of your problems. This is true in that the brain is the seat of codified thought-form, and it is readily seen that each of you has disturbing events codified in the memory banks which you constantly react to. However, the brain is not the seat of consciousness.

Realize then that your auric field is the fourth dimensional part of you. It is the part that contains all the information used in the Divine Process from which ALL is created. Therefore, ALL inventions, all progress, all solutions to all problems reside in your auric field. Your auric field is the fourth dimensional sounding-board of thought. It reflects the universe and you.

Questioner: If this is true, then how can one understand personality and its obvious inequalities; and if it is not a question of personality or innate ability, then why do so few discover new ideas?

MaYaRa: Let us reframe the second part of your query. In your earth terms there are no "new" ideas. Everything IS created. Thus, there are only qualities of knowing by degrees: Ignorance, Faith, and Wisdom. The arrogance of the altered-ego comes from the belief that it uniquely possesses knowledge. How can this be, beloved, when all is given to you already and all you need do is work to reclaim your heritage by opening to the genius within?

Personality is a direct function of I-dentification. You are who you think you are, and are not all that you could be simply because your receiver/transmitter tunes only to the area and set of energy patterns in a fraction of your auric field, preconditioned through the magnetism of memory. Remember that the Divine Pro-cess works as a sine wave and must push/pull frequencies of thought-forms through themselves. In other words, personality is a feedback loop or circuit which is focused on a narrow bandwidth along the auric field and connected to the constellations. Over time, this produces a crystallization of frequencies, entrapping you in a web of artificial memory and forming the inertia that retards your true evolution. This is why you must incarnate so many times. Unfortunately, this grip of "personality," as you term it, can only be dislodged by a severe shock through any number of life's traumatic scenarios.

The seemingly "gifted few" are a result of a combination of past-life preconditioning, environmental impact and training, which can deeply ingrain a more automatic pattern of consciousness. We shall examine past-life preconditioning more fully in Chapter 10. Suffice it to say that the conventional view of psychology toward environmental impact cannot begin to explain the so-called supernatural, paranormal, and scores of extradimensional phenomenon.

Throughout the ages, great Masters have taught that all embody the potential for Master-hood regardless of station in life; but alas, that teaching has reverted to yet another three dimensional hierarchy, manipulated by a selected few.

Those of you reading this document are presumed literate and even intellectual. Make no mistake, beloved, the Genius Frequency is equally available to all. It is the Great Pleasure of THE ONE to create roads and ways beyond number that lead back to infinite Light and Love. Be assured that creation is designed for ALL to exist in joy, prosperity and freedom, as co-creators of the same.

Questioner: Do thought-forms exist only within the auric field; and if so, how can they be transmitted at great distances, if each auric field resides so close to each individual?

MaYaRa: Please forgive our preponderance to digress, but your queries indicate that much background material is needed before a true understanding is gleaned.

The answer to the first part of your query is simply, no. To even examine the function of thought is a function of consciousness-awareness. The auric field IS awareness. Thus, every form of creation has some degree of awareness which magnetizes thought-forms of like frequency.

You may regard the human auric field as a special organ of fourth dimensional mind due to its higher resonant frequency. Your brain is a three-dimensional storage device that orchestrates the primal memory banks as it channels various energy fields for purposes of building, maintaining and harmonizing the vast complexities of the social organizations of organs, forming the vehicle through which higher intelligence may evolve earth minds. Let us continue laying the foundations of this study for the purposes of understanding the workings of thought-forms as living entities. You will see what power is within every entity.

The auric field is a four-dimensional lens, as the eye is a three-dimensional lens. Therefore, it would be inappropriate to regard the objects perceived by the eye as residing only in its fluidic chamber or created within the optic nerve. Thus, it would be inappropriate to say that thought-forms reside only within the auric field. A thought-form can occupy infinite numbers of auric fields simultaneously, as an object can occupy infinite numbers of eyes that perceive it. Therefore, it is not accurate to say that thought-forms reside anywhere. They are fourth-dimensional objects. In fact, they are everywhere – the universe is made of them.

Unlike a three-dimensional object, thought-forms are living entities. You are, in fact, a collection of living thought-forms. The laws and mechanics of procreation are as valid for thought-forms as are the myriad life-forms that reproduce into the splendor of your world. LIFE BEGETS LIFE, THOUGHT-FORMS BEGET THOUGHT-FORMS. You may always be assured, beloved, that whatever you witness in the physical realms has an exact parallel in perfect synchronicity to all other realms. Just as life-forms produce, reproduce and evolve new life-forms in a proclivity of abundance, so too, thought-forms expand and grow, craving life. It is one of the primary laws of THE ONE CREATOR, powered by Divine Love and existing in GOD-MIND. In the LAW-OF-ONE, all thought-forms are destined to recapitulate the entire process of creation. How could it be otherwise, beloved? There is no other process. But there are many artificially created subdivisions of the Original Impulse.

All of this indicates the tremendous responsibility of a co-creator with the inherent powers to create and perpetuate thought-forms, which inevitably manifest as life-forms. Your ancient teachings are full of methods and warnings about how to discipline the mind in a virtual ocean of thought-forms, and what will occur if these methods are not practiced.

These teachings are born of practicality from living in a three-dimensional material dimension, which traps thought-forms in its powerful electromagnetic field of gravity. If the thoughts of an embodied entity had no bearing upon one's destiny, there would have been no reason whatever to devote so much time and energy to this facet of the teaching. Let us now review some simple mathematics regarding thought-forms and perhaps you will agree that you have a significant role to play in the consciousness of your planet.

The average human produces and/or incubates some 50,000 thought-forms per day. Quite a progeny for a day's work! This works out to some 18 million thought-forms per year. Now, contemplate that some six-billion humans are embodied presently within the earth plane. Since even science has to admit that energy is mass and that thinking requires energy, it becomes rather obvious that the energy must be converting into mass on some level of reality. The serious nature of this reality and its power to manifest conditions upon your earth cannot be ignored. Its potential for the worst imaginable disaster or the most beautiful and joyful existence the earth has ever known becomes an individual/global choice! Your world will change, one thought-form at a time.

The state of mind of most humans upon your plane at this time, with your greatly expanded world view, is to slump into the posture of apathy, helplessness and fear, while the Light of THE ONE radiates from the centers of each one of you, overflowing and pouring forth into the world the raw material of Light which you, by your own choice, expend as you fashion it into living thought-forms, creating the reality that you witness and experience each moment – thought-forms that you continually project onto the field of awareness that reflects what you think the world is – thus becoming the world.

So if you entertain the notion that there is nothing that you can do to improve your life and the condition of the world, think again! Pay attention to what you are creating as a co-creator – 18 million thought-forms per year. Each is a living entity that you have incubated and imbued with the free Light of THE ONE bestowed to you, berthed into the flow of life through the birth canal of your transmitter, which pulsates the glow of that thought-form in your auric field. This, in turn, resonates and ignites all similar thought-forms in every other auric field through the extremely low frequencies of earth resonances. What are you thinking, beloved entities? What are you giving birth to? What do you I-dentify with? Helpless indeed!

Each of you operates a powerful mind in the fourth dimension, regardless of your level of consciousness. Join with us in thought for the liberation of all suffering. That is all we ask. Your thought-forms are alive. This is not merely an esoteric exercise. It is a Divine Process, which every co-creator shares, regardless that many are blind to the power of THE ONE in self.

You can prove this if you choose to take responsibility. You do not need a book. Open your hearts to the brilliant power that each of you are. There is so much that you can do. Tune into the Genius Frequency, and all life will be yours again. Do not wait for agreements from a darkened society. Your brothers and sisters need your help – your thought-forms of love, healing and forgiveness. It matters not whether you are famous. It matters not what you have done before. It matters not if you are *in* a position of power. You ARE the position of power.

The Golden Rule of living is not an idle philosophy. It is the law of the fourth dimension. The fourth dimension is the mirror reflecting thought-forms as blueprints of life to be. Thinking precedes doing. Think unto others the Love and healing and forgiveness, and the rest shall follow. Be selective in what thought-forms you give your portion of the life force to. Take responsibility for the thought-forms you project to others, for they are also reflected back into your being through the mirror of the auric field. The justifications for hatred are totally unfounded, artificial, and can only reflect back to the inner soul of the doer, the thinker of those thoughts.

A grand cycle of the stars is closing and a new one being born. Awaken from your slumbers and co-create your new world. Your influence is significant. Any thought-form that you create or incubate through I-dentification is transmitted with quantum forces through the addition of new frequencies of Light pouring into your solar system at this moment.

I-dentify with your true natures of LOVE-LIGHT/ GOD-MIND and your thought-forms will heal and strengthen the world and reflect back into your body/soul the same. The fate of your earth family, the children of the earth hangs in the balance.

In the beginning was the Thought. From the Thought came the Light. From the Light came the Word. And from the Word came Form. You cannot live the principles of Divine Process if you are creating and incubating thought-forms of judgments and fear. These reflect into your body, pitting you against yourself as the monstrous face of hypocrisy looms and jeers at you from the mirror of your world. Then how shall you escape your self?

So start from the beginning, the PRIMAL CAUSE of all creation. Create and sustain thought-forms that resonate with the power and life force of THE ONE and all will follow, to your most exquisite surprise. And know that you are not alone. As you awaken you shall meet more co-creators. There are far more than you realize.

HEART OF HEARTS

"THE TRANSFORMER"

*"Cosmic knowingness
is yours for the taking by opening to
the Genius Frequency of
unlimited thought."*

Questioner: There are thousands of books on the subject of chakras or the seven energy points in the body. Can you add to this information, and would it be appropriate to single out any one of
these points as the most important?

MaYaRa: This query is the most amazing thus far, in that it asks
us to recapitulate and reiterate some 10,000 years of teachings in a
few pages. It is rarely the "facts" that achieve true knowledge,

beloved, but rather the process of thought which opens minds to a higher frequency of understanding.

We begin our digression much like your archaeologists, who must dig through much undesirable material before an artifact of revelation presents itself. We have discussed briefly the reflective nature of the human mind, the seat of perception and thought, as it functions within the auric field. Let us now further examine the refractive nature of mind, common to the animal and insect world as well as the human.

The knowledge we may "add to" this subject is, to view it in a more unified perspective, a more holistic vision. Therefore, it is paramount to perceive these "chakras" not as energy points or vortices but as seven complete minds possessing receiver/transmitting (or what we term transceiver) functions with the capacity to act independently, as well as in concert.

It is for the above reasons that communication with Higher Intelligence is considerably dimmed when your consciousness-awareness processes low frequency thought-forms. That is, what was once pure consciousness in a free state, must be divided into separate functions of awareness of that consciousness, while simultaneously compressed into a thought-form which reflects aspects of THE ONE. In other words, a price is paid in order to individualize that free consciousness by dividing it into itself, in the Divine Process of manifesting THE ONE into Many Ones.

It has always been known by the Masters that the fantastic scheme of creation is the ultimate act of infinite Love by THE ONE; and "risky business," as you would term it, for the many, who could get quite lost, in their own sense of power given to them out of that Love. Yet the rewards far outweighed the risks. In addition, an ultimate fail-safe mechanism was created, known to the ancients as the Alpha/Omega Program of Redemption.

In our earlier exercise, you created four directions with only two lines. Then you added only one more line to produce six directions. And by placing yourself in the center, rather than at the outside of the spinning wheel, you suddenly apprehended fourth dimensional thinking. From this perspective, it was much easier to understand the awareness of consciousness, as perceived by the reflection of thought. As you study your chakras, use this method to examine the true nature of each center.

Mind is a holistic process. That is, if you refract or divide it, it does not become a part of a whole, but rather it becomes a replica of the whole. Therefore, each chakra is a complete mind unto itself, fully capable of independent receiver/transmitter functions, yet with the inherent and powerful capacity to work in concert with the larger organism or mind.

When you reflect a part of the whole (mind), however, you only perceive a fragment or partial equation of the whole. Thus, as we stated earlier (Chapter 2), the animal kingdom, being primarily refractive mind, exists in a very pure state as it must exist in the holistic microcosm of Divine Mind. However, the human kingdom, existing primarily as a reflective mind, can exhibit all sorts of violations due to its preconditioned tendency to focus on only part of its reflection. That was not the original plan, however. By no means does this suggest that the animal kingdom is superior to the human creation – although the purity of the animal awareness has been worshipped by many cultures. Only the reflective mind is capable of co-creation and was the greatest gift of love given to man.

With the above information in mind, we shall refer to the chakras as mind-centers. Each of these mind-centers is complete unto itself; and together, these are connected to, and form the auric field through color bands of intelligent energy frequencies. Actually, there are eight mind-centers plus four that operate in even higher dimensions of consciousness. However, we shall concentrate on the eight since most earth dwellers focus on the first three.

Each mind operates on a frequency of thought with a corresponding color and sound. Thus, the human consciousness embodiment is based on the octave, each mind-center being one note of that octave and each note being composed also of an octave, and so on. Together, these mind-centers compose the over-all tone or frequency and color of the auric field, determining the quantity of awareness and the quality of consciousness, depending upon how you have developed them. We shall further expand this subject from various perspectives later in this segment. We should like to concentrate now upon the second part of your query concerning the relative importance of the mind-centers as they pertain to the human scenario.

We may begin by considering that the ultimate completion of an evolving being in the earth realm is its ascension, whereby the entire being physically, mentally and spiritually is transformed or quantized into an extremely high Light frequency. This cannot be accomplished unless the entity fine-tunes every mind-center to its highest and purest pitch. The ancient Far Eastern teachings are quite accurate in tracing the movements of energy through a proper evolution. However, much confusion remains as a result of the ritual and dogma centered around the religious institutions which may speak the truth, albeit with the unfortunate addendum that each is the one and only way back to THE ONE. In light of this earth-realm situation, we should like to stress the area or mind-center that contains the key to achieving this evolution in your present space/time.

You will find in the Far Eastern teachings, a stress laid upon the sixth and seventh mind-centers corresponding to the medulla oblongata and the pineal gland or third eye area. Our purpose is not to argue the validity of the teaching, for it is quite correct in that it designates these areas as primary transducers of cosmic energy which scale down the frequencies for distribution through the spinal network. However, for all intents and purposes, we view this as "putting the cart before the horse," as you term it. The teachings quite correctly diagram the movement of energy, or as we term it, the ascension of frequencies through the octaves of consciousness.

However, in the many perspectives of the modern intellect, stress has been laid upon the "mystic" areas of the brain, rather than the balance of harmonics so necessary to awaken the dormant functions of these splendid organs of perception. Thus, in your age, mankind, for the most part, wishes to skip a step or two with the hope of passing the competition in an apparent race to enlightenment. Thus, in this segment of our document, we shall shed what light we can upon the entire octave of mind-centers, while stressing THE most important note to be sung, as it were, in the octave of your evolving consciousness.

That note is the fourth mind-center located near the heart. From this point forward, little that is news to you will be revealed, and this is precisely why work needs to be accomplished in this area of your lives. Man is moving with such incredible speed through consciousness programs, in this the final chapter of the Omega cycle, that the most recent teachings on this subject, as revealed by the Master, Christ Jesus, seem to you passé. Mankind is anxious to get on with it – to the "high tech" part of the teachings – so that he may fire up his third eye, so to speak, and blast off for parts unknown and come back to start another religion.

Now, this is not a religious document, by any means. It is a metaphysical compilation of insights, designed to open the doors of perceptions through the use of seven levels of understanding, via a most rigid beast known as the intellect. It is an exceedingly difficult and challenging task, for which we are joyful to be of service. Perhaps we may reach some of you. Reaching even one would be great cause for celebration – that is how precious and important this work is. Thus, we shall push onward, using the greatest truths, from wherever they may be found, to weave a tapestry of light for your benefit and ours.

As we proceed, lay aside all thought-forms of limitation and confusion, so that you may learn what you seek. Lay aside the polarized thought-forms of church and state, for the truth that sets you free is everywhere about you and within you. As we proceed, we ask you to fully open the mind-center of your heart, for that is the mind-center that we shall address with emphasis. The final result is that each individual must experientially discover the great cosmic truths that will liberate all suffering. No religion, no government, no book, no embodied or disembodied entity can do it for you; nor should this ever occur, for it would be a false enlightenment.

There is no need to encumber the data processing of your receiver/transmitter with lengthy proofs concerning the validity of the heart as power point and seed crystal of Divine Process, a compressed thought-form in a pure state, providing the primal, sustaining pulse of Love. Suffice it to say that even the most pragmatic, common sense approach reveals a source of energy with a life of its own as evidenced by the fact that any other organ of life may be damaged or removed, including 90% of the brain, and yet survive. However, without the heart, only a few seconds of organic life are sustained.

Questioner: Could you explain how our technology has demonstrated brief success in mechanical heart implants and transplants, and how this relates to the heart as an energy source?

MaYaRa: The brief success that you describe is just that: brief. For a three-dimensional understanding that views the heart as merely a pump, is in itself faulty. In the early aeons of evolution, the heart, as you now know it, did not exist; for if there is anything to be termed a pump, it is the lungs and not the heart.

In the primordial mists of time, the movements of the expanding and contracting lungs sufficiently moved and oxygenated the blood by hydraulic displacement and convection currents. With the rapid cooling of the earth's atmosphere and new energy requirements needed to propel the body from danger (after the "fall"), the organ of the heart, once a large gland sensitive to the concentration of life force centered there, began to enlarge under the strain, and eventually assumed a function to assist the now laboring mechanism of breath.

We point this out so you may better understand that what we understand as "the heart" is a point of Divine Mind power centered there, which is the original mind-center containing the mental attributes of Divine Process in its purest state. Because it was a mind-center, rather than a pump, made of flesh, that pulses the life you have come to know in material reality, we advise that no machine implanted there can ever have lasting benefit due to the interference of the wave harmonics generated by the remaining seed crystal.

In order to avoid confusion in our visualizations we shall term the true point of life giving power as the Heart of Hearts so that it is not regarded merely as muscle tissue - although the study of the physical heart proves a most fascinating subject and actually supports what we are about to set forth. Let us now sketch an overview of the seven mind-centers before we concentrate upon the Heart of Hearts.

Each of the seven mind-centers is a complete, thinking entity with a specialized awareness, special duties to perform, a history of its own particular evolution, a memory bank, a communications system capable of transmitting as well as receiving data and thought-forms, and its own defined area of the total auric field of the individual, giving it the capacity to be aware of itself and its environment. Now, this may seem fantastic to you, but as you develop your abilities to use the Genius Frequency, you shall discover even more fantastic truths.

Each mind-center is powered and sustained by a specific frequency of the Divine Ray. You are, in fact, a multi-channelled energy station that houses seven complete mind-centers of functional awareness, each being a receiver/transmitter matrix of sentient intelligence. It would be accurate to liken each mind-center to a galaxy within the totality of a universe: your being. Hopefully, the material thus far has at least begun to make clear the tremendous gaps in understanding through your traditional medical sciences. One can dissect tissue until the end of time, but until the true nature of mind is understood, there shall be no lasting cures with these primitive methods.

Each of these mind-centers are tuned to a bandwidth of frequencies streaming into them from Universal Mind. What makes the mind center of the Heart of Hearts so powerful and special is that it is tuned to the Primary Frequency, termed by you as Love. In other words, your heart has a mind of its own, composed of a seed crystal of the pure primordial Light of THE ONE. Each of the other mind-centers are specialized through certain sub-harmonics and ultra-harmonics of the octave of creation, which form your bio-organism and its other dimensional bodies of light.

It may become clear at this point that the tuning of any of your mind-centers to a purpose that excludes this Primary Frequency results in entropy and decay in the area of receivership. Therefore, the denial of this Frequency within the mind-center of the Heart of Hearts results in the attraction of yet more destructive thought-forms, even though the heart lovingly continues to supply the life impulse to the very thought-forms that may eventually destroy its local process.

Likewise, the denial of love of self, transmitted as thought-forms of self-hatred (or hatred of others – it is the same), clouds and blocks the life giving nourishment to the heart muscle from the Seed Crystal resonator. It is a curiosity, indeed, that you refer to this as a "heart attack," as if it is the heart that does the attacking. It is the entity who attacks the heart through the summoning of destructive thought-forms from the other mind-centers. This process may work in the same manner for each mind-center and the results form the platform for either health or disease. You can now see, beloved, that even organic life is a study in mind, rather than tissue.

You see, Love can neither be limited to a type of moral conduct, nor can it be dismissed as a romantic inclination. Neither can it be limited to a fraternal or maternal instinctual drive carried over from the primates, although the latter is perhaps closer to the truth in that it reflects a relatively pure form of the life impulse frequency. It is unfortunate that rarely is an attempt made to be objective or scientific when defining the term Love.

Due to the tremendous power of this life force and its all-pervading, omnipotent qualities, its definition remains elusive and, at best, is described as an aftermath of emotional thought-forms, which it evokes. Unfortunately, most of these thought-forms are tainted by opposing forces of polarities inherent in material creation. Thus, a redefinition is in order.

Love is a Divine, Universal, Cosmic energy principle, a primordial still point, through which the electric polarities of creation interchange, reverse, and begin again renewed. If there was ever anything in the universe that was taken for granted and only superficially understood, it is the frequency of Love. All of this becomes clear when you open to the Genius Frequency. LOVE HAS NO OPPOSITE! Therefore, Love has no beginning, nor has it an end, nor has it death.

But a definition in a book is only an abstract, a guidepost at best. By all means, contemplate it. As you do, the obvious proofs will begin to open your eyes. Think. Feel. Your heart contracts and expands to the rhythm of an ongoing, independent power that manifests as both polarities, yet is neither. It takes no sides, for if it did, life would cease. And even when one heart stops beating, the Power does not stop, for hearts continue to beat forever.

The frequency of Love is a continuous catalyst for the impulse of life, though it is reduced to the sub-harmonics of the earth's biosphere, which is presently leaving its entropic half-life function and entering a centropic wave-form of "a new heavens and a new earth." This greatest of Powers even supports those life forms indifferent to its profound reality. What greater power can there be!

It is time for an exercise. We feel that this segment of our message is so profoundly important that we shall change our format temporarily. Thus far, we have designed the format of this material to engage the reader to use his or her intellect as a key to opening the other mind-centers. We appeal now directly to your Heart of Hearts, asking that your intellect merely follow along openly. Read, and if you are distracted for any reason during the reading, start over and try it again so that you retain the entire exercise as one thought-form.

We are going to journey into the fourth dimension to find the greatest of jewels, the Heart of Hearts. This is not in any way a fairy tale. What we describe to you in this passage is the way we perceive a human body in this dimension. Relax. Ready?

As you read this, gently monitor your body posture, checking for any kinks or strains. Start with the skin. Notice any excess pressures and, if necessary, loosen any restrictive clothing.

Next, monitor the musculature. If you discover any tension, massage the area gently with your fingertips. Fingertips of every entity emit high frequency healing rays. In this moment, your heart is pumping vital energy into your hands and out your fingertips. Use them like combs to smooth the energy field around your body, recycling the radiations of that frequency called Love back into the system. Your auric field begins to glow more radiantly as the harmonics of the healing frequency smooth out some of the tangled lines of light.

Go deeper, now. Let your consciousness explore the remarkable creation within you. Remember when you were a child and you were enthralled with nature, awestruck by the massive beauty of the trees, knowing somehow that they are alive and they love and protect. You have four trees within you made from the same blueprint. Go deeper. Examine the four trees within you: the arterial; the veinal, the lymphatic, and the respiratory. Trees of Life. Rivers of Life. All the trees are made of light. Think of that. All the trees are made of light.

Notice that the trees are glowing in different color spectrums and they radiate this light throughout your body. You are now seeing in the fourth dimension. You even have access to the fifth dimension. There is an additional source of light inside your body – like a forest on a summer morning. Notice the morning light streaming through the branches of these intertwining trees. The trees and its branches radiate their own light. You are enthralled by this awesome creation.

As your new vision adjusts to more subtle detail, you notice transparent, iridescent light where there would normally be shadows. Even these iridescent areas pulsate with each surge of Life Force generated from the area of your heart. Looking deeper, you focus on the branches now. You see liquid rainbows coursing through thousands of rivers that branch into millions of tributaries that branch further into billions of tiny multicolored, glistening lakes, like an endless landscape of jewels. They are moving like water as they wash against the underside of your skin.

You are floating through this incredible universe of life and light. You stop, now and then, to gaze. Everything is functioning perfectly. You notice that it is far more beautiful than even a tropical rain forest or the most impeccably maintained botanical garden.

As your new senses adjust to the fourth dimension, you notice that each hue, as it shimmers, generates its own light; it also generates an accompanying sound-tone. These sound-tones hum and blend into a soft cacophony of shifting harmonies as they exchange, one with another, corresponding colors and harmonics like oceans of stringed instruments.

You begin to notice, as you float through this wonderland, that there is an area within you where the sound and light emanations originate. You become aware of a source within you, beckoning you with an irresistible attraction. You begin to float towards it, through this incredible garden of light. Nearing the source, you begin to see powerful golden rays that crisscross, penetrating the spaces between the iridescent colors like a crystal sun penetrating the canopy of a rain forest: single and multiple rays streaming through the branches, forming thousands of cathedral windows pouring dappled light patterns upon the surrounding trees. Floating closer to the source multiplies this effect geometrically, and the sound is filling your senses.

You are aware of your location as you move toward the heart area. Suddenly, you move out of the thick, luminescent forest into a clearing where you witness the most spectacular sight, sound, and feelings emanating from a swirling sphere of light. You are overwhelmed with euphoric feelings and irresistibly drawn toward the sphere of undying light, which is a thousand times brighter than the sun. Exhilarated, you realize that the light does not hurt your eyes. You sense that its power is unlimited as you are bathed in the most beautiful, powerful love and affection you have ever imagined.

The radiations of this frequency are irresistible. It beckons you to enter its sphere of nourishing affection and total security.

You find it impossible to believe that you can feel any more joyous and loved than you do this moment, yet the feeling increases as you float into the sphere of light. You are carried and surrounded and permeated with healing sounds calling to you from the center, the source. The desire to move to the source of this sound is overwhelming. Moving into the center, you begin to hear even more symphonies and choirs playing and singing indescribable songs of lifegiving energy.

At that moment, the door to the inner chamber slides away, revealing a brilliant, pulsating, crystalline center. You can't resist the feeling of well-being, affection, welcome, and the rapture of it all, as you glide into the chamber. For an eternal moment, you become one with this celebrating star-birth of love, light and wisdom.

Tears of joy suddenly stream from your eyes, cascading into liquid rainbows as you remember how it all started – your true origins embrace you. For the first time in so many, many lifetimes, you remember your connection to All-There-Is. The power is awesome. You feel like a great star breathing life-giving power into your planetary children. You can't believe how you could have forgotten this splendor, this connection to all life, and it to you.

From within this chamber of life, you see the relationship of this source of life to your heart. You see how your heart is the first joyful recipient of the immense and loving power that you are now experiencing first hand, and you sense that it dances to the rhythms of this source, rather than beating. You sense that it lives forever. You are filled with powerful feelings of praise and thankfulness for all that you are, for all that has been given you.

Sensing an opening above you opens a new feeling of connection to all of humanity. You can't wait to bring the news of this discovery to all those beating hearts upon planet earth who forgot their origins and the power that lies within them, calling for a celebration of life. Moving up through the opening into your wind pipe, you bring the news as you radiate light, healing and purifying everything in your path. Arriving in the area of your brain, you bathe it in the healing light still emanating from your consciousness. Your pineal gland senses the powerful, nourishing rays of the light and begins to blossom like a flower in the long-awaited spring initiation into life, spilling the sweet nectar of awareness into the brain and it, too, begins to remember how it all began.

As you continue to ascend to the top of your head, you arrive at a golden pyramidal gateway that only opens in the presence of the high quality, life-giving light that you carry. Emerging from the majestic gate, you glimpse your earth and all life upon it with new eyes. You see a tree glowing in multi-colored raiment, seeing the same energy matrix of frequencies that you experienced in your body. You see that the tree did not produce it, rather it grew into its matrix just as you grew into yours. Rest for a few minutes in this feeling and awareness, and give thanks for the life of all.

You have just visited the Heart of Hearts. May you never walk in the feeling of loneliness and hatred again. Use this exercise upon retiring for the night or upon rising or any time during the day. Try this every day for seven days and the results will astound you. Although you relied heavily upon your imagination to visualize, there shall come a moment soon in your time that you will truly experience it. By imagining, you are preparing for the reality of the experience.

If you have ever wondered what energy powers your heart to perform the Herculean task of moving tons of life-giving fluids through your body every day, relentlessly, without sleep – now you know it is the Heart of Hearts. Notice it more often and realize that every single entity carries this Light, regardless of their choosing to deny it. Work with this mind-center consciously and you may heal yourself and others, for ALL healing springs from this well. The Heart of Hearts is the well, the Divine Spark within each of you.

Contemplate the form of your heart. It is no accident that it resembles an inverted pyramidal structure. The form follows the function of the spiraling pyramidal energy dynamics that power it, while adapting perfectly to the organic needs of the entire system. In the heart, the principles of the receiver/transmitter are easiest to see: expansion/contraction; receiving/transmitting; a unification of polarities that echoes the LAW-OF-ONE that emanates from and IS the Infinite Point of LOVE-LIGHT/GOD-MIND.

Questioner: I can see how the heart is a receiver/transmitter. But can you explain further how it is a mind-center or thinking mechanism?

MaYaRa: Now, first let us examine an overview of the functions of five of your seven mind-centers. We are reviewing five for the reason that the first five chakras, or mind-centers are directly connected to and have parallel physical attributes. In addition, we shall continue to refer to the total electro-physical system of the body as a bio-computer. The primary reasoning behind this is that the intellect can accept this "technical" approach with minimum resistance – considering that the majority of intellects are stuck in the limiting attitude that it knows what it knows and cannot know what it doesn't.

We have the outstanding challenge of proving, via the intellect, that it knows more than it thinks that it knows. We shall start with the following digression to clarify the inherent flaw in the intellectual process which blocks the proper understanding to the answer which you seek. For all of you already know the answers. However, it takes certain combinations of thought-forms on various levels to trigger that knowing. Thus, in actuality, we supply the new mental patterns, the template; and you supply the answers.

Now, the altered-ego screens information pouring into it. This screen is the intellect. One of the distortions that it creates is that it shouldn''t trust any thought-form with which it is not already familiar, regardless that such a thought-form may liberate it from suffering and confusion. This is restrictive feedback that forms a closed loop, precluding the expansion of awareness that could lead to further consciousness evolution.

The fact is that each mind-center receives, processes, and transmits data and thought-forms to the other mind-centers through the medium of the auric field, so that vast amounts of knowledge are available to form the awareness of the totality of your being. In other words, it is already there, waiting to be accessed. You do not have to look "out there" to some distant horizon to find the answer to any questions. Your mind-centers are like portals of multidimensional awareness eagerly processing universal data, waiting for the access code to admit them into your consciousness. This is analogous to the computer which will not yield information within its program unless proper access codes are entered.

Taking the analogy of the prism again, we shall demonstrate how and why the frequencies from the life sustaining Universal Mind are divided spectrally as they enter the organism. However, this is more than an analogy. The mind-centers or chakras are indeed a prism, dividing the spectrum frequencies of Universal Light into sub-spectrum intelligence.

All of these spectrum-frequencies are intelligently aware – they are intelligence as energy. Therefore, wherever this intelligence is concentrated, (i.e. the mind-centers of your biocomputer), there exists a point of thinking – intelligent awareness. In your physical system of intelligence, the seat of this mind is the Heart of Hearts. The seed crystal of life is located there. Therefore the seat of intelligence is the Heart of Hearts. All other mind-centers depend upon this point of power for their survival in the physical, as well as other, dimensions.

You may ask why all this complexity is necessary. Why the division of The Ray into all these component parts as material manifestations of THE ONE. Creation is designed to share the infinite Love of THE ONE. To accomplish the realization of this awesome gift of life and realization of the Joy of THE ONE, to fully realize IT and live IT and focus IT in a self-conscious, individualized awareness of IT, and to be a co-creator with IT, thereby sharing totally in IT, is to fully understand the nuances and aspects of THE ONE.

The purpose of your transmitters is to add your own spectral energies to the Spectral Emanations of THE ONE, and transmit these back into the universe for THE ONE to rejoice in, which in turn sends even greater spectral emanations of joy back to the co-creator; and so on, forever. The surplus generated by this process is used in creating more universes to create more life and so on, forever. It is the most beautiful plan imaginable, is it not? Are you not yet realizing that you are far more important to the Creator than you previously thought? Indeed, you are. You co-create by your very existence.

The information that we have outlined in the preceding segment of this document regarding thought-forms should take on new depth with a greater understanding of the seven mind-centers. You can now comprehend that creating and incubating thought-forms, a function of mind, is multiplied to the seventh power. That is, each mind-center, being a mind unto itself, is capable of creating and incubating thought-forms. For example, the sexual mind-center magnetizes, holds and transmits thought-forms of that quality and frequency, while the third mind-center of the "will" can incubate and transmit thought-forms of manipulation and control. Each mind-center can magnetize thought-forms separately and together.

Understand beloved, this can only occur due to the free will given by THE ONE to the co-creators. And for all the blame laid upon THE ONE for creating such a miserable world, the truth of the matter is that the co-creators would like to shirk their responsibility for having bungled such a perfect plan. You may see then that there is no wrath of God. There is only the upsetting of the critical balance of such a finely-tuned system, created by those who sought glory for themselves through control over others. It is that simple. Undoing the mess is not so simple because so many dimensions of life are thrown off balance: any corrections made to one dimension from on high, without surgical precision, can annihilate large portions of the universe.

Questioner: Knowing your preponderance to digress, I would like to ask for what purpose, then, is free will?

MaYaRa: May we suggest that the preponderance of which you speak is largely due to the nature of the question asked. At times we perceive one query surrounded by an additional ten, and we attempt to answer as many as possible, regardless of whether you are aware of them.

However, together we might restrain ourselves somewhat in deference to your editor, who may at this point consider the launching of this manuscript, airborne into the adjoining room. All editorial considerations aside, beloved, you may ask as many questions as you please on any subject, and we shall be joyful in trying to make them fit.

Now as to the query regarding "free will," we perceive it is born of a compassionate attempt to second guess mass-consciousness and you are quite correct in assuming that this type of question enjoys the popularity of confusion. So we trust that you will not be "put out" as you term it, if we fairly assault this viewpoint. It is strictly academic and is one question in a large array of moot points generated by third dimensional thinking.

Before the God-Mind of THE ONE contemplated ITSELF, there was no universe as we know it. Therefore, there were no entities existing to agree or disagree with existence. You see the futile reasoning behind the question? THE ONE CREATOR created the universe from the substance of DIVINE THOUGHT.

What else could the universe be made of? Since every particum of energy-matter is literally made of the same Divine Substance (then), without free will, THE CREATOR could only create puppets and machines, which would hardly be a Divine Plan.

The Divine Plan of THE ONE, then, is to send portions of ITSELF to develop into an independent likeness of ITSELF, unified by the LAW-Of-ONE, which is the singular, Causative Factor creating ALL-THAT-IS in the first place. Free will is the only way to guarantee this unified independence. THE ONE CREATOR is not a puppet or puppeteer. Each unit of ITS consciousness in the form of creation possesses the same qualities as THE ONE in micro-scale. Therefore ITS creation cannot be puppets. Is this enough for you at this time, beloved?

Questioner: Yes. Thank you. It was a difficult question to answer.

MaYaRa: Recall that you requested through contemplation to have your questions answered. You did not request to know what questions to ask. However, we are making excellent progress thus far. Remember that all is connected, all energy, all thought-forms. Thus, any question will lead back to THE ONE eventually. You have chosen a most difficult task, beloved. Asking questions is far more difficult than answering them, for the latter is always inherent in the former.

Each of you micro-universes has the answers to questions yet unasked. When you feel confused, in the vise-grip of the limited altered-ego, go to that place: your Heart of Hearts, where the perpetual masterpiece of creation is playing and singing and dancing and painting and sculpting the sublime existence of abundance and prosperity and joy, in the original thought-form of LOVE-LIGHT/GOD-MIND, which is your beginning and answer, without, end to all questions. Permit us this further digression and watch how it finds its way back to the fundamental question at hand. For the analytical process is intellect. It is not mind. It is a product of a fragmented altered-ego, a portion of the mind connected to physical process.

Your studies have shown you that just one of the cells of your body contains enough information to replicate an entire body, down to the last hair upon your head. You may liken yourself to a cell of your universe. Therefore, you do indeed carry all of the information necessary to create another one. There is nothing that your universe can do or be, that you cannot do or be. This is a profound truth. Cosmic knowingness is yours for the taking by opening to the Genius Frequency of unlimited thought. Do not waste your precious time and cause pain to your being by judging yourself with the limited altered-ego.

Just as one cell contains the information of the entire body, so too, each particum of light of each subdivision of the Divine Ray from GOD-MIND contains all information of creation. It is only the angle of perception that differs. Therefore, each of your seven mind-centers thinks. Each possesses all of the information contained in your universe, yet focused through a special lens of perception which utilizes a certain color of the Divine Ray for purposes of maintaining its contribution to that creation. The great advantage of your prismatic natures is that each of you can Know THE ONE in seven different ways, in seven different dimensions at the same time.

This leads to another big question. Why were you created and why on earth? You were created through the desire of THE ONE to share in the joy of creation. The decision to imbue flesh and blood organisms, products of local creations, with power of Divine Consciousness was yours! It was never the intention of THE ONE to entrap the Divine Sparks of consciousness, so loving-ly created, into such a limited expression.

But free will that "short circuits" the process of creation is free will without restriction. The results were quite messy indeed.

Thus, the promise was made to rescue that portion who elected to engage in and failed this dangerous experiment. However, certain procedures are first necessary so that other dimensions of creation are not destroyed just to isolate a renegade group. Be that as it may, the final result is that those who transcend this powerful entrapment are forged with an additional strength of spirit that could not otherwise be accomplished. In other words, you may use this situation to develop very special honors indeed. At any rate, you are doomed to succeed.

Thus, a very unique situation has been created whereby the entrapment of consciousness in matter affords the opportunity for a "hands on" experience of unequaled rewards. Mankind is in a unique position to directly imbue elemental matter with the Light of THE ONE, which your very existence accomplishes in every breath. You may walk upon the earth and consecrate from within every molecule and species of creation. In short, the fine opportunity is yours to create perfection from imperfection. Another benefit is that only with your earth bodies can you witness and directly participate in the splendor of nature as a husband and friend to its forces. Through your earth bodies, you can focus the Divine Ray upon the elements and transmute them into the Higher Light that is unique and imperishable.

Consciousness thus imbued with the blood of the earth creates the effect of light striking water and is prismatically divided into spectrum frequencies, dividing the complete mind into separate minds which grow and maintain earth bodies. It is your job now to recombine those separate minds into the One Mind with which you were gifted, in the freedom of co-creation, in the beginning. This is a splendid plan, not nearly so difficult as you have made it out to be.

Do not delay your work any longer. You possess seven mind-centers, complete receiver/transmitters, awaiting your command as an overseer of their activities. They do not control you, if you choose not to be controlled by them. Listen, feel, see, learn and contemplate what each of those mind-centers within your primary mind or oversoul is revealing to you about your God-Nature. Study their special functions. Study your Heart of Hearts, for it specializes in processing the driving power of the universal pulse of the frequency of Love of THE ONE to all of creation. Then you shall have the power and insights necessary to transmit an enhanced form of the Love Impulse back into the earth, as all life is elevated to the Genius Frequency.

Christ, the Master, walked upon the earth plane in a body of flesh to (among other cosmic reasons) reverse the beliefs of the vast majority of humanity who ran about lamenting that it was impossible to gain mastery over the seven minds of the human body, that they were hopelessly trapped and at the mercy of one or more mind-centers of organic creation as represented by certain minor deities who, each in their own way, mastered only one mind-center and used it to dominate the others. The point of the teaching of this great Master – continually missed by the vast majority of mankind – is that the key to this mastery over the other mind-centers is to ally oneself with the Original Seed Crystal of Divine Mind located in the Heart of Hearts. Only from this mind-center, this point of power, can thought-forms of eternal life and joy be manifested.

It was at great risk that the pure thought-form of The Christ entered so deeply into the material realm as a body named Jesus. The dangers mentioned above of spirit being crucified to the space/time cross of earth organisms was no less a reality for Him than it is for you, as evidenced by the numerous "temptations" that he endured. That is what made Him the most powerful teacher the earth has ever known. He was given no special circumstances. In fact, He chose the worst scenario so that those entities who suffer the worst could not say, "Of course, it was easy for Him, for He was God and I, a powerless human, have problems far greater."

It is a fact that The Christ, walking among your people as a human is what so confused the high priests who only looked for outward signs of royalty and were convinced by their altered-egos that if there should be a Master Savior it should be one only of their class.

Yet the Master's life demonstrated the awesome splendor, power, peace and realized potential of the human spirit, mind, and, most definitely, the human body by shifting the total focus of existence to the mind-center of the Heart of Hearts. By harnessing this most powerful frequency of life, the dead were raised by literally reorganizing the cellular integrity of the so-called corpse through the outpouring of this infinite reservoir of regeneration. By shifting the focus of all receiver/transmitters or mind-centers under the direction of the Master Seed Crystal, He was able to cure the sick without laboratories, scalpels, drugs, or cobalt guns.

He demonstrated that thousands could be fed from a few scraps of organic matter by the recapitulation of the Divine Process of similitude, resulting in instantaneous cellular cloning activated by the same Ray that powers the heart. The restless winds and the untamable oceans rested peacefully in the auric expansion of protection generating this frequency of life.

These so-called miracles were not accomplished through the other mind-centers. No, it was not through sex power, brain power, will power, third eye power, psychic power, kundalini power, or nuclear power. We shall repeat this yet again. This was accomplished by orchestrating the seven mind-centers of the body into a Spectral Emanation of the Primary Seed Crystal of life. Read the exercise given again. Set the ugly, faceless cynicism of the altered-ego aside as you attempt this. Each of you has this Primal Seed Crystal. The mind-center of the Heart of Hearts is the temple that houses the Seed Crystal of your being, the living principle of THE LAW OF ONE.

As you experience the truth of what we teach, you shall come to realize that the model of an earthly Christ was not, and is not, designed to overwhelm you with magic or shame you with a crushing guilt, or for the purpose of leading you to fall into blind worship, denigrating yourselves into an even more wretched, helpless, and pitiful existence than before this great event took place. Obviously....OBVIOUSLY, it was designed to prove that the potential is in YOU.

Why do you suppose these seeming miracles were performed through a physical instrument (body) identical with yours? Reason. Think for yourselves. The power of a Christ does not need a body to prove anything to anyone. If it were blind worship that was intended, the Christ could have easily manifested as a colossal vision of an angel or an animal or an insect or an amorphous blob, for that matter, and you would have fallen in awe and worship just the same.

Questioner: How should we regard the other Masters and their teachings?

MaYaRa: You may regard them as Masters. Each of them drew upon slightly different variations of the same source of power from the Primal Seed Crystal in the Heart of Hearts. The entire genealogy of Buddhas, Boddhi Satvas (such as Kwan Yin), and Krishna share in this continuing effort to align humankind to its source through the powers of the Primordial Seed Crystal in the Heart of Hearts. They all have had their parts to play as they emerged from higher dimensions to bring Light into the earth mind of men. In the linear, historic time line, as well as in the hierarchy of cosmic dimensions, The Christ – as personified in Jesus after His anointing – is the Teacher of Teachers.

You may also consider, in your conventional, historic references that the teachings of the other Masters were designed to organize and clarify the prevailing thought-forms of the times.

To all of the above, you may consider the fact that the older teachings have had much more time to be distorted for various institutional purposes. Therefore, the Christ teaching, as lived and taught by Jesus, is the updated version, as it were, that speaks and demonstrates the procedures of eternal life to the modern world as the last word, the last teaching before the end of time.

We do not wish, at this time to pursue this beautiful subject as the thrust of our document. It is deeply unfortunate that discussions of this sort, regardless of the clarity and truth of it, evoke hostile sentiments, as instigated by competing religions of your present day. However, we shall devote more of this segment of the document to what many of you so aptly term, Christ Consciousness.

The beauty and the difficulty of this teaching is that one cannot speak of the philosophical teaching and techniques without speaking of the life of Jesus, the embodiment of Christ Consciousness. He is the Master and embodiment of the Heart of Hearts as a living, total consciousness power with which all things may be accomplished: all problems of every dimension including technology. For this reason, it is fairly impossible to properly treat the subject of this segment of the document without speaking of this Master of all dimensions, up to THE ONE.

You see, all the technical examples conceivable may be given of the physics of this mind-center and reasons why it should be cultivated, but the actions taken to achieve it are in the Christ Consciousness, which cannot be analyzed – only lived.

The logic of what we are saying is this: the third dimensional altered-ego has taken control of the definitions that qualify your perceptions of world and personal reality. The single most important word to be redefined is Genius. Genius, in no uncertain terms, is to be equated with the Heart of Hearts, and no other mind-center or physical organ. To the altered-ego this may seem odd or even preposterous. But the altered-ego is a function of the first, second and third mind-centers.

Proof of Genius residing in the Heart of Hearts cannot be the result of some – and very aptly termed – "double blind experiments." Consider this: If you had the ability to heal the sick, raise the dead, control the elements, walk upon water, appear in more than one geographic location at one moment in time, spontaneously clone cells, speak in 27 languages simultaneously, accurately visualize future events, communicate directly and consciously with star intelligence, and finally raise yourself from the dead by reassembling and transfiguring cellular integrity and composition to a frequency high enough to literally ascend, body and all, into another dimension, would you not be considered a genius?!!

Should the above scenario not be the definition of genius? How long can you cling to the altered-ego's puny definition of some person with a higher than average I.Q.? – someone who claims the dubious distinction of possessing the uncanny ability to manipulate abstract data to a greater extent than most. Add to this the final absurdity that suggests a genius is born into the world, a product of genetic mutations which accidentally develops in a family lineage and environment that leads this freak of nature to an appropriate line of work – almost always in the scientific community.

And where does that leave the rest of you? Waiting with baited breath for some genius to explain your world to you, in a language that is designed for you not to understand.

The altered-ego has erected a fierce defense of energy blocks, composed of third dimensional thought-forms, to separate the mind-center of the Heart of Hearts from the mind-center of the intellect, for obvious reasons. These are the same subconscious reasons that manifest this fact as separations in church and state.

For if Genius, as we have defined the term, were to become a wholesale reality in your society, of what use would your thousands of institutions be?

From this perspective, then, the actions, teachings, life styles, philosophy, and yes, even the nuclear physics and biophysics of Christ Consciousness, open fully another dimension – the Original Dimension – of human existence. It also clarifies the muddy waters of moralistic interpretations.

Understand that the altered-ego imposes the same three dimensional limitations upon every thought-form. Therefore, one of the greatest tragedies of modern thought is that such a teaching is relegated to some obtuse reference to a concept of historical morality which dilutes the pursuit of true human potential to a thin, vaporous ideology of an impractical, impossible utopia. This also creates, for those predisposed to pursuing moral issues, a platform of self-righteousness from which they feel justified in seeking out an opposing illusion of immoral creatures who must be eradicated, punished, or both. Thus, to the altered-ego, the interpretation of Christ Consciousness has fostered a deep psychological superstition and has become, as a harbinger of witch hunts, crusades of war, terrorism and persecution.

We shall examine this word "moral" yet again in another way, for its importance cannot be stressed enough; and if you think that we mince words here, we suggest that you find this word in your book of definitions (dictionary). It is defined as perceiving life as good and evil. This is precisely the problem in categorizing Christ Consciousness as a moral teaching. Christ Consciousness is not a moral issue. It is the unfolding of the Primordial Seed Crystal of THE ONE within each and every human entity so that they are collectively and INDIVIDUALLY in resonant attunement with the Frequency of GOD-MIND, in which every entity may exhibit and manifest the powers that HE demonstrated. "GREATER THINGS THAN THESE SHALL YE DO!!"

It is time to wake up, beloved. Dispense with the morality games of the altered-ego and get thee down to the business of evolving your Christ Powers. Weed out the words from the gardens of your vocabulary that feed the polarity of the altered-ego, for words arrange thought-forms into beliefs. Words are real and alive. That is why we are making such great efforts to redefine them, or discard them, if they are inherently faulty or antagonistic to your ultimate quest of understanding, knowledge and wisdom.

Questioner: Is there another word that we can use besides "moral?"

MaYaRa: VALUES. Simply, values will do for now. There is little inherent polarity in the thought-forms of opposition associated with it. It connotes a condition of desirability by degrees, without the need for the dangerous game of opposing thought-forms. Thus, something may be more or less valuable, or even invaluable, but these are not opposing. It is a question of desirability of a value for the degree of accomplishment of a goal. The "value" of this splitting of hairs, as you term it, shall become much clearer as we progress, for this shall be a recurring theme in this document.

Unlocking the Primordial Seed Crystal of Christ Consciousness in the Heart of Hearts is the great sword that the Master Jesus spoke of: "I come not to bring peace, but the sword." Not a sword to carve up human organisms as literally translated by the moralists. It is the sword that carves up archaic traditions and institutions upon which the entire human kingdom is built. Breaking the seals of consciousness of the seven mind-centers is a dangerous thing to established order, for it opens the possibility for even an illiterate, poverty-stricken, socially ostracized entity to manifest genius.

You may at first thought believe that the world would embrace one who might emerge from city or desert with powers to heal, without thought of reward. You might hope that one who would walk into a nuclear physics laboratory with no "formal" education and reveal the secrets of proton spin coupling and electron wave transfer to ultraviolet velocities, opening new horizons for biogenetics, would be greeted with celebration and open arms. But contemplate how the altered-ego would view such true genius.

It is happening NOW in your space/time singularity, as well as in the other dimensions of reality. That is the sword: the shocking realization that the powers of mind do not reside in the physical brain; that, indeed, true genius is a frequency of mind, the power of Christ Consciousness, that is not even located in the region of the head. It is in the Heart of Hearts – And ALL OF THE POWERS OF THIS GENIUS ARE GIVEN FREELY TO THOSE WHO ASK IN THE NAME OF THE ONE!!! Is that not the sharpest of swords?

THE MANY AND THE ONE
"THE TOTAL BIO-COMPUTER"

> "Present with you,
> in your now moments,
> are the echoes and shadows
> of multiple incarnations, as related and preserved
> by multiple mind-centers."

Questioner: What is the major stumbling block in Western thinking preventing us from truly comprehending and proving the validity of ancient teachings?

MaYaRa: The answers to this question are extremely complex. However, this an appropriate time to begin an overview of the technology of thought, laying the foundation for the next segment of this document which shall reveal even more profound insights. For now, let us begin with a general examination of the nature of mind.

The entire mind-set of Western thinking is predicated upon analysis/reasoning, based entirely upon the sensory domain of the altered-ego of which the intellect is the primary tool. As you shall see, the entirety of this dimension of thinking has little to do with the true function of mind as totality of being.

If you are sensitive to your thought processes at this moment, you will sense an instant resistance to the above statement, which simply proves the strength of the defense mechanisms set up by the altered-ego to protect what it knows and to reject what it does not.

The thinking process of the altered-ego is inherently flawed because it filters data based upon three dimensional frequencies before the intellect dissects and analyzes it with tainted faculties of reason and logic. Unfortunately, this entire system of data processing heartily rebels when the same thinking process is applied to itself. This is a sad truth of third dimensional thinking dominated by the altered-ego because it demands that its system of thought be used to understand only a reality that is seemingly outside its functional domain. Thus, the altered-ego has much to say about virtually every object in the universe, but not from whence it came.

The altered-ego regards itself as the be-all and end-all of conscious mind. Because it operates on a very narrow frequency, all attempts to understand higher mind or multidimensional mind is, of course, thwarted. Scientific analysis and its system of proofs demand that there is no consciousness beyond material existence, because it allows itself to prove only that which is outside itself – fundamentally impossible. This provides the perfect defense, protecting itself from the cleansing processes of the pure-ego.

When the altered-ego is analyzed by higher frequencies of consciousness, such as that governed by pure-ego or soul-ego, which every entity has, the foundation of its entire domain is questioned. However, true consciousness, true mind, is the master of the altered-ego since it created the altered-ego in the first place and shall always have dominion over it.

Questioner: Why is it that our scientific way of thinking seems to discover so many new things?

MaYaRa: Because scientific analysis is usually redeemed by the natural synthesis of the Light force which quickly reassembles dissociated facts and fragments of life into a pattern familiar to the altered-ego. Due to the natural, creative Processes of mind, the facts and observations of the experiments spiral into a new pattern, leading to various so-called "discoveries" for which the altered-ego takes credit, boasting further confirmation of its system of thought.

Discovery manifests on all levels due to the deep desire of the researcher to break out of the altered-ego's system of thought, which has entrapped it in hopeless ignorance. It is at that point that the research inadvertently taps into the fringes of the Genius Frequency and suddenly a new theory or proof is offered, only to be quickly "accounted for" by the altered-ego once again.

When you begin to truly perceive the totality of your being as meta-energy, or Light-energy, the need for your science to remove some entity's brain and hack it to bits upon a table – which is also meta-energy – becomes rather foolish at best. We shall tell you straight away and without embellishment: ALL LIGHT IS MADE OF CONSCIOUS THOUGHT; ALL UNIVERSES, INCLUDING THE MATERIAL UNIVERSES, ARE MADE ENTIRELY OF LIGHT; EVERYTHING IS LIGHT. Therefore, the secret of consciousness, mind, and all matter can all be ascertained by the study of only one subject: LIGHT.

The beauty of this message of Truth is that since all of you are Light, the only real research is to become conscious of self. Thus: KNOW THYSELF is the axiom of all true evolution and you don't have to chop into pieces your material bodies to do it.

However, this document is addressed primarily to the intellect, since it is the primary perceptual tool used in comprehension on the material plane in a society such as yours.

Since the intellect has a special thrust in Western thinking, we shall use it to begin the analysis of its own larger consciousness domains, which prove so painful to the altered-ego. So we will now endeavor to view your system of consciousness as a total bio-computer, comprised of multiple minds and bodies of adjacent and nested dimensions, forming a more truthful picture of the total mind, reflecting its perfect potential and predilection toward super intelligence, super health, and super communication with Cosmic Intelligence in the Genius Frequency.

In the previous segment (Chapter 3), you saw the self-imposed limitations that result in focusing the thrust of your awareness through mind-centers other than the Heart of Hearts. To attain the proper understanding of your true potential, it is necessary to perceive the bio-computer that you are in terms of energy fields and patterns of consciousness rather than objects isolated in space/time. For, in this expanded definition, you may see that the reality of you is a multidimensional vehicle capable of transmuting the electromagnetic spectrum-energy-patterns of material planes into higher dimensions of Light.

In order to understand the nature of yourself as a total bio-computer comprised of seven minds and five bodies of patterned energy of intelligent awareness, we will briefly state the fundamental process of Creation. The Primary Ray of Creative Intelligent Thought is subdivided prismatically into component rays which coalesce into areas of appropriate color frequencies that create, resonate with, and drive their seemingly separate functions within the bio-computer.

The Primary Ray spirals into the mind-centers (see Chapter 3) creating a spinning motion or energy vortex, that in turn spin the secondary energy points, giving them life, just as your solar logos spins the planets that surround it. The only mind-center containing a pure Seed Atom of the Primary Ray is the Heart of Hearts. Since the mind-center of the Heart is the only place where a pure point of the Primary Ray is to be found, this can be the only point from which the other mind-centers are propelled. It would be just as foolish to consider any other mind-center as the driving force as it would be to consider one of the planets of your solar system as such.

A planetary mind within the solar system cannot revolve the sun around it because the sun is a primary ray or seed crystal within its solar body. Scientifically speaking, you have not discovered this Seed Atom or Crystal, but this shall be forthcoming. However, this by no means necessitates waiting, nor does it preclude information preserved in other dimensions accessible to all of you who ask from the Heart.

In the history of your earth, worship of "many gods" was tantamount to perceiving the universe through the different mind-centers of the human body. Each civilization has had its turn exalting one or the other of these mind-centers or planets within its total body. And for each civilization, a partial equation of entropy led to their appropriate demise. Without exception, the Masters of Light periodically worked upon the earth and demonstrated stupendous powers of wisdom and healing by focusing in the Primary Ray or the Seed Crystal of man's true image. They operated in the Genius Frequency, maintaining resonant contact with the Primary Ray. And when they departed the planet, earth-man merely made gods of them, adding yet another to the growing list to be worshipped and fought over.

Have you not ever wondered why these great Masters worked through the same type of organic bio-computer that you are? Or why they did not float around the planet as spheres of light or bolts of lightning? It is because the image of man, even as manifested in earth, contains the Adamic Seed Crystal of a higher order of THE ONE.

Reason this: If the human-form on earth or the bio-computer, as we term it, was the miserable, disease ridden animal that you consider it to be, the great feats of the Masters could not have been performed while working within such a form. The teachings were to prove to you that when any total human bio-computer is opened and tuned to the Genius Frequency, and all of the mind-centers are in synchronous resonance with the Primary Ray of the Heart of Hearts, the energy of Cosmic Intelligence can manifest a most splendid, joyful and prosperous life, free from disease, war, bondage, fear, limitations, ignorance, confusion and hunger.

Thus, the teachings of the Masters are unanimous in instructing those on earth that any mind-center taken out of context with the Seed Crystal of the Primary Ray results in a partial equation of life – in entropy and destruction of the integrity of the system.

So, every entity existing in earth is mind-forming-body. It is for this reason that you have so many contradictory opinions. One moment you like something; in the next, you dislike it; and in the next, you may be disinterested or even indifferent. To finalize the confusion, each opinion is prefaced with "I," or "I am." Thus, you utter: "I am religious." "I am atheist." "I am afraid." "I am happy." "I am hot." "I am cold." "I hate you." "I love you." In addition are the things that "I" did, that "I" want, that "I" said, etc. If you tallied up your "I's" for the week, the numbers would be staggering. If you tallied them up for the entire year or for a lifetime, you might explode in frustration. There is a good reason why the psychiatrists on your earth are so well off.

Much of this confusion is due to the use of your language, comprised of a most inanimate symbology. For this reason, we are compelled to redefine and create words in hyphenated form to convey a most animate reality. As it is, you are faced with the task of articulating the vast input of seven mind-centers pouring oceans of data into memory banks conditioned to filter information in a linear time base through the functions of the altered-ego, with a language fundamentally analytical rather than synthetic. In other words, your intellect, which is virtually synonymous with language, is conditioned to take things apart, and when it tries to put them together again, there are always a few "screws" missing. The missing screw is the relentless, non repeating spiral of time. Thus, you throw the old watch away and purchase a new one. You may throw one of your organs away and purchase a new one. You may even throw your mate away and purchase a new one. You may now see how the same linear thinking process pervades your entire lives.

The totality of your being is comprised of five bodies and seven minds, in nine dimensions. Your analytical language is designed to take things apart. Then you are expected to explain yourselves – you, who are seven minds and five bodies – with a language that can only take things apart in three dimensions. When you begin to see that your language and your intellect are one and the same, the confusion begins to clear in the Light of your master-ego, the original, pure ego, before it was altered.

To clarify this confusion is to increase the frequency of your total bio-computer. To begin this process, simply pay attention to how the altered-ego controls and defines the mundane affairs of your daily lives. Try to count the number of times you hear and say the word, or rather the symbol, "I" in any given day. It is used more often than any word in your language. Why? Because of the desperate attempts of the entities to unify themselves without the slightest regard for the fact that they are Many-in-One. It is no wonder that there is, what you term, an "ego problem" upon your plane.

Questioner: Are there other languages of earth that lend themselves to this concept of the many and the one?

MaYaRa: There are other languages which are more unified in their expression of a multiple being such as Sanskrit and Hebrew, the king of them all being the pictograph. But these are considered unscientific by Western thought, regardless that science has discovered great truths which bear testimony in ancient languages. This would not fit the linear scheme of Darwinistic, evolutionary thought which is also a product of the altered-ego, even though bioengineering and molecular biology have discovered an exact correlation between the ancient, universal symbols of the 64 Chinese hexagrams which form a perfect diagram of the 64 amino acids or codes of life. Nonetheless, we shall take as a most glorious challenge this attempt to elucidate, through your language, the Many-and-the-One principle of your beingness. For the time is fast approaching when science and religion will marry in the celebration of THE ONE, with undeniable proof. In the meantime, let us preview these amazing "discoveries" yet to be discovered.

You have been conditioned to judge yourself as mentally or emotionally unstable when experiencing conflicting thoughts or feelings. The altered-ego uses this self-inflicted insecurity and loss of self-esteem as an inducement for fear-oriented flight or fright syndromes. The universal question, "Who am I?," born of a need to focus human thought within its source, becomes, instead a dark cloud fraught with irreconcilable differences in its existence, breeding despair and clinging to a system of death and entropy.

The mist begins to clear when the entity realizes that it is natural, indeed, within the designs of creation, to possess seven minds. However, what is not natural is for these mind-centers is to be at odds with each other. The first step is to recognize the multiplicity of mind-centers within the total mind. When this is accomplished through the master or total mind, the entity may effectively harmonize the resonating factors of interaction between the mind-centers through the unifying principle of the Heart-Mind. When you succeed in creating this resonance, the total bio-computer will be tuned to the Genius Frequency.

Questioner: How can this be accomplished?

MaYaRa: We reiterate: Pay attention to, rather than avoiding, the conflicting "I" statements within the framework of your expression as an individual. When you discover discrepancies, an automatic awareness of separate mind-centers will begin to present itself clearly, opening the channel to the master-ego which will, in conjunction with the Heart-Mind, bring forth specific exercises raising the entity's cellular frequency. For the Heart-Mind strives to harmonize discrepancies and conflict because the latter are antagonistic to the Life Impulse.

For example, the entity may discover that it feels great love for someone, yet cannot express this love verbally through the Throat-Mind. Or the entity may find itself attracted to someone without deep love or perhaps even with feelings of antagonism. The entity could find itself manipulating others with its will power though another of its minds is compelled to act compassionately. There are millions of these conflicting feelings, thoughts and actions in the life of an average earth dweller. The entity will find that each of these conflicting ideas is preceded by the symbolic expression "I." Further, the entity will discover, through this simple exercise, that the altered-ego "I"-dentifies with each and every "I" proclamation to the very jeopardy of the total being.

Now, the function of the intellect is to justify the conflicting "I" proclamations as part of the altered-ego's defense mechanism. One of the greatest illusions that the altered-ego perpetrates is that this function of "I" exists within the physical brain and body, giving the illusion of the entity's solidarity and individualism. Thus, it tenaciously and desperately proclaims itself the defender of the entity as it attempts to serve the conflicting needs of the various mind-centers.

The entity may begin to comprehend the extent of this di-lemma. For when the many conflicting "I's" use the powers of the intellect to justify their separate existences, a breeding ground for neurosis and a host of other psychological dysfunctions manifest, for the entity is at odds and often at war with different parts of its one-being.

Thus far, we have examined the altered-ego as a factor within the framework of the Western mind. Now that a foundation has been established, let us begin to examine some variations on this theme of the total bio-computer and its minds within mind. Do not succumb to the attempts of the altered-ego to dissuade you from exploring these thoughts on the grounds that they might not be true and they have not been scientifically proven. You may ap-pease it by telling yourselves that if there is no truth in all of this, it certainly cannot hurt you. But if there is, it could help a great deal on a personal level in these final days of the earth. Removing the restricting and limiting functions of the altered-ego is the first grand step in tuning into the Genius Frequency.

As the entity removes the artificial functions of the altered-ego by feeding the intellect stimulating, high frequency informa-tion, the entity begins raising the frequency of its total resonance by loosening the grip of I-dentification with conflicting beliefs locked within the individual memories of the seven mind-centers. The entity will find blissful moments appearing in the most unex-pected moments in its life, for in that moment, the war with self will be equalized in a peace that renders the warlike altered-ego useless.

In those moments of increasing frequency, the intellect no longer is saddled with the maddening task of justifying opposing views that serve only to fragment the entity. For possibly the first time in lifetimes, the entity will unite with its master-ego to per-form its true function for which it was originally designed: to conduct and orchestrate the symphony of its many minds into true individualization, as created by THE ONE ultimate composer.

Composing the electromagnetic mind-centers of the physical bio-computer is a force field, containing the reflecting mind of the master-ego, that has the capacity to apprehend the ultra-spectrum intelligences that work throughout universal creations. When it is tuned to the Genius Frequency, it can communicate with these intelligences, emanating from THE ONE, as it processes pure energy data for use by the other mind-centers of the bio-computer in conjunction with healing, regeneration and the evolution of each mind-center toward the harmonious resonance with the Higher Creative Forces. It receives and transmits them to the other mind-centers according to their needs at any given moment. Ultimately, YOU are the conductor of such power.

FUNCTIONS OF THE BRAIN

The brain has two functions. Its primary function is to receive and store information from ganglia of sensory extensions known as the senses of the ears, eyes, nose and mouth; and communicate these findings with the other brain centers in order that appropriate actions be taken to preserve the integrity of the organism. Essentially this function of preservation operates on the same frequency as the elements of which it is made.

The secondary purpose of the brain is to store back-up information from the other brain centers in the event of a short circuit. For this reason, it is the fashionable trend of academicism to declare that 90% of the brain is inoperative, which means they are at a loss to explain its functions. Since multiple back-up copies of magnetic life patterns are stored in various places throughout the physical bio-computer, it becomes difficult to pinpoint a specific function in that location and that is precisely the purpose of its design. This is because there are overlapping memory banks that can take over a function in the event that another is damaged.

Thus, the mind-centers, to an extent, function as support systems for each other. This is accomplished by molecular imagery in the expression of facets of total mind as material creation. The total bio-computer, that you are now occupying, is an awareness machine, designed to examine in detail aspects of creation through an individualized point of pure God-Consciousness spectrally divided. This molecular imaging coalesces in organic development as a collection of fibers on different scales.

The fibers continue to bunch into a complex of nerve ganglia surrounded by a spinning vortex of Life Impulses that operate on a specific frequency and color spectrum of the Primary Ray, imparting the neural networks and the synaptic sparks to facilitate the storing and transferring of memory. Thus, the ganglia become glands or very specialized brains. These brain-glands cannot think any more than the central brain can think. Memory cannot think. Only a higher function of mind – in this case, the vortex of frequencies spinning around the ganglia – can think. All of these fields taken together produce the auric field where actual reflective thought occurs. Only when the symbolic reference of "I" is centered in the Heart of Hearts are these various mind-centers united. Only then, can you speak as the I-AM.

It may be helpful at this juncture to contemplate that the universal symbol "I" represents the spinal column, which when vertical becomes an antenna and conduit connecting the earth mind to the seven human minds to the galactic minds of THE ONE.

Realize that the altered-ego and the intellect is founded on the brain functions of memory, not on mind functions of thought. The physical network of the brain is a replica of the star systems that formed the patterns for its holographic development; therefore, it contains an inherent memory as represented in its molecular imaging of its origins. Only your higher mind, or Master-Ego, under the unflagging sustenance of the Heart-Mind, can create the time/space for this memory to be released as pure thought. The altered-ego is far too busy with the sensory input magnetically attracted to the entity by the memory banks of past experience.

We shall now briefly touch upon the seven brain-mind-centers and their functions within the bio-computer. They are, in order of creation:

1: Heart-Mind

2: Brow and Regenerative Minds

3: Solar plexus and Throat Minds

4: Crown and Sexual Minds.

We have listed all, save the Heart-Mind, as pairs for a specific reason: the others were created as simultaneous pairs. A tree does not form its entire root system before it sprouts the trunk. Half of a leaf does not grow first, followed by the other half. This pairing throughout creation is issued from a center point or Heart of Hearts.

Now, each of the mind-centers or glands receiving its initial input of energy-spectra function as a time/space portal. Thus, you have:

1:Thymus-portal (heart)

2:Thyroid-portal (throat) /Adrenal-portal (solar plexus)

3:Pituitary-portal(brow-third-eye)/Lyden-portal (intest)

4:Pineal-portal (crown) / Gonad-portal (sexual organ).

Further, each of your seven mind-centers is a vortex of spiraling energy powered by a subset of spectral emanations, producing living colors that resonate with the specialized intelligences, combining to form the archetypal blueprint of light that projects the holographic thought-form of the Adamic Image into meta-matter. They are as follows:

CROWN-MIND = VIOLET TO PINK

PINEAL EYE-MIND = INDIGO

THROAT-MIND = BLUE

HEART-MIND = GREEN

SOLAR PLEXUS-MIND = YELLOW

INTESTINAL-MIND = ORANGE

SEXUAL-MIND = RED.

These colors are approximations in your terms and are not to be understood as the solid colors of crayons or paints. They are transparent, refractive color-bands that are permeated with the blue-white light of the galactic logos, and the golden-white light of THE CHRIST. Every entity has these colors in its being in varying degrees of purity.

The seven brain-mind-centers of the total bio-computer prismatically radiate their particular energy color or spectrum from an infinite source, both inward and outward. Intelligent energy, moving inward through these mind-centers reaches the energy portals or glands where they radiate outward specific color codes at varying angles of intersection, forming a living matrix or grid of energy that continually transforms molecular combinations, holographically filling the mold or blueprint of its function to create, for example, the organs of the body.

THE ONE contemplates: A Primary Ray is issued into infinity, simultaneously in opposing directions, whence it subdivides into sets and subsets of opposing lights in perfect balance with itself as it spirals into centropy towards freedom of perfection and returns to the Source. Thus, when the entity acts upon low frequency thought-forms locked in one of its mind-centers, and the altered-ego I-dentifies with them by proclaiming "I am" to its desires, a partial equation of life is formed, creating unbalance.

When unbalanced, the mind-centers are not synchronous with THE ONE I AM. Since the mind-centers are so polluted with deep enfolded memories of injury and destruction, I-dentifying with the Heart-mind, as taught by the Master Jesus, THE CHRIST, is the only effective means by which the Adamic Image in the Primary Seed Crystal can be "redeemed," restoring the entity to its former glory.

Each entity has tremendous effects upon its planetary body and atmosphere, because each is a biosphere of thought-forms occupying a large area of earth-mind, even though it is in a compressed, material state. The earth-mind is an extension of the total minds of each entity. It is not the opposite, as many naturalists believe. It was the human family in the form of Adamic Creation that brought mind to earth. The earth is a brain and brains cannot think, because brains are structured memory and memory cannot think. Only mind can think. You are the earth's mind.

Mind is the responsibility of man. The earth reacts to the turmoil and destruction of unbalanced thought-forms, just as your individual bio-computers react to them. Thus, the earth develops ulcers, cancer, AIDS, nervous breakdowns, etc., because the masters of thought upon her (man!) I-dentify with thought-forms which upset the balance of light.

Do not be overwhelmed by this, beloved readers. For it is only language that is faltering under the weight of a much greater reality and the altered-ego is not of sufficiently high frequency to resonate with this truth. When any entity resonates with the Genius

Frequency, the perception of the next dimension opens to its eyes of mind.

In a moment, a heartbeat, any of you could "see" with fourth dimensional perception, the infinite force-field lines radiating from the Seed Crystal of the Heart-Mind and connecting the other mind-centers through the polar axis of the spine, forming arcs of light, otherwise known as the auric field. Each entity is a biospheric replica of the galactic mind, indeed, a star-mind. Each entity is responsible for what it thinks, just as it is responsible for any material creation which those thought-forms bring into the world.

The arcs of light form an eggshell-shaped energy field where the connection is made with the seven mind-centers as they leave their points of power and join the auric field and return. The integrity and belief system of each mind-center is reflected in the auric field to form color bands of frequency comprised of all like thought-forms resonating within the memory banks. This color scheme "reads" as electromagnetic frequency dynamics that create the attraction and repulsion of other entities and circumstances, and through quantum resonant induction becomes a large area of earth mind.

Questioner: Can you explain more about thought-forms affecting health?

MaYaRa: The degree of health and well-being of the many minds as one mind depends upon the continual transmutation of energy, not only for specific functions but for overall integrity of purpose.

The molecules of organic matter are formed by and maintained through energy grids creating patterned webs, pathways which assemble the molecules into cells, which are charged with additional electromagnetic patterns of what you feel and think about your life at that moment as each cell is formed and moves to its destination. Your organs are maintained by this process. They can even be completely rebuilt.

However, if the entity's thoughts and feelings are antagonistic toward life (this includes any other life form), the matrix and webbing are distorted, producing cells which are alien to the system because they are partial equations of the life force. When the many "I's" do not recognize each other, a state of alert occurs, producing stress, thus overloading the immune functions.

Not only do the organs or tissue originally in need of maintenance or repair receive none, but the additional strain of antagonistic cells creates a situation where the organs begin to die. However, when the seven mind-centers operate in harmonic resonance, each with the other, the blueprints untwist and undistort, resuming the original blueprint of the Adamic Image contained in the Seed Crystal of the Heart. This is how all healing takes place, including the so-called miracle cures, as well as those claimed by conventional medicine.

Questioner: Are each of the mind-centers a separate dimension?

MaYaRa: No. However they can merge into harmonic overtones and frequencies which can function directly in other dimensions.

Each of the energy portals or glands are separate crystal points of light, coded in pyramidal geometries. It is the geometry of the pyramid that creates the spinning energy vortex, so well known to the ancient Masters. Thus, a rainbow spectrum is generated from the sustaining blue-white to ultraviolet. The solar spectrum is of the yellow-white frequency, essentially of a lower order than the human light. In this sense, each entity has another dimension, another universe, operating in the same space. The third dimensional color frequency resonates with the solar frequency, while the fourth dimensional color frequency resonates with the galactic mind. The original design of human creation is patterned after the galactic mind and is of a higher order and frequency than the solar system in which you now reside. In the closing of the cosmic cycle, those who choose to raise their frequencies shall again reign over the solar spectrum and not be subservient to its lower frequency ray.

Questioner: Why is there so much difficulty in balancing the seven mind-centers?

MaYaRa: This is only problematic in the terms and parameters of the altered-ego. However, a brief examination of the mechanics of the earth bound mind-centers, in an historical sense, may shed some light upon the shadow areas of understanding.

The confusion lies in your multitudinous incarnations in earth plane existence. Aeons ago, when the mind-centers were thrown out of synchronous resonance with the Primary Life Force, it seemed a simple matter to incarnate within another time-zone-circumstance to provide a slightly different scenario of the human drama for the purpose of achieving the balance again. An entity, who over stimulated or abused one mind-center at the expense of the other, could use the new scenario to restrict one mind-center and use the free energy to rebuild the damaged mind-center – only to be thrown off into another imbalance.

On it went for some 36,000 years, in this most recent solar cycle. The incarnating entities began to lose their conscious contact with the blue-white frequency of galactic mind. Slowly, the yellow-white frequency of the solar logos began to dominate, as entities became conscious only of the food-chain mentality of this solar ray that must consume itself for its survival.

False teachings began to flourish, matching the lower frequency of third dimensional awareness, describing how each entity was a puppet and prisoner of the solar and planetary forces (minds) that the entity must appease in order to continue its existence. Thus began the long spiral of entropy and decay, shortening the life span and creating shorter cycles in which to recreate the necessary balances. More and more entities began to vie for self-serving positions, that others may serve them in deranged entrapments of self-glory.

Thus the incarnations continued, the odds against balancing the mind-centers and reestablishing conscious contact with the life sustaining Intelligence of THE ONE increasing with every revolution of the earth. Billions of entities were ensnared in the spinning webs of space/time illusion, until those souls and the very earth cried out in a great pulsation of sorrow and suffering. In response to this cry and as the last adjustment to the etheric balance of earth mind – created by human mind – the Christ Consciousness, embodied in the vehicle of the Master Jesus, penetrated the veil of confusion by using the power of all seven mind-centers in a perfect state of resonance with THE ONE to reestablish the resonance between earth/human mind and galactic mind to break the bonds of the solar mind on earth.

With this backdrop of your history, you may perceive the futility of I-dentifying with the altered-ego through the intellect. Through all of your lifetimes, which for all intents and purposes are beyond counting, a perfect, total record of every experience is recorded in the astro-genetic double helix; and therefore, programmed into the structure of each cell, otherwise known as cellular memory. This means that each of your mind-centers possesses a holographic memory bank of the experiences that affected that particular mind-center. Each is a history unto itself.

So, present with you in your now moments are the echoes and shadows of multiple incarnations, as related and preserved by multiple mind-centers. In light of this, there is little wonder as to why the intellect succumbs to madness when confronted with the question: "Who am I?" For these reasons, what was once Intelligent mind became the intellect and what was once the Master-Ego became the altered-ego, as it apathetically surrendered to the forces of the solar frequency of the food-chain mentality. Thus the philosophy of "eat, drink, and be merry, for tomorrow you will die," became its new paradigm of life.

Questioner: Can rebirthing and regressing techniques correct these imbalances?

MaYaRa: To an extent, they achieve excellent results for temporary relief from some of the more recent and obvious traumatic thought-forms blocking energy flow. However, if you were regressed and rebirthed every day of your life for the next 10 lifetimes, you could not relive 1/10 of your experiences. All experience lives in the eternal moment of now.

The totality of being for each entity is, in the now moment, its experience. Therefore, events and experiences have little meaning or effect when taken out of context with the eternal moment of now. The little gains achieved by these techniques are instantly subverted by the conflicting rationalizations of the intellect under the supervision of the altered-ego, forming yet another partial equation of life. The intellect merely creates yet another Pandora's box, as it were, by supplying yet more reasons to support the original thought-forms creating the blocks to higher frequency consciousness.

The intellect, via the altered-ego, does not have the capacity to allow you to accomplish true evolution because it functions as a separative, past-tense mechanism of memory. By its very nature, it cannot permit your consciousness-awareness to exist in the present tense. It does not have the capacity to catch up to the *ongoingness* of forever that the total bio-computer exists in. Each entity, as a bio-computer, a bio-mind, travels with the earth around the sun in excess of 17,000 miles per second, in relative terms. Add this figure to the speed of your solar system that travels in excess of 100,000 miles per second, the total is roughly the speed of light as you calculate it in relativistic terms.

How fast is your thrust into forever? How long will living in the past of yourself allow you to experience the splendor and joy of this adventure? With such great effort and pain, you succeed in recreating a mere moment of some past life experience; and when you awaken, you are mystified by yet another illusion. It may be far more mystifying to contemplate how many miles slipped by in that "now" moment while you relived the past. Where were you? Why are you there – when you could be here in the Genius Frequency of the eternal present – where the universes of infinite Intelligence, within the mind of THE ONE, are forever unfolding new beginnings into which you may expand.

You have always possessed the power of transmutation of energy. It is a gift. It creates billions of new cells with every heartbeat. The perfect image of you NOW is preserved in radiant energy in the Heart of Hearts. Only from that mind-center can the unconditional love of THE ONE issue forth into the other mind-centers to transmute the past injuries and abuses into perfect healing. Only there exists the one pure, unpolluted, all powerful Atom – Adam! – of THE ONE. Only there, in the eternal presence of NOW, can unconditional Love be found: to ultimately forgive, uplift, relieve and heal the many imbalances of the past in THIS moment. Only from the Heart of Hearts can the world be changed.

Beloved, you do not have the time to go back. You have all tried that and failed countless times. Indeed, you do not have to go back, regardless of what injustices have assaulted your being in any of your mind-centers or lifetimes, the powers that you abused, the atrocities that you committed in ignorance or greed, the love withheld by others or tortures you have endured at the hands of the enemies that you attracted, who were also tortured beings. You can be sure that every one of you lived and died these moments in your lifetimes, and in that respect, you are not unique.

Is it not accurate to say that the only lifetime that you would like to uncover and "relive" is one in which you were rich, powerful, influential, popular, wise, worshipped, cared for, loved unconditionally, and/or just important in some way to the scheme of things? Do not waste your precious time, beloved. Be assured that each of you has had more than a few turns at the helm. There is soon coming a day in your time when you shall recall every single experience. You are not strong enough to handle that with your present fixation in the altered-ego. For now there are more important preparations for you to accomplish so that you do not hurl yourself into the past to begin again in the next cycle.

What would become of you should you uncover one of your lifetimes in which you were a murderer, prostitute, slave master, henchman, executioner, torturer of the innocent, prophet of false teachings, corrupt official, dictator, or... shall we continue? The point is that you were all of these and if you uncovered one of these lifetimes you would quickly shut the book and perhaps live the remainder of this lifetime in mortal guilt. Perhaps you might even consider taking your own life, which you may painfully uncover in some future day upon the regression table. But do not wallow in the low frequencies of guilt or of the past.

Just look at those who are living those lives NOW. Do not judge them, beloved. Cultivate the higher frequencies of forgiveness – deep, unconditional forgiveness. Yes, the Christ came to open the doors to the Heart and usher in the new age of peace. And yes, the Christ brought forgiveness in the name of THE ONE. But, not even Christ can forgive what you cannot forgive, beloved entities. This is a most serious and profound truth for all human kind. You must follow the example and forgive. As you do, remarkable events will fill your lives with joy NOW, not in some past/future that can never become now.

How long can the human family justify the hatred of others – which is really self-hatred – who are presently enacting the above scenarios, when all have played these parts? These are hard words against an intellect that strives to justify the ignorance of the altered-ego. But if this were not a truth, beloved, none of you would be experiencing your predicaments. For these reasons, billions of entities are incarnating at this time for the purpose of cleansing and balancing the mind-centers at the end of the cycle – the Omega Point.

Through the Heart-Mind, this dilemma can be expediently solved. Through it, you may gain access to the unified energy field of the total bio-computer. You shall command the respect and co-operation of every mind-center. You will develop the will power of a true Co-Creator; the melodic, golden voice of an inspired orator; the wisdom of a great Master; the regenerative capacity to feed your bodies from the nutrients of the stars; the capacity of the crown of your being to communicate with the Highest realms of the Masters of Light, working through THE ONE; and the sexual vitality to transmute and restructure your own genetic code, freeing you from the atmosphere of the earth. The only lifetime worth re-living is the one in which you exercised all of the gifts from THE ONE. If you choose, you may return to this glory.

To pass judgment upon your world family is to pass equal judgment upon the histories of your mind-centers. To condemn any is to condemn self. Allow each of your mind-centers to experience their true powers once again. Embrace all of the experiences in those memory banks and forgive them, by your own powers of for-giveness. There is no need whatsoever to relive them, unless you can transmute them. There is absolutely the need to forgive them, free them, love them. Take the tremendous, unwavering Love Im-pulse that powers the Heart-Mind and channel that energy, that Intelligence, that Genius Frequency into the other mind-centers to heal them. Create your own exercises that you may use every day, so that when you close this book you do not close your heart with it. Place the crown of the glory of THE ONE within you, again, upon the total bio-computer that serves you. Resume your evo-lution of true centropy, where there is no sting of death's illusion to cause you fear.

When these things are accomplished by each of you, the question, "Who am I?," shall be forever answered. You shall wear your I AM presence as a cloak of Light and invincible protection. The "lost arc" is the arc of Light that emanates from your true image as a co-creator. The key to the Genius Frequency is there. When you open this final door of your lives, you shall stand in awe of yourself and the worlds of creation, for you shall KNOW that you are not only the many, but you are also the ONE.

COSMIC INTELLIGENCE
"VERSUS THE INTELLECT"

> *"Every entity has the potential, yea, the innate
> ability to live in Christ Consciousness,
> to walk and communicate with
> THE ONE directly."*

Questioner: If it is appropriate at this time, I would like to ask that you explain in greater depth the way you define the intellect as a product of the altered-ego, how it relates to the auric field, and what part the physical brain plays in this process?

MaYaRa: We realize that we have done little to appease the altered-ego since embarking on this journey upon the ship of GOD-MIND, and we ask your forgiveness for any discomfort you may have experienced.

The irritation that you experience at times when you are trying to "make sense" out of this material is noteworthy. For it indicates one of the many defense mechanisms of the altered-ego that can block any thought-forms outside of its programming. Since this programming is not centered in the Heart of Hearts, the Primal Seed Crystal, it has the incredibly futile job of trying to remain balanced on the circumference of life's spinning wheels. It is as if you were walking a tightrope while someone persistently attempts to hand you a million dollars. Your response is to scream for him to get away, scowling indignantly at his seeming ignorance of your situation, which is to survive until you reach the end. Only after reaching the end, you might ask to see what he was trying to give you.

In the same way, then, the gifts of freedom and eternal Life are offered to the tightrope walker of the altered-ego so overcome with the fear of falling or not surviving or not making the most out of its "one shot," that it rejects all thought-forms save those that it has been programmed to incubate and create.

For all intents and purposes, you may regard the altered-ego in its entirety as a body of defense mechanisms one upon the other, layer upon layer, building armor and walls around its territory, whether that territory be information, emotions, beliefs or physical matter. It is little wonder then, that any reference to the altered-ego or to the intellect or to one of its weapons of defense, in terms less than worship, will evoke resistance ranging from mild irritation to mindless cynicism to outright violent disagreement.

For the above reasons, it is extremely important to monitor your resistance to new information of any kind; and it is imperative that you remain open to new, constructive thought-forms by remaining centered in the mind center of the Heart of Hearts. For when you are centered there, you may examine any truth in the light of your highest interests and you shall not fear being misled by destructive thought-forms, regardless that they be thickly cloaked in illusion.

As we continue with our exploration into the dimensions of God-Mind, be secure in your heart and remain open to the gifts that are being offered to so many areas of your life. It is not even a matter of believing what you read on these pages. The important thing to remember is that every entity has an unerring guidance mechanism through the Primordial Seed Crystal or Atom of Intelligence in that entity's Heart of Hearts. Weigh all knowledge upon its scales, beloved. For the intellect may indeed be easily tricked and manipulated, but true Intelligence of THE ONE in each of you shall never be deceived in that special golden light on your true path. Study openly and enthusiastically as a child would explore the wonders of nature. Struggle not with the artificial fears of the altered-ego imprisoned within the dark walls of ignorance.

Now, it would be advantageous to outline the difference between the functions of the brain and functions of mind. Though this will prove shocking to the altered-ego, notice that there will also be a part of you that is strangely attracted to this higher reasoning. Remember that every new idea that you examine openly will be one brick removed from the walls of defense of the altered-ego. Each time a brick is removed, the golden Light of wisdom will pour in upon you like water upon the desert. Remember also that the window of Light you create in that wall is only one. There are thousands more that your open mind will create.

The physical brain, then, is simply a central or mainframe computer. It uses microwave frequencies to ignite or charge an infinite supply of photons, the primary building blocks of light, and therefore, matter. Each of the billions of photons are charged by a specific, quantum induction of electromagnetic patterns that encode each into a spiraling energy bundle, or matrix, much like your ribbon of DNA material. The result is that each charged energy bundle of photons renders a snapshot, as it were, a replica of your entire being in what may be termed the YOU-NOW in the eternal Now Moment. All of this forms a complex of electromagnetic and electrochemical patterns and bundles. To save space, we shall refer to this as the synaptic matrix.

This matrix is not only stored in the brain tissue as electrochemical imprints which are activated through coordinate points in the auric field, it IS the brain tissue. Brain tissue is structured memory. Once this memory matrix is created, it can be evoked again by any number of means, two of which are environmental impact and thought-form resonance generated from self or otherselves.

As you mature, this impact and resonance (programming) forms a continuous feedback loop which fixates your awareness in one tiny spot upon the auric field, and a definition of who you are and what reality is for you is crystallized within the very tissue of the total organic system.

This outlines the answer to your query. We shall now explore more specific, as well as more general, information regarding this most fascinating, beautiful, and fundamental aspect of creation.

Each photon bundle or synaptic matrix is a microcosm integrated within the cellular structure of the physical body which conforms to it, affecting the functioning of the total bio-computer as well as reflecting, or more precisely, projecting through resonance, the awareness of this combined blueprint of you-now in the auric field. The crucial difference in these two processes is that the brain stores only codified experience of the past and the auric field encompasses fourth dimensional mind which can operate in past/-present/future dimensions.

You are, in effect, continually recreating the thought-form of yourself, exactly as the cells of your body are continually re-creating replicas of themselves, for the purpose of overcoming entropy (the process of matter disintegrating back into light to be created again). It is important, then, to understand that the physical cells are imprinted with the encoded matrix of what you think (your thought-forms) at any given moment. This has profound implications on your health and well-being of the moment, which, of course, is your past and future.

With this background, then, you may see that the altered-ego, of which the intellect is a part, is a direct function of the brain that only stores synaptic matrices of past scenarios. You may also see how the feedback loop of consciousness is an encoded past scenario, reflected or projected onto the screen of the perpetual NOW moment of the auric field through resonating harmonic fields which connect you to all other harmonic fields and all other auric fields.

If you had any doubts concerning how an entity creates its own reality, perhaps they have been clarified. For the feedback loop of the altered-ego is not merely an abstract definition of an I-dentity problem. It is a veritable broadcasting station to the world via the auric field of what you think and believe. By the same harmonic resonance, other auric fields broadcasting similar frequencies of thought-forms are attracted to each other to produce the reality scenarios which convince the altered-ego of its veracity. That is, what it knows – i.e. the past – is constantly validated through present and future experiences, ad nauseam.

Since the synaptic matrices in the brain are fairly polluted with unbalanced thought-form scenarios depicting trauma, insecurity, fear, doubt, jealousy, resentment, and the like; it is little wonder that the altered-ego is such a limiting, if not maddening, affair. The past is perpetually recreating itself, and all of this is reflected in the physical body. If the feedback/reflection is pleasing, the altered-ego is filled with boastful pride. However, if this feedback/reflection of the past is painful or revolting, the altered-ego is quick to justify blame, judgment, hostility toward the reflections of itself in the world, and/or the ultimate in victimization by declaring a happenstance reality – "things happen to me: Life is a series of accidents."

Questioner: Can this situation be rectified through the systems of thought that teach one how to reprogram the mind?

MaYaRa: There are many upon your earth plane who have discovered this truth to one degree or another; and quite logically have adopted and prescribed various methods of what is termed re-programming, for purposes of overcoming the vicious cycle of the altered-ego.

This is an excellent start, as this method can, to a degree, create and begin new feedback loops of awareness as it rearranges and restructures many of the insidious thought-forms encoded within the synaptic matrices. The result is an improved self-image, which is reflected in the auric field where it may resonate with other auric fields containing similar thought-forms. Thus, the entity attracts different, new situations and circumstances rather than the same past situations. As a side effect, the physical body will reflect and eventually manifest this new programming as a noticeable, healthy improvement in the integrity of its functioning. This re-programming technique may seem to hold the ultimate hope for improvement in circumstances, but as we shall see, it leaves much to be desired. There are two reasons for this.

First, you would do well always to remember that the primary law of the altered-ego is resistance to new thought-forms – and to the altered-ego, everything new or different is alien and threatening – with its characteristic brick wall of defense mechanisms. These defense mechanisms are designed to filter (through the intellect) all new information which threatens its functional continuity. Thus, it alters all information and thought-forms to fit the preconditioned brain cell patterns or synaptic matrices (memory). And even if one succeeds in breaking some barriers, through persistence and repetition of a new thought-form, or program of thought-forms, the altered-ego will rapidly build another brick wall of defenses around the new programming to justify its actions, with encoded thought-forms pulled from ever deeper layers of past events.

Secondly, all reprogramming techniques attempt to influence the altered-ego by inducing a thought-form program from the surface or outside the brain matter onto the synaptic bundles (memory banks), resulting in a pressure differential due to a polarity shift in the electrochemical balance of the previous thought-form to be changed. For if there were no previously codified thought-forms, there would be no need for reprogramming. Bringing pressure to bear is an apt expression.

Since the altered-ego is extremely sensitive to these pressure differentials, and since the physical cells are also impregnated with an encoded imprint of your beliefs, the new information being forced upon it triggers an attack against an invading force, which also manifests as physical distress signals – regardless of a reprogramming suggestion that is beautiful and constructive. Thus we are handing a million dollars in small bills to the tightrope walker, or breaking and entering a home to repeatedly suggest that the occupants change their color scheme.

All past thought-forms reside codified in the physical brain and the physical cells of the body, and the altered-ego is the guardian and personification of those memories projected onto the auric field and reflected back from the world. It is not difficult to understand, then, how an entity can live lifetime after lifetime locked in past events. This forms such a powerful, binding force through the feedback loop of the altered-ego that it usually requires a severe shock to the system to effect a permanent change or feedback loop of awareness.

Indeed, most entities, through an inner desire to break out of this painful pattern, will manifest just such a shock, in the form of accidents, disease and/or trauma of every conceivable nature.

Although the end result of liberation through disconnecting human past and reconnecting to the past/present/future of GOD-MIND through the Genius Frequency is well worth the effort, the time and amount of suffering generally experienced is not necessary. How this is accomplished will be revealed to your inner nature as we continue to expand our study of creation and its Divine processes. Relax, and enjoy the journey into GOD-MIND.

Questioner: Can you explain more about the relationship of the brain and the mind, and how certain thought-forms can be much stronger than others?

MaYaRa: We shall answer the second part of your query first.

The number or density of photons that create the strength of a given thought-form depends upon the amount of energy, as feelings of emotional desire, resulting in a certain field-strength, giving them a higher charge than the surrounding thought-forms. Thus charged, the collection of photons form a pattern, mathematically and geometrically encoding an idea into a thought-form, a living intelligent entity in the fourth dimension.

Possessing a magnetic charge, the photons instantly collect and organize themselves into a holographic form, an encoded copy of which is etched into the electrochemical replica composing the brain. Another replica is etched upon the cells of the body and moved to an organ or region of the body most receptive to that frequency; and yet another replica resonates in the auric field through harmonic induction, resulting in the final broadcast to other auric fields the nature of who and what the entity is. However, it is only at the stage where the replica ignites similar patterns upon the auric field that the entity becomes cognizant of the thought-form as object – witnessing the experience generated by the living thought-form reflected from the world reality.

For the above reasons, no two entities "see" the world exactly the same, nor should they. For an example, let us take the perception of a tree. The eye perceives the tree, but it does not "see" the tree. The eye is merely a lens for the brain that focuses a specific and narrow range of frequencies upon brain matter which retains the encoded replica, so that a reference can be made as regards sensory objects.

In your elementary studies of biology, you are correctly taught that the retinal image is upside down. At what point it becomes right side up is still a mystery. That is because true perception is a function of mind, not brain. Optically, it makes perfect sense that the image must be projected through another lens onto a surface to reverse the image. That lens is the auric field.

The brain, through inconceivable associative cross-referencing assembles a composite image of the desired or triggered thought-form scenarios, and through the powers of consciousness-awareness are projected upon the auric field. It is at this point that you are cognizant of the tree in its upright perspective. You see, it is the entire body, the entire being that "sees" the tree. The tree would remain hopelessly upside-down in the imaging of brain matter without the surface of the auric field, since the eyes are merely an extension of the brain's sensory functions. Thus, the auric field is the true eye of perception.

The same is true of the other three sense organs, whose job is to receive samples of the material plane for chemical storage in the brain tissue for reference and orientation of the physical body. However, no more thought or reflected consciousness can be produced by this chemical repository than can be produced by a mineral, plant, or animal. Thus, it is the auric field, forming a concave lens, which perceives with the addition of mind.

Questioner: Could the process of identification be a factor in the perceiving, and could you explain in less technical terms how the altered-ego affects this perception?

MaYaRa: We shall use the example of the tree.

It is simply that myriad judgments are made by the intellect in its vain attempt to describe the tree, each different for each individual. Some will perceive it as living intelligence, others as six cords of firewood, or 100 two-by-four boards. Yet others will perceive it as friend and some as a mere obstacle to be removed. What prevents the entity from perceiving the essence of the tree is only the limiting descriptions of it provided by the intellect, a product of the altered-ego which is a compilation of chemically encoded perceptions, as documented by the entity's past sensory experience. Things look different when living in the past.

Since the brain is simply the archive of sensory experience and the altered-ego is its guardian; the ability of the entity to perceive with the entire auric field is severely limited, for the auric field possesses information for which the altered-ego has no reference. The final result is that the altered-ego is the force that convinces the entity that it has no personal connection with the tree or any other creation outside it.

Questioner: Wouldn't it be extremely confusing to see life in this way?

MaYaRa: You are correct to an extent.

The narrow frequency band of awareness in which your altered-ego is designed to operate has the importance of assisting you in maneuvering your physical bio-computer through the maze of objects that surrounds it. This is a question of merely possessing the perception that works best for negotiating your auto vehicles or any other physical movement.

When the potential of your consciousness is open to the Genius Frequency, you have the power to shift consciousness-awareness to any frequency you choose. As it is, you are trapped in 1/10 of the realization of the indescribable beauty of your world and all universes, as well as the ability to interact in the other dimensions where the solutions to all of your problems lie. It is not

1/10th of the brain's capacity th which we refer. It is 1/10th of the auric field's perceptual powers.

The nature of the altered-ego is designed to fixate you in this minute 10% awareness of consciousness and convince you that the narrow frequency band composing the sensory organs is all that there is to life, or at least all that you are capable of perceiving without the use of expensive technology to which few have access. It further restricts the entity by internalizing the fear of what it perceives and suspects as the unknown. The latter is interpreted as death or total annihilation, to be feared at all costs.

Questioner: How then does the auric field provide the function of perception?

MaYaRa: Using our example of the tree again, you can see how the photons are charged with the tree's being. After it is sampled, it is instantly projected or, more accurately, amplified by harmonic resonant induction. These photons vibrate corresponding tones and colors in the auric field. Thus, the perception of the tree within a certain frequency is reflected. In reality, death is merely the change of the frequency of perception, withdrawing the prismatic functions of the bio-organic computer that enables you to interact with matter on an intimate level.

Questioner: How does memory work in conjunction with the auric field of perception in our daily lives?

MaYaRa: First we shall explain this in more or less technical terms and then we shall begin to review more practical examples, explaining how these processes work in your daily lives. For at that point, the entity shall have a fair grasp on the technology of thought-forms as consciousness.

The material explaining memory is sufficiently documented in your scientific research and we have added material to this concept of knowledge to clarify what academic research has not revealed. The crucial difference as set forth in this, and many other teachings of ancient origins, is that perception in its cognizant, conscious awareness cannot occur in the brain. The brain can only store codified samplings of sensory experience as memory for recall.

The brain cannot create thought any more than your computers and their programs can create thought. Memory is not thought. Nor can memory create thought. Only consciousness in Light can create thought. Although memory is made of light, it cannot of its own accord create thought, due to its codified state. It takes the conscious Light of free-awareness, or the Genius Frequency, to free the light trapped in memory so that it can be expanded, changed or recreated. If light is not released from the thought-forms encoded in memory banks and cellular memory, and/or if the angle of perception within the auric field is not changed, a continuous feedback loop of recurring events will persist. The altered-ego I-dentifies with this feedback loop.

Now, with a general background of thought-form and consciousness technology in place, let us begin to explore different aspects of these processes as we visualize their functions.

Back to the tree. As we have stated, the photons are not only charged with the encoding of what you perceive as the tree, but each is charged with an encoded replica of your total being at the moment of perception. Thus, a holographic thought-form is created which, because it contains your personal information as well as that of the perceived object, is magnetically attracted to the entity's bio-computer by harmonic resonance. Like attracts like, so you retain the total composite holograph in memory banks of a combination of you-and-tree. We have explained, yet again, why the Masters teach that you are the tree and the tree is you. That everything is a reflection of yourself is more than a philosophy or myth; it is a most definite, literal, reality.

What is termed the associative mechanism of mind in the academic study of psychology is an accurate concept that we should like to expand. We shall also attempt to clear any ambiguities concerning our statements regarding mind as a function of awareness and consciousness outside the physical brain. You will see that the brain exists IN mind.

We have established that the brain stores holographic thought-forms composed of photons, arranged into a charged pattern: a synaptic matrix. This memory storage system of the brain is far more powerful than all the present computers of earth added together. However, it is similar in that it cannot process this memory without a program. Your present program is, unfortunately, your system of education and indoctrination, a function of the identification process of social-consciousness. It can be stated, with a fair degree of accuracy, that thought-form-replicas locked within the chemical brain are dormant until activated by a program that uses an appropriate portion of the auric field to perceive what it remembers.

It can be seen from the above statements that more information within the same frequency rarely, if ever, solves problems in life created and perpetuated by the feedback loop of the altered-ego. It only provides more reasons to support its limited and basically faulty programming. The brain has the capacity to group together all similar thought-forms into a holographic scenario according to its programming which, when resonating with the auric field, electromagnetically attracts similar scenarios that without fail are experienced again until some change is implemented in the programming.

What is termed a belief system can be one or more of these thought-form scenarios forming the patterns that continually glow in the auric field, magnetizing exterior circumstances and locations into the entity's life and confirming them as personal reality. Thus, we are not stating that there is nothing in your heads. We are stating that the processes of mind take place outside the physical brain, but within the auric field.

The associative mechanism of mind is a physical process of the brain, making it far more potent than any computer hardware presently built. Thought-form scenarios codified as patterned photons continually rearrange themselves as new ones are created. So the physical brain does far more than add a piece of information onto the tail end of the last entry. The sum total of every thought-form you have accumulated in your many lifetimes changes in its totality with each new entry and like the tree, some thought-forms become the leaves, some the bark, etc., forming a total living entity.

However, the processing program of the altered-ego operates very much like present-day computer hardware. It searches for and organizes thought-form data in a linear fashion, totally ignoring the fourth dimensional dynamics of the brain and the fifth dimensional dynamics of the auric field. Tremendous capacity and potential of consciousness is thus bypassed by the inferior programming of the altered-ego.

The fact is, that in any given moment, every thought-form created during all lifetimes of the entity exist within the memory bank of the brain as a total and unified holograph. It is a living entity unto itself. Would you like to "see" that entity? Given this explanation, it is doubtful that there will be a long line of altered-egos waiting to see it. Yet every entity inherently knows that this is true and the guilt and suffering associated with destructive thought-forms attracts more of the same until fear of the growing, malformed holographic entity within begins to surface as every type of psychological disorder. Yet even when the circumstances in life bring these thought-forms into experience to remind the entity that it is still present within, the altered-ego merely labels ever new forms of pathology, as the books on the subject multiply like tadpoles in a spring pond.

The altered-ego is, therefore, the programming itself, relentlessly maintaining the feedback loop of memory into the eternal present moment of human life experience, creating the continual verification of the way life is to you and the way you are in life. Once this process is crystallized, sometime in puberty, the aging process rapidly accelerates due to the entity's sudden awareness that not only will the life experience never change, but the partial life equations are introduced into the new cells producing disease of all types.

The futility of the awareness that life is an endlessly repeating scenario within a finite span of time, ending in a horrifying unknown, is in itself enough to cause the bio-computer to begin self-destructing. The altered-ego, in the futile attempt to maintain the illusion of its evolution in time, seeks distractions that give the illusion that it is changing, that it is futuristic. A true definition of the intellect is an increased self-awareness program of the altered-ego's linear tracking system producing, at best, partial equations in contrast to the totality of consciousness.

This fragmented consciousness, ultimately, creates the thought-form of a partial entity which, by definition, must perish in the scheme of past survival. The intellect, then, as vast as it may become to an individual or society, is not synonymous with true or Cosmic intelligence, which is conscious awareness pervading all things and events as past, present and future simultaneously. The intellect, born of the awareness of the sensory extensions of the physical brain, is deeply entrenched in past events as dredged up from the memory banks, creating the illusion of evolution – an illusion built upon ever more clever ways to justify the past events and experiences by recreating them in various new disguises.

For these reasons, we have defined Intelligence as a holistic, unified field of thought pervading every atom and providing an open-ended universe of creative energy, capable of conscious participation in simultaneous events in at least seven dimensions. From yet another angle, Intelligence may be defined as the original program of universal mind.

By contrast, the intellect is a subset of the quantum energy fields of Universal Mind trapped in the binding process which compresses Light into matter, which is exactly the same as structured memory. All material creation by virtue of its polarized existence must oscillate as a pendulum within its Alpha and Omega cycles of expansion and contraction. Thus, material creation, in toto, is a fragment of the whole truth of creation and therefore, the fragmentary truth of every physical entity in the material plane of existence.

The axiom of all creator-gods is I AM THAT I AM, a divine expression of Universal Intelligence. You can begin to see the disastrous consequences of living a partial truth such as I-am-that-I-was or I-was-that-I-am. Through the limitations of the altered-ego the integrity of the bio-system is subverted as photons of light realign and rearrange themselves to form an incomplete, fragmented entity. As you shift from the partial truths of the intellect, as directed by the altered-ego that breeds thought-forms of fear and annihilation through the concepts of separatism, toward the unifying domain of Universal Intelligence, you are tuning into the Genius Frequency where healing, peace, prosperity, and joy are the foundations for true evolution.

Questioner: Is it true that we use only 1/10 of our brains?

MaYaRa: Your scientific community has made this statement of "fact" quite fashionable. In a day and age where most entities are disillusioned with the promises made by an arrogant technologically-based civilization, it appears that this statement is offered as a convenient excuse for the shortcomings of the system and is a clever way of admitting defeat, while subtly suggesting that a retarded and ignorant majority is to blame for the failures of the elite.

Yet the supporting arguments for the "90% unused brain" are glossed over. If this statement is true, then what happened to the other 90% ? If you have it and don't use it, why? If you have it and it is not necessary, where did it come from? If you had it and lost it, where did it go, why did you lose it, and how could your society appear to be so advanced without it? If you did use it, what would happen? If Darwinistic evolution is a fact, then such a capacity having evolved for no apparent reason would completely refute the theory of "natural selectivity." If the brain capacity evolved suddenly in the ancient past and then became dormant, it would indicate that you are devolving! Realize that institutions have collective altered-egos which mindlessly defend their vested interests. Thus, it is properly the mind and not the brain that you use 10% of, and as we have outlined in the previous segments (chapters 3 and 4), this is compounded by the holographic interfacing of all seven brain/mind-centers – making it virtually impossible to isolate a specific area or boundary between functions. Each is part of all in the holography of life.

It may be stated at this juncture that the answer to this quandary is that humans use 10% of the auric field that is visibly illuminated by conscious thought. We shall examine this in greater depth in a later segment of this book. For now, it is sufficient to understand that the auric field is a shell or force field, resulting from the meeting of two forces: electromagnetic attraction, and a combination of thermodynamic and high-frequency light radiation.

These two opposing forces take place in the fourth dimensional pressure zone of equalization, just as the skin of the body is the third dimensional pressure zone forming a shell between the tendency of the body to expand against the compression of the atmospheric weight of your environment. Relating to the skin, any substance – and relating to the auric field, any thought-form received or transmitted – must interact with this barrier. As you see, there are laws of physics in the astral lane. Perhaps this concept will serve as a tool of understanding as we continue our examination of the intellect and Intelligent Mind.

The altered-ego is the third dimensional lord and master of sensory data. Since all sensory data, at best, can occupy only 10% of the auric field's capacity for thought, and since your system of education and indoctrination is primarily, almost exclusively, third dimensional, there is little wonder why this "lord and master" could only identify the brain as that which is partially used.

With this strategy, it can then promise that its technology will "someday" develop a suitable brain so you can throw away the old model and buy a new one providing, of course, that you can afford it. This game has been played for millennia upon the earth plane. It has been the solemn duty of all earthly hierarchies to "brainwash" its people into believing that the lot of them are inferior mutants and sinners dependent upon the few who magnanimously sustain them from oblivion. Thus, the people chant, "God save the king, God save the queen, God save science." The fact is that each is responsible for saving himself.

The point here is that every entity has the potential, yea, the innate ability to live in Christ Consciousness, to walk and communicate with THE ONE directly. Do not be confused by the bantering of the altered-ego designed to render you an earth slave, chained to the third dimensional sense world. If a part of you wonders why the altered-ego would go to such lengths of deception to render you a helpless victim rather than truly developing a better life for all – which it self-righteously claims – then think again. What need has any entity of such a limited system if ALL can walk in the all mighty power of THE ONE?

The fears of the altered-ego regarding the loss of its beloved institutions are absurd and completely unfounded. For even Jesus, walking as the Christ upon earth, studied many treasures of the earth. Thus, there shall always be a need for certain specialties of thought and study. Through the Christ consciousness using 100% of GOD-MIND, great advances will bring all areas of thought under the common goal of perfecting all life.

Questioner: When considering how deeply entrenched human awareness is in the altered-ego, not only on a personal basis, but worldwide, it seems that only a few will accomplish the goals of higher consciousness. It has proved so in the past. Why should it be any different now?

MaYaRa: A very poignant query. If you choose to remain open to our communication, we fully intend to reveal a most profound, exciting and hopeful reply.

For now, we ask you to contemplate the entirely unique phenomenon in which you are engaged at this moment. For you, and thousands of other entities, who choose to continue the efforts in the search for truth by directly going within, great accomplishments are flourishing. In the very near future in your time, tens of thousands and yes, even hundreds of thousands will joyfully engage in communication with the higher intelligence working with THE ONE. Higher frequencies than ever before are pouring into the earth-body/mind from the inside out and eventually all will be engulfed in this frequency.

The tremendous changes upon and within the earth at this time attest to this fact. Erratic weather and psychological and physical changes indicate that the old order of the altered-ego, regardless of how long it has been entrenched, can be uprooted in a heart beat. Those that choose to upgrade their spiritual/physical unification in THE ONE shall reap benefits untold, in comparatively short periods of time in this lifetime. Those who accept responsibility for their lives and work to elevate their consciousness and the consciousness of those around them in the Name of THE ONE will engage in great acts of healing, teaching, organizing and quickening this higher frequency into a peaceful world order – not the political world order by war.

The information of higher knowledge, such as that given to you and thousands of others at this time, is being released at unprecedented rates, as authorized by the Higherarchy governing the evolution of universal systems. We are at the cosmic threshold of the Omega cycle of rebirth and re-creation. This teaching, as well as others of the same and higher frequencies, is designed to familiarize all entities who choose to know about their higher natures and the processes that govern them, so that they will not be fearful of the changes that are building.

Armed with this knowledge, they may walk in the Light of THE ONE and in turn, ease the fears of those with innocent hearts, as well as those bearing the passion to be a part of the new earth, regardless of their histories. By understanding these higher teachings, a joyful wisdom will replace fearful ignorance as the most intimate thought-forms of all entities are magnified. When dreams become so vivid that they begin to manifest in the waking state, what will you do without this higher wisdom?

Realize that the totality of your billions of thought-forms trapped within a lower order of light exist through the holographic functions of creation as one total thought-form, just as your physical body forms one body comprised of millions of cells. Taking this one step further, the thought-forms and the physical cells are all thoughts forming reflections of the entity who bears them and gives them life. So for you who have been tormented by your feelings of insignificance, know that it takes only one thought-form of the proper frequency to change the world significantly. No one can save you. You must choose to be chosen.

We invite you to join with the 144,000 ascended Masters of this universe and the millions of Masters and guides who work with only THE ONE to bring forth the changes, peacefully and joyfully. It cannot be done without you, for you are physically there and are the only ones who can directly influence the elements of earth-mind through your precious bodies. All of you have guides who are waiting for you to find them. Together we shall build a new world of Light in the Light of THE ONE.

Questioner: What is the most effective way to hasten these connections and how is the Genius Frequency to be understood?

MaYaRa: We shall briefly answer the second part of your query first, as this is a subject to be treated in more depth in later segments of this document, if you choose to continue communications.

The Genius Frequency is within you and without you on all levels of creation at all moments in all dimensions of universal intelligence. It is a frequency of golden Light connecting every atom to every other, providing an instant and continual web-work of communication in all realms simultaneously. To resonate with this frequency is to open conscious contact with the totality of your auric mind, connecting you to the true powers of Co-creation for the benefit and eternal life in the Light of THE ONE for all.

The most effective way to "hasten," as you term it, the conscious connection with your guides through resonating with the Genius Frequency is not to hasten at all. All beings aboard planet earth feel the "time crunch," however. It is only the panic-stricken altered-ego that is desperately trying to work out its sensory survival. Oh yes, we have seen so-called enlightened, new-age entities, who at this moment are stealthily planning their defenses from the changes to come to your planet. For many of these entities are still in the grip of the altered-ego's plan to serve self at the expense of others. However, their plans will be divided within, for the new frequencies cannot support the lower frequencies. All of those who choose to elevate the planet and those upon it shall be instructed as to when and where they should move, and when and where they should stay.

The most effective means to begin or improve communication with Higher Intelligence working with THE ONE, is to be still: To sit in the calm and peace within each of you that connects each of your mind-centers. Be still. Contemplate and meditate. Read works of high frequency, then meditate and let your own truth surface, and only then take appropriate action. Call upon your inner Light within the Heart of Hearts and command it, in the name of THE ONE, to permeate your being, illuminating the darkness of the altered-ego. Let the fears of sensory thinking melt into a knowingness of your eternal nature and the glorious future being prepared for those who consciously follow their inner guidance, as you seek the highest truth for you to act upon in your now moment. Do not look far, beloved; for you are the Light of the world.

The purpose of all of this is to create a space for higher frequencies to circulate. This occurs automatically, to some extent, when you sleep, although the act is not a conscious decision and even then the altered-ego is busy at work to ascribe every possible sensory explanation of what is occurring. Dreams that you remember usually do not make sense because the low frequency altered-ego makes a super effort to translate each very high-frequency experience into a sensual one. Thus, by a conscious effort during waking hours to suspend at least some of the functions of the altered-ego, such as the intellect, a true intelligence frequency may resume its work to realign and heal the entity. Your dreams will begin to speak to you, coherently.

It is a matter of temporarily disconnecting your attention from its ceaseless evaluations of the status of the physical machinery. The altered-ego lures you into a fear that if you stop paying attention to the echoes of its memory banks, trouble will certainly be waiting for you. The term "paying" attention is most appropriate, for the entity pays heavily for not attending to the higher frequencies which regenerate it.

Try it: Take this moment to close your eyes and begin to relax into the higher frequencies of Light, and you will feel the tremendous push of the altered-ego to remind you of "so many things to do." If you succeed in relaxing, it sends out stronger fear signals to win your attention again, for it cannot function without your attention.

Many have been misled by some teachings claiming that to properly meditate, one must achieve a mindless and thoughtless state of oblivion. This sets up another fear cycle which may be dispelled by your consciousness light. The truth is that your entire bio-computer is a thought-form. You were thought into beingness. Without the process of thought you could not exist. Therefore, know that the notion of thoughtlessness is not only misleading, but absurd. However, it is quite possible and very desirable not to think, insofar as thinking is related to the intellect. So it is not this fearful matter of seeking oblivion, but rather of seeking a pristine moment when the channels to your mind centers are clear from their usual distortions, static and diversions, so that higher thought-forms can be received on the Genius Frequency – unpolluted and undistorted. It is a moment more powerful that you can imagine at this time.

Questioner: What is an effective meditating technique?

MaYaRa: There are as many techniques as there are individual entities who meditate. Any form of meditation raises the primary frequency of all seven mind-centers. What you are interested in is the highest results. Thus, some experimentation on the part of the entity is not only suggested, it is mandatory based upon the unique nature of each entity. Stilling the mind is a necessary step. But the Genius Frequency is not a mind game. The Genius Frequency is Cosmic Intelligence.

Meditation is simply the balancing of the seven prismatically divided mind centers. The balancing process then must be individually tailored for each entity. Whatever technique the entity uses, the objective is to achieve harmonic resonance with the Genius Frequency, connecting all to all, which has little to do with the intellect and everything to do with Cosmic Intelligence. We feel that it is far more important to educate each entity as to the processes of consciousness, so that the objectives are clear. For the details and specifics of each entity's liberation is a very personal matter and not for another to prescribe.

Questioner: Would you give a more detailed explanation of the seven mind-centers?

MaYaRa: Within the auric field of thought, located in seven ascending positions within the physical body, are seven complete mind-centers that directly create and maintain clusters of glands and organs representing their functions. The free energy of awareness associated with these centers are very well-known through Eastern teachings as chakras or spinning vortices of energy. What we endeavor to add to this fundamental truth is that each is to be regarded as a mind unto itself. For some, this may seem to be a subtle play on words, and for others, this may be impossible to comprehend. However, you shall see the wisdom of this concept as we proceed in our examination.

The functions of each mind-center are similar to those of the brain. Each contains a preset portion of the Adamic Blueprint for initial form and function with a particular quality of life force, activating earth elements to form a particular area of the body. The complete blueprint for the original Adamic, or human image is located in the Heart of Hearts. None of this is as strange as it first may seem. For in each of these six locations in the physical body resides a concentrated complex of nerves or ganglia which any earth doctor can verify.

We say six because the seventh mind center resides on the top of the head as an invisible fourth dimensional nerve center. So, each of you possesses, physically, six brains complete with its original memory template and accumulated memories of the entity's activities and thought-forms, relating to that particular domain of life on earth. Each brain center is surrounded by a spinning energy which connects it to the auric field, forming a color band of awareness enabling the process of thinking to take place in that medium of thought. These brain/mind-centers are consciously aware memory banks manifested in form appropriate to their functions. What you term the brain is no different and possesses no capacity to think as reflective consciousness.

There is one difference, however, in the function of the brain located in the skull cavity; and this difference explains the discrepancy discussed in the earlier material (of this Chapter), concerning some 90% of the brain's area which is unaccountable in scientific research. That is, the brain serves as a "back up" memory bank. The supposed oversized brain stores duplicate memory holographs of the lower five brain centers. This becomes evident in events where the organism is damaged and the composite memory can be supplied one to the other for repair. Thus, it is seen that when damage occurs in an area within the domain of a brain/mind-center, the original and karmic patterns of memory can be supplied by the other.

You have many examples of an entity who has no apparent "mental" activity or what is also termed "brain dead," yet the body continues to function. You have also examples of entities whose organs have been damaged, yet the backup memory patterns in the brain sustain it and assist in the rebuilding process and substitution of functions, one organ for another. Without this interactive cross-referencing of independent brain centers, the slightest damage would result in instant death of the physical body.

The original function of this "extra" capacity of the brain is to concentrate the total thought-form memories of all the other brain centers into a physical location close to the higher Cosmic Intelligence which has the ability to alter the molecular frequency and composition of the other brain centers, so that they may all receive the regenerative Higher Cosmic Intelligence enabling the entire physical body to move in and out of other dimensions. However, to accomplish this, the color bands or thought-form frequencies of the auric field must be in harmonic alignment, creating a perfect vertical energy flow from the first brain center to the last.

All entities possess this capacity via the amigdala complex. The altered-ego, however, has usurped this function of the brain for the purpose of expanding sensory data. This explains your three dimensional sensory expansion of technology.

With the above conceptual schematic in mind, we may proceed with some earthly examples. In order to build and power an elemental body in a dense material sphere, such as earth, a very powerful atom of pure Light, termed by us the Primary Seed Crystal, containing the pure Light Image or the Adamic Image of Man, is projected as a point of pure Mind of THE ONE and located in the Heart of Hearts. The next event is the division or refraction, prismatically, of that point of pure Mind into brain centers driven by certain color tones that have specific qualities and functions to perform, which become their domains of operation. These operations are used for the purpose of manifesting that quality of mind through the Adamic Image as material reality in the third dimensional dynamics of creation.

Now, every activity that an entity is involved in is influenced by one of the domains under the jurisdiction of a mind-center appropriate to its function. Thus, all thought-forms, appropriate to the function of a particular mind-center, direct that activity. However, you are still the conductor of this orchestra.

The vast majority of activities engaged in by human entities at this time are influenced by only one or two brain/mind centers at any one time. For example, a sports activity might use only intense willpower in conjunction with brain centers that control specific motor functions. A career might demand only the intellect and willpower. The expression of physical love would only use the sexual brain center with portions of willpower and/or imagination formed from past memory locked in that particular brain center. Granted, the effects of any of these or other activities can be powerful and often seem quite fulfilling. Recall the grandest moment of your life and it would only be a minute fraction of the joy that is possible for you to experience by opening to and tuning into the Genius Frequency.

The great joy of tapping into the Genius Frequency can only manifest when ALL of the mind-centers are activated and harmoniously used together. The power from this total unity is so tremendous, so awesome in its scope, that words utterly fail to describe it. This unfathomable power would command respect in all sectors of all galaxies in all universes. It can be readily seen, then, that no entity ever can possess this power unless all the mind-centers are united in harmonious, powerful, high frequencies termed "love" in your language. If it were possible to unify all mind-centers in any other frequency, as you might imagine, the universe would rip itself apart in total annihilation in an instant. Regardless of what type of powers are promised by those who teach partial equations of life, they must, by the inherent law of Love in the universes, result in self destruction, suffering and death. This Law is made clear to every co-creator by THE ONE.

Every biologically incarnate human enters the wheel of life through the celestial mind-energies, termed by you as astrological signs, and it is no accident or mindless myth that has designated these power sectors of angular velocities as a collection of animals. We shall explore this portion of galactic consciousness at a later segment of this document. For now, understand that we draw your attention to the fact that, generally, each human embodiment is endowed with an unbalanced energy spectrum. That is, each has entered from a previous lifetime with energy concentrated in one mind-center, revealing a lack or weakness in the entity's makeup. This is termed by you as personality or character and you are taught to live with it or fight against it. Rarely, if ever, is the entity taught to balance these mind powers.

Cosmic Intelligence leads to the "Mansion Worlds of the Father," referred to in your ancient book. These are other dimensions of existence which are your inheritance. The Genius

Frequency is the key to unlocking the doors of these Mansion Worlds. Each entity is a personal mansion, given as a gift to explore intimately in the experiential reality of a segment of creation. The intellect is a closet within the small room of the altered-ego, shutting you out of the treasures that lie within. Not to use the key of the Genius Frequency to unlock the doors within is to live a partial equation of life fraught in fear and needless shocks of death transitions. Your mansion was created for you to have the great, joyful adventure of discovering the treasures, created by THE ONE, the ALL-THAT-IS, so lovingly given to each of you.

Look at the countless examples of entities that have developed only one or two of the mind-centers. Study the lives of those who only develop their sexual, will, vocal, intellect or psychic powers. You will find, without exception, incomplete, fragmented equations of life, of the totality of their mind-centers – so many incomplete and tragic stories of unfulfillment and suffering, of rich and poor alike. Yes, examine all the teachings of the pseudo-teachers running about your planet preaching: Develop your mind power; develop your sex power; develop your voice power; develop your muscular power or develop your psychic powers. Each of these are related to one of the mind-centers. They teach you to remain locked in one small room of the altered-ego; and by believing in it, you deny yourself the right to true health, prosperity and holistic joy that THE ONE has designed for each of you to celebrate.

The divisions formed by refracting the pure Adamic Seed Crystal into seemingly separate minds are in fact there, not only for the purpose of building and maintaining a physical thought-form, but for the purpose of studying and recognizing the different aspects of Cosmic Intelligence, as it reflects itself in the material creations.

The purpose of this examination is to bring to your conscious awareness the understanding that the same processes of the altered-ego that operate in the so-called "outside world" are those that operate within your being. Moreover, that which is "outside" is a direct result of those processes within. It is too easy to condemn the condition of your world, believing that you are helpless to affect change within and that by changing yourself you cannot possibly affect the world at large. This is precisely what the altered-ego creates. However, the solution is not to simply shut down the altered-ego or the intellect. It is, rather, the unification, balancing and synchronous resonance of the many mind-centers into one mind-center. This is the true work of I-dentifying with the eternal energy of LOVE-LIGHT/GOD-MIND that streams into your Heart Of Hearts. For that is the only location in your physical being where you may apprehend the God-Energy before it becomes polluted by the other brain centers, containing the contaminated thought-forms within their memory banks.

Go into your Heart of Hearts, into the Seed Crystal of your pure energy being and command from your highest power that the other brain centers be unified in the Cosmic Intelligence that will set you free and prepare you for the new energy of Light that is now pulsing into the center of your solar logos and every planet to uplift you. This will occur only if you so choose to carry on as a Co-Creator with THE ONE.

Command, do not ask, that your mind-centers operate on the Genius Frequency. The persistence in this most important matter shall open the secrets of the stars to you, revealing the glory that you have always been and ever shall be. There shall be no problem that you cannot solve, for the Universal, Cosmic Intelligence will be instantly available; and the many entities of the Light (not of the technological space gods) will communicate their help to you and assist you in the co-creation of an existence, even in the material world, of true freedom and Light.

Cosmic Intelligence is not a mind game. It is Life. It is the creative process that formed the universes of which each of you is a micro-replica. The history of your lives in earth bears witness to these truths. Every ruined civilization has tried to control the world by concentrating and worshipping every mind-center, save the Heart of Hearts. The results are always the same because a partial equation of the Life Force can only produce entropy and decay.

If you have built your world around one or two mind-centers, you will live in fear because your inner knowingness has calculated the factors of entropy leaving you with little hope for a better life. The altered-ego seizes upon this fear and pushes you relentlessly to defend its limited outlook, always painting pictures from its polluted memory banks of imminent annihilation, serving as the primary motivation for the food-chain-mentality.

The earth is moving into a fourth dimensional paradigm where a partial life-equation can no longer function. All who cling to the fearful vibrations and frequencies of the altered-ego will find themselves in a world consisting of thought-forms that manifest as stark reality within moments after they are conceived. That is the "hell" described in your ancient book, although the interpretation has been distorted for the purpose of controlling other entities. These events do not occur due to any wrath or vengeance from THE ONE. These are a natural breathing cycle of the universe as it evolves. The only "hell" that exists is one of choosing to cut oneself off from the threads of sustenance from THE ONE by not making the effort to evolve with the universe into the Light.

Actually, NOW in your time, the cosmic doors of perception are opening freely for all who choose to step through. In a moment, a heart beat, the Genius Frequency can channel energy that you simply cannot imagine through the intellect. Now is the time when all have the natural boost of Cosmic Intelligence to carry all into the age of Light. Now is the time to practice being a co-creator in the scheme of life: to dream and plan a perfect life; to warm up "behind the lines," knowing that very soon you shall be called into play.

Even now, your deepest thought-forms are manifesting before your eyes. What will you be creating when the power of Light intensifies upon and through your planet? If this boggles your intellect, it most definitely should. For the intellect is founded upon limited, third dimensional judgments, and cannot handle the higher frequencies of Cosmic Intelligence. The intellectual structure will explode as it confronts the incredible reality-events to come. In the meantime, the intellect shall judge itself into oblivion.

You, beloved, are the lights through which Cosmic Intelligence will pour, if you choose to prepare yourself for this momentous event. No one else, not Jesus, Buddha, Krishna, nor even God, THE ONE, can do this for you. It is your responsibility to contemplate, choose, and act to prepare yourselves. We repeat that this is neither a fairy tale, nor a metaphor, nor idle philosophy; but is an event in progress at this moment in your time and rapidly consummating into the final adjustments of Omega.

If you choose, you may command, by your highest Light in every breath, that your mind-centers be unified in the pure Light within you. You may wake up to the music of the spheres and write your own symphony of Life, and receive the untold joy in beholding the myriad life forms dancing within your song. That is what Cosmic Intelligence is about. To awake in the morning of multiple blue-white and golden stars of wisdom within you, illuminating the universe with your being as your individual essence of THE ONE becomes the space for new worlds. This is a critical time in the cosmic timetables. You may be a part of this, if you unify your mind-centers with the Genius Frequency. Indeed, this is why you are embodied at this fortuitous time in creation.

THE BRAIN

"A HOLOGRAPHIC UNIVERSE"

*"In the Genius Frequency,
you go beyond the fragmented,
partial equations of life that block your
understanding of the totality of your being."*

Questioner: How can we best begin to realize the totality of ourselves?

MaYaRa: Although the totality of each entity is something that cannot be described directly in your language, it most certainly can be experienced by every entity. The entity needs only to open itself to its highest purpose by beginning to take stock of all the qualities and quantities of thought-forms that it embodies. The so-called positive and negative qualities of each entity, in a grand perspective, are merely polarities of a micro-universe of oscillating elec-

tromagnetic pulses. The vast majority of entities have been indoctrinated by education and environments, created and governed by
the altered-ego, to believe that each is a finite, limited creature.
There is another part of every entity, deep within the memory
banks, that knows this to be false teaching and misinformation. In
reality, every entity knows its origins. Thus, it is a question of
memory, of remembering.

How does one go about remembering? Passing the low frequency functions of the altered-ego and its functions, of the intellect and its varying degrees of sensory logic, is the first step for
those who have been indoctrinated by Western thinking. This may
seem like an impossible task at first, but you would do well to
know that the simple act of reading this material, the ancient books
or any literature of a higher operating frequency than that of the
altered-ego, bypasses the altered-ego. You will know when this is
the case because the Heart-Mind will crave the information, the intellect will be overwhelmed by it, and the defense mechanisms of
the altered-ego will be screaming at you to stop wasting time with
such myth and fantasy and get down to the practical, everyday
business of surviving.

A word of advice to the reader will be in order at this juncture. When studying any material, concept, teaching or technique,
observe your reactions. The entity may learn which mind-center is
concerned or activated in some way. If the entity should be reading
a religious document and come upon a passage taking a stand a-
gainst all types of sexual activity, there is a very good chance that
a hearty rebellion from the first chakra or mind-center will be the
result.

In this simple example, it would be clear that the sexual
mind-center is involved. The point of this is that there is a very
refined consciousness of a high frequency that each of you possess,
but with which you do not resonate. It is neutral, open, nonjudg-

mental, clear, yet discerning and most intelligent. It is located in the Heart of Hearts.

Understand that all beliefs are under the control of the altered-ego. Thus, whether you believe or do not believe what you see or hear is not necessarily an indication of the truth. This is the most common flaw and trap of the altered-ego. So many entities are drawn to finding the light on their path and are stopped short, either by believing what they are exposed to or not believing it. Either way, it is a judgment call by the altered-ego and the entity may not change or may even lose the way altogether. It is imperative that you discover the truth for yourself. This is not to say that there are no higher or universal truths and that all truth is totally relative to the individual. The latter is a definition of ignorance. The truth is not something that can be agreed upon or disagreed with by the altered-ego. It is a living thought-form that increases the overall frequency of Love/Light within the entity, promoting a sense of awe and well-being. If the entity finds itself arguing with another or itself about any truth, be it a personal truth or a Universal Truth, it can be sure that the altered-ego has waylaid the attempt at enlightenment.

At a later time, in your time, we shall expound upon the above statements. For now, we shall get on with some very exciting explorations into consciousness, as we make the assumption that those entities who have read thus far are undaunted by material that exceeds the frequency of the altered-ego. The adventure of Life was meant to be joyful.

Here are three steps for those entities who are encumbered by the intellectual function of altered-ego:

1. Study material of a higher frequency than that of the altered-ego, in order to bypass its conceptual limitations.

2. Visualize higher realities in a contemplation of high frequency material, in order to increase the frequency of the perceptual apparatus such as sacred geometry.

3. Use the functions of imagination to feel the realities of those visualizations. Always prepare yourself with an internal, centering contemplation, such as that given for the Heart of Hearts (Chapter 3), before exploring the illusion of external realities.

Let us then begin a contemplation and visualization of what appears to be a universe beyond. We make this arbitrary distinction because some entities may find it difficult at first to see that the external universe and the internal universe are the same, each existing in the other, each directly influencing and creating the other. Some entities claim that they are not capable of visualizing. This is a limited precept of the altered-ego and has no foundation whatever. The simple, elementary act of drawing a square upon paper cannot be accomplished without the ability to visualize.

There are many academic programs on earth that include studies for the appreciation of a subject such as music. You may regard the following as cosmic appreciation. Read slowly, if necessary. Stop often to close your eyes and visualize, and then reread. Again, it is not a matter of believing or disbelieving. It is a matter of raising the frequency of perception by stretching, as it were, your faculties for comprehending and experiencing a greater truth for YOU. Knowledge cannot become wisdom, unless it resonates with the Heart-Mind in the Seed Crystal of pure consciousness. Let us begin by freeing inner consciousness from the limited intellect and letting it soar like a great bird into the mind of THE ONE. Relax into your innate knowingness that you are a Light. Open your mind-centers to the highest truth. Ready?

As you gaze into the heavens on a starlit night, realize that this stupendous display of Light bodies exists also during your light-time. Gaze into the blue biosphere, during this light-time, and realize that the billions of star-bodies and the galactic information network ceaselessly communicate thought-forms to all regions, to all dimensions, in all forms of time/space and space/time. Visualize these simultaneous events to whatever degree to which you are comfortable, and then "stretch" to include concepts that you do not immediately comprehend, such as orbiting solar systems.

Take the time to familiarize yourself with the dynamics of your universe, knowing that the same processes of creation are active within you. Let each concept, each word, become a pictograph or thought-form scenario which spirals through the illusion of space/time in the dynamics of illusion of motion within the stillness of GOD-MIND. Construct a Nautilus of knowledge.

Visualize the planets revolving around the solar logos within the edge of your galaxy. Now, begin to visualize your galaxy as a living, intelligent entity in cycles of breathing – of expansion and contraction, as well as in an orbital configuration.

Now, visualize the five circulatory systems of your body as an expanding/contracting, ebbing and flowing of life giving liquids of light through miles of tubes and billions of chambers that pulsate in sets and subsets of capillary action, powered by the chambers of the heart, centered within this universe of intelligence, organized by the seven mind-centers of spiraling, electromagnetic and geomagnetic energy vortices of light that communicate with and coordinate infinite numbers of wave and particle geometries.

Next, visualize the particle organizations within your body and "see" how the systems take form from thought into the shape of various organs and glands. Stretch your inner perceptual powers. "See" the millions of similar, yet completely unique molecular patterns of each of these organs formed from the light-geometries, known as hydrogen-oxygen-nitrogen-carbon chains, creating an intelligent network of consciously interactive reflections of a projected image.

Visualize the individual, atomic "solar systems" that form the specific valences necessary to create the bonding process that attracts "sympathetically resonating" earth elements, locking them in angles of intersection, forming shapes of frequencies that you sense as water, amino acids, DNA, RNA, tRNA (messenger RNA): all made of light. See the electrons whirling through their infinite space, at the speed of light, creating a space/time for light to coalesce

*into matter. And know that anything that can
travel at the speed of light, is light!*

*Understand all of this in terms of light-
energy-waves. Stretch your inner auditory perceptions. Hear the sound-tonal vibration from
each atomic solar system, each tuned to a
specific harmonic of an octave. See the waves
pulsating, oscillating, expanding into ripples
that also intersect at angles, forming trillions of
sound/color tapestries. Within this tapestry,
each intersecting ripple of sound/color forms a
harmonic resonant point, setting up a galaxy of
electromagnetic pulsars, quasars, white holes
and black holes acting as energy portals, transmuting energy, information, consciousness into
other dimensions within dimensions and universes within universes.*

*Now, switch to your "normal" vision.
Gaze upon that galactic starscape again. As you
perceive those heavenly bodies, know that you
could not see them if they were not connected to
you. They are not objects that you perceive at a
distance, but rather a continuous stream of
consciousness filling all space between you and
it. Those liquid orbs, your eyes, are also
spheres, for they were formed by the same intelligent bodies that produce the modified, dual
nature of Light from The Mind of THE ONE.
Only motion creates the illusion of space and
time.*

*But there is a Light from which the light
of material worlds is generated. This Light is*

only invisible to the elemental eyes of earth. It is not invisible to the inner eye of consciousness. Switch to your inner eye and behold the Spectra-Light filling all space with the frequency of Genius, of all-knowing communication with all dimensions. It creates its own tapestry of thought intersecting at harmonic resonant points that ignite and sustain the stars. Visualize this Omnipresent Light radiating in all directions, meeting Itself at points that form stars that reflect the thought-forms of THE ONE. You exist within and are a tapestry of Light and light-related energies in an infinite matrix of angular velocities and intersections, forming oceans and rivers of pyramidal, crystalline life. The so-called void or space is, so to speak, "solid" with the energies of Light creations. All objects that you perceive are points of light intersecting as points of conscious energy. The center of each object is the center of every other object.

Hold this tapestry of light in your inner vision. Reread the exercise until each of the pictures you form during the reading can be added to the other. Feel the reality of that vision. Remember your Light Body.

Now, look at the objects in your room and another entity or animal or any life form that may be present and imagine the universe within that being. Go inside it. There is another galaxy. There is more Light. Eternal Light!

"See" what you are missing? Do not leave the interpretations of this stupendous reality to the scientists, religious administrators and academicians of the world. The universe IS consciousness-awareness and you are obviously part and parcel of that universe. Therefore, you are a consciously aware universe in your own right. Consciousness-awareness operating on the Genius Frequency is the only scientific instrument necessary to unlock the secrets of the universe. The consciousness of the Genius Frequency, which holds together the tapestry of you, is all that you will ever need. For it is LIGHT-LOVE/GOD-MIND.

Take the time every day to visualize the tapestries of light. Even a few moments has profound effects upon the nervous system. When you exercise your consciousness awareness in this manner, the Genius Frequency opens by degrees. When that occurs, the feeling of connection with the universe that you are is generated, and a vast system of universal data is accessible to your mind in the waking state.

In the Genius Frequency, you go beyond the fragmented, partial equations of life that block your understanding of the totality of your being. The intellect, as defender of the altered-ego, has worn you down and convinced you that a few know and the remainder do not. This is an absurd limitation of your light. Every entity knows everything inherently, because it is everything. Everything is a form of Light and all Light is a form of consciousness. Consciousness is aware of itself. Each of you is Light consciousness perceiving itself and its unfolding into and out of itself. How grand and exquisite you are! How sacred and wondrous Creation is!

Questioner: Can these visualization techniques be used in place of meditation?

MaYaRa: They are used simultaneously with it. The above technique is a contemplation. Meditation and contemplation are two half-waves creating a full cycle, just as two half circles are required to produce a sine wave when extended in time. Thus, all "either/or" situations are a gross limitation upon awareness, lowering the frequency of consciousness awareness by not allowing it to complete its natural wave function as light. One cannot be fully accomplished without the other. Meditation is a balancing function of the transmitting portion of the bio-computer, and contemplation is the same for the receiver portion.

One meditates to still the rampant and repetitive thought-form dialogue roaring in the oceans of earth mind, including the cellular memory banks of the seven mind-centers. Thus, while in meditation, it is also necessary to contemplate the awesome scope of Creation, creating a clear space in the receiver functions of consciousness, freeing these to apprehend the totality of your being. The transmitter then becomes passive and the receiver becomes active. There is a self-organizing aspect to this process. The mind-centers begin to align with the Genius Frequency and the entity begins to feel the infinite quality of being ONE.

Questioner: Would it be appropriate, now, to explain in more detail, the use of the term "nodal-points?"

MaYaRa: Indeed. As we attempt to formulate the complex mechanics of the universe in this limited syntax, we suggest that the following material also be used as a contemplation. Contemplation is a powerful tool of consciousness-awareness perception that, coupled with imagination, bypasses the intellect. Thus, the entity may increase the overall resonant frequency of the bio-computer, regardless that the entity does not immediately comprehend intellectually. The total mind field shall easily retain the information and loosen the limitations of the altered-ego's belief systems through a higher order and frequency of thought-forms. Meet this Sacred Process half-way and it will work for you..

Now, waves within waves, radiated and received by heavenly bodies, including every atom of your being, in every direction, form "nodal-points" of angular intersection where they cross
each other, forming an holographic image. Everything that you
perceive, all the life within and about you is a holograph of Divine
thought-form projections manifesting into form within matrix
fields, the tapestry of intelligent energy.

In this same process, the totality of every entity, as well as
each atomic unit of this energy, produces wave-form and particle-
mass, radiating in wave frequencies that intersect and communicate with all other cosmic waves issuing from the Mind of THE
ONE. Further, you and your fellowman radiate and receive in the
same exact manner, so that the transmitted and received thought-
forms intersect to create nodal-points, or events, that you experience as reality.

Form and function follow each other in the pyramidal geometries of your circle of life, so that all appearances taking place in
your perception of it are actually a cross section or slice of a conic
section of pyramidal frequencies, as revealed in the crystalline
nature of the blood cell. In other words, all so-called objects in so-
called space are holographs formed by the multi-projection properties of conscious light waves intersecting to form nodal points.

Again, in a slightly different way: the Rays of life-force
move through, with, and against themselves, exiting a resonant frequency that takes on an individualized consciousness, becoming a
point of intelligence within a membrane of tension. This is the
basis for cell formation and the collective mind of the auric field.
The membrane is reflective and refractive, thereby forming a resonating micro-replica of cosmic functions that reflect the universal
life force, as well as contain it as individualized awareness that
becomes consciousness when it becomes aware of itself. Thus,
there is no need to search some eternal "distance" to understand

who or what God is. You are a replica of the entire, cosmic process of the Mind of THE ONE.

The variance of life forms, that originated as thought-forms, are due to geometric digressions – or what your scientists term "fractal geometries" – of atomic and molecular structures assembling at points of resonance within membranes of tension, created by holographic imaging, or standing wave forms manifested by thought. In other words, the Creator God "appears" in as many fractal forms as there are possible combinations of geometric angles of intersection – Infinite life.

Thus, even in a seemingly hostile, ammonia-based environment, the Creator's Mind will ultimately be reflected and refracted within consciousness bodies of intelligence that embody whatever form is best suited to balancing its functions in a particular environment. This may help you understand how it is possible for conscious life to exist on and within all planets, stars, and star systems. **The Universe is pre-seeded!**

The holographic standing wave sets up convection currents within any given environment, and the predominant molecules or waves organize along those lines of force, creating a new bonding pattern and organizing them into a new form of life. This briefly explains the infinite combinations of life and thought-forms existing within a given universe. It also explains why the present earth dogmas of evolution of the species are partial equations of life. For even in some instances of happenstance, spontaneous combinations of life forms, the law of Sacred Geometry does not change. Due to the nature of projected universes, evolution develops from the top down, not from the bottom up, as is supposed by current dogma.

Happenstance creation of lower life forms only occurs as a byproduct of thought-form combinations that do not take into account the total equation of the Master Plan of THE ONE. All of you, as creator-gods, share the creation of these by products which appear to be happenstance, such as diseases, as well as discoveries. Thus, the altered-ego assesses its own byproducts from partial life equations and comes to the "logical" conclusion that it lives in a happenstance universe that was accidentally created and will accidentally disappear. In higher orders of universal creativity, every thought-form issued is balanced as a replica of the total equation of life. Thus, there is no byproduct of happenstance creation to off-balance the perfect energies of God-Mind.

Again: each of you is a holographic, standing wave form; a thought-form composed of intersecting, geometric-energies that form billions upon billions of nodal points of power with sets and subsets of Light frequencies, identical and simultaneously interactive with all other identical orders of energy throughout the universe. In other words, there is no space or distance between you and the action of any other point in the universe. This is why the Masters continue to teach the understanding of the "eternal present" of the now moment. Only in this NOW moment can you resonate with the Genius Frequency and in that eternal moment lies the experience of ultimate freedom to receive and transmit, not only thought, but your entire being, flesh, blood, mind, and all into other dimensional realms.

The illusion of separation between life forms and thought-forms is due to the membrane tension of various frequencies or "veils" of light that form around it, trapping more light, as it expands against the greater part of itself, giving that particular holograph an individuality through which it may be cognizant of itself as a reflection of its creator.

The Original Program of creation provides each human entity with a capacity to resonate with the Genius Frequency, so that it may inhabit the elemental spheres, yet remain in contact with the Master Plan by piercing the "veils of light" in order to balance all

thought-forms, thus creating no destructive, happenstance byproducts of partial life equations. By a type of self-hypnosis created
by the altered-ego, these pathways of communication were made
dormant, leaving each entity to flounder in the happenstance byproducts of local creation.

With help from the Masters, under direction of THE
CHRIST, the innate Genius Frequency is now being increased
from the Source in order to assist any entity who chooses, to
systematically "pierce" the veils of light that block the return of
consciousness to The Source. For those who choose to make the
effort and call upon the assistance of the Masters, the power of the
Genius Frequency will rejuvenate their bodies, open their conscious communication with Higher Intelligence, and liberate them
from the limitations imposed by the altered-ego acting as a "veil"
of lower light frequencies. This is possible because THE ONE continually creates, without end, an open-ended universe of Infinite
Joy.

This systematic "piercing" of the lower frequency light
veils is attained by the accumulation of quantum energy field-
charges, to a point of critical light-energy/mass, as the seven mind-
centers of each entity unite. This critical mass of the higher frequency of Genius can be ignited when all brain-mind-centers are
balanced in the Light of the Master Blueprint of creation.

Upon earth, each entity witnesses only the image of a
thought-form and not the process. You hear the music but you do
not "see" the orchestra. Contemplating these high frequency concepts prepare the altered-ego for the shock of revelation when
these processes of Divine Creation are "seen." For if you were
suddenly to see the totality of creative processes forming your narrow view of reality, the altered-ego would be so severely shocked
that it would begin destroying the physical body in order to shut
down the revelation. This teaching and the exercises within it will

prepare the bio-computer to accept higher realities without damage by increasing the frequency of awareness by degrees.

Incorporated in the design of the human entity is the similitude of THE ONE, which is the capacity of the human form, or image, to contain a quantum thought-form charge of Light, producing critical light/energy-mass that can transmute its own form, as well as any other life form of lower orders of creation. That is why your eyes resemble enlarged amoebae and your arterial system resembles a tree, etc. For the mind-center that created the holograph that you experience as "tree" and "amoeba" is you: the part of you that reached critical light/energy-mass within its manifold creation as it bonded with other subsets of intelligences (elementals) to form the animal kingdom.

Questioner: Would you explain in more detail why our present conception of evolution is incomplete?

MaYaRa: Present accepted theories of evolution do not explain radical, rapid shifts in life forms such as a "newly discovered" species, nor does it explain the enigma termed, "missing link." Minor shocks to the altered-ego, as in an unexpected revelation that upsets commonly held beliefs, is instantly defended and justified by the altered-ego. Instant and extreme pressure is brought to bear upon the existing dogma, which must be swiftly manipulated to protect the status quo.

The type of "missing link" sought is one that attempts to bridge the gap, explaining how lower life – thought to be accidentally created – evolves to more complex, superior intelligence, suggesting a linear tracking of time in a third dimensional understanding – forming a partial life equation. What this vast network of misinformation cannot afford is to ask very obvious questions: Could it be that humankind made a quantum leap, somehow slipping through a linear time frame through a fourth dimensional time-base and back? Indeed, could the sudden appearance of a species be, in fact, an indication that creation of life forms could originate outside the manipulation of a hostile environment which threatens to kill by its violent nature or sheer indifference to the life it supports? And, could it be that the entire concept of evolutionary dogma is 180 degrees off the mark?

A link shall be found, but it will in no way support the limited theory of evolution, as it now stands. The link shall be proof through ancient artifacts, technology, and intelligence within the earth, that humankind is a Divine Similitude, a Divine blueprint, a holographic projection of Divine Consciousness into the earth's environment.

The similarities between various organisms upon your plane of existence are just that, similarities. When God Consciousness projects image and similitude into a sphere of intelligence, it must, of course, take a form based upon the geometries prevalent within the energy field into which it expands. Thus, the building blocks of the carbon chain give rise to similar "forms" created by different thought-forms from the mind of man. Further, any creatures unearthed that appear to be human-like are actually degenerations of a once perfect being or the root-races that evolved through the blueprints of life created by the local creator-gods. The natural order of Life has been tampered with.

The phylogenetic recapitulation of ontogenesis (the fetus in various ancestral animal states) is actually evidence of an holographic projection attracting earth elements that reflect the image and similitude of a preexistent Divine Man, predating even earth. The visible animal likenesses are a manifestation of the cooperative earth-mind that perfected the specialized "parts" or organs within their domain to create a high capacity organism for the purpose of housing a consciousness creation from an origin other than the local universe. It is a process by which fragments of the Creator God meet and dwell within Its own creation.

The Divine Blueprint of Adamic Man is orchestrated through DNA and RNA, which are molecular reflections of encoded Light. It is a spiral of Light-encoded meta-matter of pyramidal geometries, shaping structure through angular intersecting energy dynamics.

The Original Program of man is a preexistent thought, existing even before the creation of earth. After the fundamental life forms were created by Adamic Man and developed into myriad variations upon a theme of creation through a specific Ray of God-Mind, the first attempts were made to inhabit the higher capacity organism composed of these perfected organs. It was calculated by the creator-god, Man, that in order for an organism of the highest complexity allowed under the restrictions of earth to contain the high frequencies of God-Mind, certain organs, such as the brain and gland systems, should be modified to transmute the Divine Frequencies in and out of the powerful electromagnetic bonds of dense elements.

Now, the brain systems were developed along the lines of a specific Ray of creation in conjunction with parallel mind-centers or domains, termed earth elementals or intelligent elements. The function of this organ in human embodiment is an electromagnetic capacitor/transmitter, designed to be a master template for the intelligences governing each specific domain of creation present within the organism.

The brain within human organisms is designed and perfected through the species/race termed Dolphin and Whale, in conjunction with humankind, from other earth-type galactic spheres. Human camaraderie with these aquatic root-races is due to the natural kinship of a portion of humanity who volunteered to embody certain functions of thought in earth elements by instilling them with light patterns that developed a high frequency organ of communication. This step having been completed, the preexistent program of man was projected, which in turn assembled the available genetic material from the animal kingdom into a temple of consciousness for God-Mind. This is why the "missing link" will never be found. The "missing link" is man himself.

As you contemplate the mind-centers or kingdoms upon and within the earth, and compare them with the kingdoms within you, similarities between the various systems and organs will be easily recognized, through the image of the form, as being of the same pattern of encoded Light Blueprints (such as the tree and the lung). If you have some difficulty in comprehending which kingdom the brain is patterned after, it is because it is patterned after a galactic-mind, not after an earth-mind. To form a deeper understanding of what type of energies or frequencies are responsible for the form and function of the brain, you must turn the gaze of your contemplation, again, toward the night sky.

Go back to the section of this segment (chapter) describing the Intelligent Energies that fill the spaces, as it were, in your heavens. Read and contemplate this again. If at that moment, in your time, there is a clear night sky, step out of your dwelling and turn your gaze upon it. Use your transmitter functions to visualize and project that information and clear the channel of the receiver function to the more subtle energy matrices that create the celestial tapestry upon the Divine Canvas of God-Mind. If your altered-ego is so rigid that you continue to believe that you cannot visualize these exercises, it would be most inspiring and beneficial to visit what you term "planetariums" and/or acquire a photograph of your local galaxy.

Using the fourth dimensional frequency of mind, perceive the spaces between the star bodies as "thick" with intelligent force fields. Assist your imagination by using the image of ripples emanating from the center of each star

body in all directions. Let your perception
expand until you become the center of the
tapestry of light. Notice the ovoid shape of your
galaxy. See the divisions of hemispheres and
the spiral arms reaching out into the vastness of
God-Mind. See the energy patterns intercon-
necting every celestial body to every other, ra-
diating like a billion pebbles tossed into a mir-
rored lake of mind, forming infinite points of
intersection.

Do not be discouraged if you, at once, cannot perceive completely. Just open the receiver of your temple of mind to the highest truth you are capable of contemplating at the moment. It shall increase very rapidly as you resonate with the Genius Frequency.

The holographic projections described above emanate from the Divine Template that provides the multidimensional Blueprint that patterns your physical brain. You can see the resemblance of this form in the center of the galaxy, forming the hemispheric poles from which four major arms are projected. The other organs of the physical body, including the so-called primitive brain, are patterned after galactic energies that are prismatically reduced through the earth's biosphere, which are filtered through the solar logos. For this reason, the structure of brain has remained somewhat of an enigma to scientists.

The human brain is patterned from galactic blueprints. However, do not confuse this with the electromagnetic predilections toward certain emotional states, as dictated by the fragmented teachings of astrology. It is important to understand that each organ of the human bio-computer is patterned after a specific energy field, holographically projected as a standing wave of intelligent energy points.

All organs, except the brain, are patterned after intelligent energy patterns within earth domains. Thus, the galactic-center supplies the form and function of meta-energy matter serving as master memory for the entire galaxy. As a replica of your universe, the brain serves the same function, while in a state of meta-energy matter in earth. Remember also, as we continue, that thought-form energy is not restricted to a form such as this. Memory is a function serving thought. Thought is not a prisoner of memory.

Consider now the development of the fetus to expand your perception of the connection that you have to all-that-is in your universe. From the first primal division of the fertile cell, as it pierces its own membrane or wall of tension through transmutation – a charged cell that reaches critical mass – a hemisphere is created from a sphere. This hemisphere resembles the form and function of the brain. This is evidenced by the fact that the head of the fetus develops much faster than the torso and limbs. The former evolves from the pattern projected directly from the galaxy.

Questioner: It was stated earlier that the Heart-mind is the primary source of the pattern, from which all else grows. Can you explain this further?

MaYaRa: Indeed, this is a truth. The confusion here originates in the space/time differential of third dimensional perception. For the pulse of life, the Adamic Seed Crystal is of the highest order of intelligence. Remember, we are describing reflections of projected patterns formed within the material planes. The Seed Crystal of God-Mind within man resonates within the first cell until it reaches critical mass and pierces its wall of tension, dividing as mirrors of itself in the plurality of elemental matter. Thus, at the moment of conception, the Heart-mind and the Divine-Mind are one, from which two are formed of itself.

In the further development of specialization, the other blueprints from various intelligent domains are utilized in a combined effort to create a temple of Light within material creation. The Heart-Mind or Seed Crystal initiates the plan and continually centers itself within the organism, thereby relocating as the organism develops. In the analogy of the tree, the roots are equivalent to the brain, and if you insist on this technicality in a three dimensional time-base, it is true that the tap root of the tree grows somewhat faster.

Realize also that your language is analytical by function of the altered-ego, predisposing concepts to seemingly continual contradictions. In attempting to describe creation with this syntax, one should use the imaginative faculty to comprehend the mirrors within mirrors that creation reflects. Thus, these simultaneous reflections cannot very well fit a linear "one, two, three" scenario of automotive manufacturing.

The Heart-mind is the first thought-form/organ to develop as a star seed. Its form is simply an expression of the Light Consciousness Program which exists as the template of human potential as God-Mind. Another expression of this Divine Template, or blueprint, manifesting in the electrochemical earth environment, is DNA and RNA chains of 64 cross-linked holograms as spiraling cubes.

The form of the brain also reflects the hemispheric shape in the first stage of all primal cell division. The fact that the shape of the brain does not evolve, as do the other organs of the bio-computer, is further indication of its direct link with the star system Intelligence which projects its pre-evolved function.

Questioner: How can these contemplations help us?

MaYaRa: It is most important, beloved, to stretch, as it were, the limits of what the altered-ego claims to know about life, for the purpose of loosening the grip of ignorance and raising the overall frequency of the bio-organism so that your higher intelligence may begin operating in a conscious manner once again.

When the Genius Frequency begins to resonate with sufficient strength in the bio-computer, you may perceive directly the atomic structure of Light that constitutes your present reality, without the misleading three dimensional instruments that produce only exaggerated sensory data. The instrument that you walk around in at this moment is a hundred million times more sensitive and powerful than the largest radio-dish, telescope or electron microscope, that only the select few are privileged to operate. Such an instrument is at your command.

When you perceive the atomic reality of Light fashioned into brain matter, you will see billions of stars moving within the space of God-Mind, forming a universe that replicates all universes. You will stand in awe of the constellations that mirror the ones in your night sky, and you will see hitherto invisible worlds of energy grids and resonant harmonics that connect you to the stars. You will realize the vast amounts of so-called space between the atoms in your brains, through which billions of intersecting points appear from what appears to be nothing, and take form, thought-form. You will see how you are creating worlds within worlds of light and how you are created from same.

But it is not enough to say that your brain was designed by and patterned after a galactic system. Realize that these energies that we refer to are living, intelligent, Sentient Beings, who operate within many dimensions simultaneously. For the universe is not merely an accidental mechanism. It is a system of material manifestations thought into existence by these Sentient Beings who express the Emanations of THE ONE into the grandeur of creation. This Hierarchy of Sentient Star-Beings project facets of their energy into the space of God-Mind, creating stars, planets, and life forms, coordinated through the Laws of Consciousness Divinity as set forth by THE ONE, THE ANCIENT OF DAYS.

Your brain, as well as the entirety of meta-creation of matter worlds, is a standing holographic wave form, or thought-form, composed of Light which generates harmonics which generate overtones, forming geometric structures from which the energy fields create atomic structures. In other words, each of you is composed into being from the same Light as the Star Beings who express their Light in three dimensional structures that function to infuse the Higher Intelligence of the Light of God-Mind directly into material creations. This is man's function in the Original Program about to be recalled.

The human brain is a vast bank of structured memory containing all the thought-forms existing before the creation of earth. That is why the large human brain remains such an enigma to science. That the human brain grew larger for species survival is an artificial distortion, created by the altered-ego in order to justify its claim to sensory reality within a food-chain-mentality. As we have stated, many species with comparatively microscopic brains have proven to be far better at survival than human beings – consider the cockroach.

The human brain is a replica of the Central Star-System whose Conscious Light is projected through a Template, modified for a particular subsystem of creation. The activities and thought-forms existing in these higher dimensions are encoded as light holograms within the brain cells and resonate with the Genius Frequency.

Thus, the human brain contains all the necessary thought-form structures in its memory banks, giving each of you the capacity to remember your origins and interact on all levels and dimensions of creation while embodied in the elemental earth. One need not die before one is liberated. In fact, one must initiate certain degrees of remembrance while in the earth, in order to focus the power of its individuality in the other dimensions. That is why so many entities come back to perfect this process. When consciousness-awareness is directed to these memory banks, rather than to those of the lower frequency thought-forms, all healing, superabundance and genius is available to all.

Questioner: Will our technology save us from the many problems that beset mankind at this time?

MaYaRa: This query is far too general. "Technically" speaking, technology is neither good nor bad. Indeed, creating a universe requires certain, shall we say, "God Technologies."

What we continue to caution mankind about is third dimensional technology with the altered-ego at the helm. In that sense, your third dimensional technology has caused virtually every major problem that besets mankind at this time and this is not the first time this course of death has been pursued.

Your techno-"logical" approach to life has revealed the knowledge (with the help of the Masters, seen and unseen) and the mechanics of the age of metal as a stepping stone to higher consciousness, not as an end in itself, for the age of metal indeed has reached its end. The irony of this so-called achievement is that revelations in research have been isolated by an elite few and the byproducts are manufactured to hypnotize the masses into believing that their lives shall be saved, if only they sacrifice them to the causes of the altered-ego.

The technology of the metal age is finished as of the year, in your time, 1936. The nuclear age, touted as futuristic by the altered-ego, is in fact a giant leap backward into the heaviest of all metals: so heavy that it reverses the life force by simulating star death, a phenomenon that occurs only when a star is cut off from the source of higher consciousness.

Questioner: But those discoveries have led to new breakthroughs in many areas of our lives, which appear to be beneficial. Can you comment on this statement?

MaYaRa: This is a partial truth, beloved. However, the polarization of your knowledge, as manipulated through the altered-ego, simultaneously produces poisons, bombs and thousands of related by-products of a death technology because the high frequency thought-forms designed for a new age were applied to the destructive age of metal.

Questioner: Then what were we supposed to do with this knowledge?

MaYaRa: In the example of the particle/wave theory, the obvious conclusion to be drawn was that if an electron, which is part and parcel of atomic structure, has the ability to occupy two different, yet simultaneous, dimensions of existence, and since everyone is composed of atoms, then is it not a techno-"logical" conclusion that every human entity possesses the same ability? Again, it can be seen from the outcome, in retrospect, that the altered-ego and its partner, the intellect, are a mass conscious limitation upon the mind's ability to exist in cosmic consciousness.

We implore each entity to begin thinking for itself. You are quite capable of performing your own research into the greatest mysteries of life, though you have been taught otherwise. There are millions of clues to higher consciousness handed down by the Masters that are admitted and verified throughout scientific exploration.

Thus, you may study science, as well as ancient teachings to reach the same conclusions, if you know what to look for. No book or teacher can do that for you. Do not wait for and eventually accept the interpretations of scientific clues or religious beliefs. Time is literally running out for you to decide on your own course.

Decide for yourselves the import of revelations, regardless from whence they come. Be not afraid that you will mislead yourselves. The Heart-mind within each of you cannot be deceived. Each of you is a genius in your own right, a friend and co-creator with THE ONE. Take the Seed Crystal of your heritage and apply it to yourself. No priest, no scientists, no psychiatrist can do this for you.

Visualize the trillions of electrons that make up your being and realize that you also possess a body composed entirely of electrons – an electron body. You have five bodies in five dimensions. Use them. Prove this to yourself. It cannot be proven to anyone else. Apply the particle/wave theory to the reality of you, and you will begin to understand that the entire dimension of your being may simultaneously exist as particulate matter (space/time) or wave matter (time/space).

The atomic structure of the human brain is a replica of the universe. It is a composite of the spectral emanations of Divine Thought manifesting organized intelligence into ever new forms of creation. Since the altered-ego and the intellect defends its right to know only what it senses, you must necessarily go beyond what is known and stretch into the Genius Frequency with an intense desire to know the higher truths for yourself. It is not a matter of awakening a dormant brain, for the brain is a memory bank which does not generate thought. Mind generates thought. Mind is consciousness. Therefore, one needs to direct one's consciousness to the area of the Heart-mind that has access to all other parts of the memory bank blocked by the altered-ego through self deception. There, a Universe awaits your ecstatic vision.

The cells of the bio-computer (your body) are organized star fields forming a resonant membrane, known as the auric field of awareness-thought and consciousness-thought. The particle/wave phenomenon is one small example of the possibilities of one dimensional universe passing through or existing within another. Each thought-form that you incubate resonates with and ignites certain memories that must interact with the Original Template or blueprint of creation. Each thought-form has frequency, mass and geometric patterns of light that either augment or destroy the Original Plan of creation for each of you, personally.

Each individual entity of the human kingdom is responsible for the reality of its life and the lives of those around them, for they are cast from the same mold. Regardless of what the world of mass-conscious altered-ego is thinking and doing, you must decide whether the thought-forms that you create, or give life to, are harmonious with or antagonistic to the integrity of your Divinely Ordered universe.

As a single cell of the body possesses the information necessary to grow another body, even to the last hair upon the head, so too, do you as a cell of the universe possess the information necessary to generate another universe. Your brain was created to resonate with the Genius Frequency in order to access its memory bank containing your true origins and the nature of creation. You are within the stars and the stars are within you. You are within THE CREATOR and THE CREATOR is within you. ALL creation contains ALL creation.

Gaze joyously into the heavens and then gaze joyously into your own body, and know that you are an holographic similitude of Mansion Worlds of Light. Know that the Heart-mind within you shall protect you in the Name of THE ONE. No false teaching can lead you astray if you contemplate every thought-form in the Light of THE ONE. When you accomplish this in any degree, you shall know the truth for yourself, not one that is taught by another for his own gain at your expense. The truth shall be yours individually, as well as universally.

Use any means available to prove that you are a truth of a higher mind, a Co-Creator of reality. Use scientific facts, metaphysical truths, religious beliefs and esoteric concepts. Prove the reality of God-Mind to yourselves. You shall never prove that you are not part of God-Mind, and you shall never prove that God-Mind is not part of you. Do not struggle with this information or any other teaching. Embrace it. Embrace the world with your Heart of Hearts and you shall never be led astray, and you shall make the truth of your being a living, conscious reality. This is the moment you have waited for these thousands of years and countless re-embodiments. Desire the truth of your existence with your entire being, and you shall find the Genius Frequency to liberate you from bondage – forever, in the Light.

ASTROLOGY
"COSMIC WEATHER"

> *"Understand that you most assuredly
> are connected to the stars,
> but you most assuredly are not controlled
> by anyone or anything."*

Questioner: Chapter 6 stressed that the brain is developed by our galaxy of star bodies. Can you explain what part, if any, the study of astrology has to offer in our quest for truth?

MaYaRa: Our intent is not to do battle with any established teachings. The result of such debating is only to pit one mind-center against another, giving rise to the defense mechanisms of the altered-ego, thereby strengthening its position by settling the dispute based upon what it knows, or rather, what it has been taught.

We shall continue to stress throughout this document that all truth apprehended by perception is commensurate with the frequency of mind that perceives it. For this reason, "truth" must be intensely personal, yet also universal. The truth is not a relativistic possession of the personality. All individual entities, whose minds operate on a certain range of frequencies, tune in, as it were, to a system of realities true to those frequencies.

All higher frequencies encompass the perceptions of a lower nature, but lower frequencies exclude the perceptions of higher reality. The altered-ego is locked into a certain frequency of sensory thought-forms, defending itself from any new information of a higher frequency. Thus, it is important for each individual, through intense desire, to focus conscious awareness upon concepts and thought-forms of a higher frequency without attempting to engage polarities of the altered-ego, such as understanding/not understanding and believing/not believing.

The study of astrology, then, is subject to many views in various degrees of truth, depending upon the frequency of mind used to comprehend it. We shall address the contemporary view of astro-logical influences, for the study of the stars is older than any system of knowledge upon the planet. The contemporary view of this ancient teaching has caused more limitations, in the awareness of your true natures, than liberation from the fetters of the altered-ego. Thus our objective, as always, is to rephrase, redefine, and raise the frequency of mind through new angles of perception formed through the contemplation of this material.

Once again, there are the usual hurdles to overcome when a higher frequency of fourth dimensional understanding is to be activated. One is the relentless limitations imposed by the altered-ego, locked into a lower frequency, demanding a linear under standing of such a vast subject. The other is the proper definitions and usage of word/symbols used in the communication of a clear vision within the mind's eye.

To properly define the function of any system of energy is to gain an accurate understanding of the intent and purpose of that system. We suggest that you review the preceding segment on the "Holographic Universe" to increase your visual frequencies. It serves as a strong foundation upon which we may build and synthesize the knowledge that you seek. With a firm grasp on the thought-forms in that material, we can proceed with an analogy, which will raise the frequency of your understanding of this complex subject.

COSMIC WEATHER

Briefly, it would be wise for you to regard the subject of astrology as "cosmic weather." This is an extremely important point. This simple analogy is your lantern in the labyrinth of astrological facts and extrapolations. Just as a weather pattern is triggered and influenced by countless solar, lunar and planetary fields of energy upon and within the earth, so too are your personal weather patterns of emotions, feelings, attitudes and perceptions. These are triggered by different frequencies within the same energy patterns, created by the shifting positions, within the greater system of the galaxy. Thus, you experience personal seasons, along with their concomitant changes and periodic exceptional circumstances. You are always in a season of your life.

To the extent that you are able to intuit or predict an approaching weather pattern, such as a storm, you change the probabilities of your immediate, "normal," course of action of thought. Taking cover in a storm is a choice, and an obvious one at that. Your thoughts and actions are not a preordained dictum which you are compelled to follow.

In our example of a storm, mundane astrology predicts that the probabilities of you taking cover are high. Conversely, the probabilities of you venturing out into the storm with reckless abandon are small, unless there is another, greater psychic weather pattern which sets up yet another counter set of probabilities. At any rate, it is not difficult to reason that weather patterns exist on many levels and dimensions, within and without each of you. Therefore, predicting probable choices made by any given individual, experiencing certain energy patterns is hardly a mystical phenomenon.

What appears mystical to most earthlings is the implied fact of action at a distance. So far, the scientific community, as a whole, abhors this concept; and the educational system has worked quite diligently at driving that point into your collective brain matter. The reluctance to accept action at a distance is based upon pragmatic reason, as well as on irrational fear. It is pragmatic in the sense that admitting to action at a distance infinitely increases the variables acting upon a given experiment, completely invalidating virtually every "proven" fact arrived at so pain-stakingly. Irrational fear appears to be a puppet manipulated impersonally by an accidental and uncaring universe.

However, if you review the previous segment of this book, your higher reason will begin to override the altered-ego's tenacious grip on the intellect. You begin to understand that you are always free to choose an appropriate course of thought, resulting in action. You may begin to realize that your "interior cosmic weather pattern" may not be the same as the exterior one. Therefore, decisions are often made by the individual that seem contrary to what is demanded of the individual, in the reflections of family and society.

Questioner: Would you explain your use of the word astro-"logical?"

MaYaRa: The purpose, then, is to draw your attention to the current use of astrology as a tool designed to appeal to the "logical" mind, in the sense that the intellect, as a function of the altered-ego, uses a limited, logical thought-process that inherently "screens out" knowledge of a higher frequency than it operates in.

The logic of the intellect, as you commonly work with it within the parameters of third dimensional thinking, recognizes only that which can be consciously illuminated with a narrow frequency of thought.

Let us briefly examine the "screening out" process of the altered-ego regarding this subject, as it relates to the reduction of a grand truth into a partial equation of entropy or an Omega point, in an otherwise ongoing mechanism of consciousness.

As the consciousness-awareness of human mind gradually succumbed to the limitations of third dimensional perception, the grand scope of the ancient teachings of the Master Messengers of THE ONE, were reduced to a mere mechanical understanding. Thus began an era of manipulation in which the sacred ZOHAR, a body of truth designed to implement man's freedom through the forecasting of cosmic weather patterns, became dogma for the high priests to use in behind-the-scenes political control. The governmental figureheads seized exclusive access to secret, magical directives, which gave them the illusory advantage and power over the enemy and the people.

There has always been ample material evidence to substantiate the veracity of our celestial ancestry. There was always the greater, invisible – to the third dimensional altered-ego – spectrum of intelligence that defied articulation in the "logical" thought process of "common" language. This greater, invisible field of energy was suspended as the altered-ego continued to ask for objective, material proof. That "proof" was not forthcoming in the past/ present time, in your time, for the only proof was to be discovered within the totally subjective experience, before any exterior manifestations were possible. Thus, the only proof that remained, to third dimensional understandings of the altered-ego concerning astrology, was the most mundane in the "logical" considerations of the material world: thus, astro-"logical."

After the negative spiral of entropy has been entrapped within an electromagnetic field, it is not easily transmuted back to its original design and function. Therefore, this grand truth, as all others, was reduced in frequency to match the consciousness gestalts of the altered-ego. Simply, the only portion of the celestial understanding that was accepted as proof was the behavioral aspects and tendencies of the surface phenomenon of character-groups. The third dimensional mind could not, after all, deny the intimate divining of its personal sensory nature by an outside agency. Thus, the entire teaching was reduced to a double-edged sword, which at once gave hope to those seeking their true connections to the stars and took away hope from those ensnared by the overwhelming maze of limitations prescribed by the "wrong sign." Thus, the soul was entrapped within its own denial and guilt.

As the altered-ego developed, it disempowered the individual to a point where it could not hope to advance without the help of those born into the earth under the "superior" astro-logical influences. In other words, the illusion of this system of thought removed all notions of self as co-creator, placing the "inferior natures" of those supposedly punished for past lives under the powers of earthly tribunals, or in the western mind, the stigma of being placed in a cold, impersonal universe that threw its blows and fortunes to those who chanced to be born on a particular day. A further dependency upon the practitioners of the "art" was created so that the fortunate individuals could consult those who would predict the "slings and arrows" on a periodic or daily basis. Thus the astrologers became the knowledgeable few – the first "stellar stockbrokers" and "lawyers" of their time.

Now, the more sophisticated proponents of astrology will balk at many of these statements, countering with more complex theories of reincarnation and karmic retribution. The significance of these partial equations notwithstanding, the unfortunate fact remains that the result of these teachings polarized human consciousness into a world of effects against an outer world of causation, directed from the nether worlds.

The original teachings of astrology were built upon the understanding of the brain as a holographic universe structured by star intelligence. The critical difference was the realization of the total bio-computer as a receiver/transmitter, rather than merely a receiver/reactor: in other words, your ability to co-create as a causative force within your universe, rather than entertaining the dim prospect of divining a "sneak preview" into a mechanized and predetermined life scenario which surrenders to either the futility of predetermined inadequacy or self-righteous superiority.

The balance is delicate and we are by no means attempting to negate what insights may be gained by the study of this subject. Rather, we communicate supplementary information in an overview to assist those who are confused or otherwise limited by the information now becoming popular in mass-mind. The reader should neither accept nor deny this or any other system of knowledge, but rather contemplate it in the Light of the Heart-mind where the truth, commensurate with the frequency of the entity's mind, shall make the appropriate life changes. By refusing to succumb to the tug-of-war by the altered-ego as to whether or not any truth should be believed, the entity shall begin to raise the frequency of its perceptions. Only then can the truth of any teaching be known.

Since all is truth on different frequencies of perception, it is necessary to recombine and redefine words in your memory banks that are attached to thought-forms through the continual repetition of a concept via the altered-ego. For example, attention is drawn to the word "logical" because it tricks the intellect into accepting information beyond the frequency of the altered-ego. Once this is accomplished, the higher faculties of mind will make proper use of the information for the ultimate fulfillment of the entity.

Questioner: Does the study of astrology provide insights into an individual's nature?

MaYaRa: If you reflect upon this statement you will soon discover that the insights you refer to are actually insights into character, or personality patterns, forming the domain of the altered-ego. These are direct reflections of the cosmic weather patterns amounting to a very superficial rendering of the entity in question. This frequency of understanding only reveals a "forecast" based upon the predisposition of an entity to react to cyclic patterns of stimuli. This, however, is not the entity's true nature. It has no more depth than to explain a "knee-jerk" response of an entity who passes through repeating energy fields, as they pass over sectors of the earth. Thus, automatic responses are very predictable.

When you examine the vast majority of entities that are attracted to astro-"logical" renderings, you will begin to recognize that deep insights are, indeed, a rarity. The initial attractions are due to an excited fascination of otherworldliness, suggested by an outside, impersonal source of information capable of revealing so-called secret aspects of a personality. But it is not long before the same information begins to constrict the entity by removing the causative faculty of co-creation given to every human ever created.

This overview can be applied to all systems of knowledge of this type, such as palmistry. If one gazes into one's palm, noticing a configuration of lines, the uniqueness of the pattern is regarded with a personal I-dentification. However, when the same pattern is viewed through the system of palmistry, the individual is confronted with, not only thousands of others with similar configurations, but thousands who share a disturbing similarity of life scenarios. Now, there is actually nothing here to be disturbed about. It is when the altered-ego begins its defense of its belief system that what may be gained, is lost.

The altered-ego at once begins a desperate attempt to validate the uniqueness of its personality, sending waves of fear and insecurity through all of the mind-centers. A "Pandora's Box" of predetermined molds begin to surface to suggest a mechanized, assembly line style of creation that also de-emphasizes the uniqueness and co-creative abilities of the entity in question. The promised preview of the future becomes an elusive, yet predetermined stamp of destiny, regardless of the entity's desire to change, as it senses an entrapment within the webs of time. What few entities investigate is the fact that one can change the physical lines in the palm by changing deeply ingrained belief systems.

Questioner: Then what is the purpose of astrology?

MaYaRa: Originally there was no purpose for astrology in the common, manipulative sense of the word. When astrology was used as a system of thought-forms, it was as obvious as contemporary man's calculation of the tides. There was no mystery and no manipulation, for it was obvious to their higher frequency perception that everything was connected to everything. The freedom to change one's destiny was as simple as looking at a road map and deciding to reach a destination by a particular route.

There was no separation between astrology and astronomy. There was no separation between church and state, science and religion or the seven mind-centers. The information was in full view for everyone to behold and partake, as co-creators.

Any facet of creation one desires to focus one's attention upon grows and reveals itself as part of the self. Thus, those who desire to gaze into the heavens of self discover infinite wonders within their beings through that particular expression – if they are not limited by their low frequency altered-ego.

In the popular, contemporary understanding of astrology, it succeeds, to some extent, in forecasting tendencies as character impulses toward or from a set of energetic circumstances. This is accomplished through ascribing star-energy-personae, as reflected in groups of organisms developing within a given time-zone-sector of celestial moments, at an impressionable moment when the being is first exposed to the impact of density containing its consciousness.

The angles of perception impressed upon the lower, or first three mind-centers are reflections of living geometries, forming a language code expressing the angular intersections of various rays of creation; which, by every second of arc, create a general as well as unique perceptual apparatus within an embodied group of probable selves.

The astro-"logical" information revealed to mass-mind, in this your time, is by no means the pinnacle of awareness regarding this subject, since it is not individually realized and must be administered by specialists. Nor is it, as many scientists would claim, a slowly evolving system of folklore at best. This system of knowledge does not appear now, in your time, as an evolutionary process born in the brain of a monkey, who one day realized that when the moon is in full circle, it had the urge to mate or thump a brother monkey upon the crown chakra with a stone. Astrology, in your time, is at best the scattered remains of a universal awareness that was once common knowledge. It was no more an obscure, secret, mystic doctrine to the ancient civilizations than is instinct to the animal kingdom. It was an obvious reality in their lives. It was the weather pattern behind the weather pattern.

Regardless of how complex the calculations or how sophisticated the interpreter, the fact remains that astrology is the science of instinct. Thus, its study has far greater value in the study of nature than in the study of man.

The beings of those enlightened days – remembering that you are your ancestors – communicated on a daily basis with star beings, galactic intelligence. The low frequency of the altered-ego of contemporary man cannot directly perceive the higher intelligence. Therefore, a secret fear of an alien force, shaping the entity's character and controlling its destiny, lurks in the darkness of its light. This alien force, to the higher consciousness of the ancient Masters, was a friendly intelligence with an affinity to the global family members in whose lineage their beings were born – long before earth was prepared for the first series of incarnations through the holographic projections of consciousness bodies.

The mass-mind of social consciousness is preoccupied and fascinated with subsets of character groups because the majority of mankind has lost its true I-dentity. Thus, many run to and fro seeking an I-dentity, regardless of how stereotyped and limiting it might be. A more appropriate use of this knowledge would be to apply it to assist in worthwhile goals for agriculture and political stability. Some are presently using it for this purpose. Many more, however, are exploiting the altered-ego's quest for death by attempting to overpower others, for their gain. The higher frequency of knowledge concerning this subject is denied access to human consciousness, for the same reasons that it was removed from the consciousness of Babylon.

Our intention here is not to minimize, nor to stifle the strides many of you are making in these noble, if somewhat limited, ventures within self. To our perception, this approach is like walking backwards up the mountain. All of the information that you may find in all books and from all teachers is but a tenth of what each of you already possess within your beings. It would do you well to contemplate this. For in doing so, the Genius Frequency will begin to open like a flower in the Light from the Heart of Hearts. You shall awaken from your timeless sleep into the dawning of your true heritage as co-creators with THE ONE.

Questioner: Can the use of astrology forecast global events?

MaYaRa: You have documented cases where animals are quite adept at forecasting catastrophic events. Have you also documented these animals consulting their personal astrologers?

The animal kingdom communicates directly with elemental forces of which the star-conscious beings are an expression. The perceptual powers of ancient astrology has been removed from your innate system of awareness due to the manipulation of others through the self-serving system of the altered-ego. At this time, even in the hands of the "experts," astrology is but a crude instrument of observation, no better or worse than a sextant or microscope.

YOU ARE THE KEY

The point we make here, beloved, is that to seek the answers to life from a source outside self is to invite the most disappointing illusions into your lives. There are no charts, no mystics, no gurus, no calculations outside self that can be useful. People of earth search madly for someone or something to save them from their own shortcomings, created by themselves and reflected in the world they experience.

Is it not far more exiting to know that every entity has a million times the observational powers of the most sophisticated machine or abstract system of knowledge? The Genius Frequency holds the key to the Divine Astrology within each of you. What outside agency could possibly articulate the totality of your being as a Divine Emanation, other than you?

It will never be to your benefit to give your power of conscious awareness away to some abstract system of knowledge that offers only power and happiness to the few born under the right "sign." Astro-"logical" definitions of your characters are no more profound than discovering the color of your eyes. As far as this teaching is concerned: if you have realized your connection to your star being intelligence, then close the book and begin your own life, rather than the life of someone past. Understand that you most assuredly are connected to the stars, but you most assuredly are not controlled by anyone or anything.

Now that we have qualified this information by neutralizing the altered-ego's duty to take sides on every issue, we shall briefly contemplate some of the mechanics of astrology for the benefit of those who have not studied it in-depth; and we hope to bring to light a few points of interest to raise the frequency of thought of the serious students as well. Many of you are familiar with the usage of the "birth chart" used as the primary tool in the forecasting of events and the character analysis of a given individual, group and even geographic loci upon the planet. These charts are particularly offensive to the mind seeking to understand the depths of creation – for the same reason that a two dimensional rendering of a holograph containing infinite energy patterns in a multidimensional universe is, at best, a partial equation of life.

Nevertheless, we shall use the primal symbol of time in eternity, the circle, to briefly sketch the basics of astrology. As we proceed, remember that each of you has all the "signs," constellations, planets and aspects – indeed, the universe – within.

Within each "chart" is placed the representational symbols of the planets and constellations as a frozen moment in time – not an eternal moment, but a static, one dimensional moment – overlying 12 sectors, representing areas of a life drama, all of which are displayed in angular relationships to each other. The polarities of material existence are represented by dividing the circle in halves which are labeled "above" and "below" the "horizon." Thus a positive and negative relationship are added to the interpretation of the total life scenario in this frozen moment.

One way of understanding this attempt to graphically still-life the dynamics of your being is to view the circle as a clock-face upon which is displayed the 12 constellations or life stations – marriage, home, career, etc. There are multiple hands on this clock, formed by the planets in various positions at any given time. The clock face, as mentioned above, is divided in half, depicting more or less the A.M. and P.M. configuration of a value commensurate with the night and the day of one's life.

General "tendencies" are first seen as the amount of "influences" which occupy the positive and negative halves of the circle. The halves of the circle can be interpreted to mean conscious and subconscious portions of the individual's awareness. The completed schematic suggests tendencies to tune into certain frequencies of awareness, in particular areas of the life drama.

These tendencies are magnified or diminished by qualities of energy recognized to emanate from each particular planet and star system. Further details of each peculiar "reading" are gleaned from the "angles" and "aspects" of the heavenly bodies that are intuited to emphasize and de-emphasize the various qualities of perception within each sector of life drama through the added discipline of GEMATRIA – sacred number relationships.

As in physical architecture, certain angles lend themselves to stronger or weaker structures, so too, do certain "angles" of energy architecture lend themselves to various psychological structures. This is true in regards to the interaction of energy patterns within the awareness of material embodiment. With all these components and calculations in place, resembling multiple sets of clock hands forming various "angles" of projection into each particular area of the life scenario, the tedious process of "interpretation and forecasting" begins; and the possibilities of interpretation are as varied as the number of entities who perform this task. Remember though, we are interested in Process not effects.

Regardless of the expertise involved in these incredibly complex calculations and intuitions, a most troubling problem looms before the entity whose chart is in question – judgments are inherent in the evaluation of the psychological architecture.

The altered-ego instantly makes judgments as to what is "good" in the chart and what is "bad," according to the same belief system it always uses when confronted with any information. Regardless of the skill, depth and good intentions of an astrologer's performance, the entity secretly continues to struggle against self in order to preserve the status quo, which is exactly what the chart is depicting. The entity may have balanced certain thought-forms by learning certain lessons in life, only to be informed that the problem is still seen in the chart.

Because of the relentless nature of the altered-ego, the entity rarely gains anything of lasting value, save a deeper I-dentification with its faults and strengths, which are not usually news. If the entity is predominantly happy or depressed about its current life scenario, it comes away happier or more depressed about the same attributes and faults. Occasionally, a precious few will emerge with a new understanding of how to balance the thought-forms of polarized thinking. A still more precious few realize that there are no weaknesses, but are only larger and smaller jewels of varying degrees of clarity and frequency with which to adorn the God-Mind within.

We speak, thus, for those who might "follow" astrology rather than for those who study the subject. There is a fine distinction in the definition of these two words. Many claim to study astrology, but in reality there is a desperate search to validate the personality through a mystical doctrine outside the self. The phrase, "born under a bad sign" is a travesty of limited self-persecution and superstition, reducing one's Divine Heritage to a stratagem of luck or to the futile teaching that suggests a bad life for those with karmic retribution and a good one for the few who are karmically chaste.

Questioner: Hasn't it been proven that each of us, through the arrangements of the heavenly bodies, possess strong and weak points within our systems?

MaYaRa: Of course, there is truth in this – three dimensional truth. The question you must ask is why there are strong and weak points in the system. Is it because of the stars? Certainly not. When an entity chooses an embodiment in any given point in time, it takes on some of the energy and perceptual biases of the "sign's" energy matrix and the circumstance on the wheel of life because it has chosen to work with a certain life scenario for the purpose of balancing itself. Once the balancing is achieved – and there is no time limit on this – that particular "chart" of life is obsolete.

There are no weaknesses. There are only unbalanced thought-forms awaiting a higher frequency Light to balance them, awaiting the desire of the entity to transmute these by the reconnection to the Divine Source of Light within the self. Even death itself can be conquered by the consummate desire to resonate with the Source within self.

Even in the "common" lives of mankind, there are tens-of-thousands of examples of those whose "charts" depicted: doomed-to-failure, sickness by grave disease or oppression by the world-at-large – suggesting the impossibility of escaping their "destiny." Yet they have demonstrated ultimate self-healing, great achievement and liberation from oppressors. Study those lives, beloved, and compare them to their "charts." This is not easily accomplished, however, due to the altered-ego's "expertise" in explaining away so many exceptions to the rules as special cases, accidents, and/or unverifiable hearsay. Yes, even astrology falls prey to the limitations of the altered-ego.

Each of you is a "special case" by the power of Light and the desire to connect with the Source within you. Thus, the gamut of astro-"logical" entanglements are dissolved in the Light within each of you at any moment you choose to give up the burden of the altered-ego and transcend all vehicle limitations – be they physical or psychological. The only true significance regarding astrology is as an "automatic" destiny for those who would do nothing to change themselves, at any cost.

From our perspective, the struggles of the altered-ego to keep one in confusion and limitation is almost laughable, if it were not for the true suffering that is wrought through the disconnection of self from Source. The logic of the altered-ego laboriously suffers to short-circuit the mind-centers through a limited belief system.

Each of you is a unique, one-of-a-kind co-creator, down to your finger and voice patterns. Could it be that one fingerprint is better than another? We are surprised that this has not become a fashionable system of judgments. After all, palmistry has enjoyed voluminous substantiation to the claims that some configurations of lines prove more beneficial than others. It is remarkable that a cult has not been formed around "thumbistry." Although, certain thumbs are considered more creative than others.

We need not belabor this point. A thorough contemplation of the usefulness of astrology as a system of liberation and of knowledge reveals a fragmented teaching, diluted through a millennia of abuse and distortion. In the final analysis, each energy pattern of each entity is originally designed with the full potential of transcendence through the Genius Frequency and nothing can take that power away, save the choice of the entity to forsake its true God-Self in the Light of THE ONE.

Thus, the chart representing the life of an entity is merely a thumbprint of a unique perception within the tablets of time, as chosen by the entity through which to view, until sufficient knowledge is gained from the experience and all partial life equations are balanced.

The "angles" forming the cornerstone of astro-"logical" understandings are a means of explaining the unique and the general perceptive colorings of a given moment in time, in which the entity first views the world. The infinite variations of "angles" and "aspects" as a result of the intersections of stellar energy patterns facilitate infinite angles of perception, reflected within each vehicle or bio-computer. In other words, these angles, aspects and patterns are not you. They are tools of perception for you to use as a co-creator. And as tools, these may be discarded, interchanged, refashioned and/or added to. Each "chart" is a chest of tools for the entity to use as it sees fit. Period.

Said yet another way: each of these "angles" in the chart may be understood as a lens of perception with a focal length that is set to perceive, more clearly or with more emphasis, certain areas of the life drama than others. The sum of these lenses of perception are chosen to begin a bio-life-drama in a three dimensional understanding. It does not constitute the totality of self! The totality of your being is not confined to any perspective or coloration of understanding within any life drama – not for a lifetime, not in the past or future and not even for a moment, if you choose to operate on a different frequency of perception.

The grand cosmic mechanism of life generation pulses, from specific to general to specific again, in an endless reciprocation of possibilities to facilitate freedom towards an understanding of your true natures, through every possible means. It forms infinite chances to liberate consciousness, not a restriction within it. The angles of perception that reveal special interests or views within the life drama on earth are gifts chosen by each entity for the benefit and enrichment of the universe, just as the multitudinous variations in physical creation reflect the endless patterns and aspects and angles of THE ONE.

In the fifth dimensional understanding through the Genius Frequency, there are no divisions of positive and negative values that can be interpreted as strength and weakness. For the gate to freedom from limitation is located within the Heart Of Hearts and in that place, all are equal, for all are in perfect balance. It is only the thought-forms created by each entity that need balancing and completing as a total life equation. In other words, there is no "chart" to be found that would define the Original Creation of perfect Adamic Man: it is a version of self, created by the entity to use its gift of power to create something or someone else of itself.

The cosmic mechanism that astro-"logical" understandings are based upon is only the flux of star energies intersecting at points in "time," that manifest a psychological architecture as a standing wave form of holographically projected patterns. This seemingly impersonal flux of intelligent energies provides not only the automatic function of continuity within an earth cycle, but is designed to power many elemental aspects of creation in the day to day running of earth as a whole. In other words, not every nuance of these energy patterns is designed for man to react. The great majority of these energy patterns sustain the animal, vegetable and mineral kingdoms. That is why the "signs" of the zodiac are depicted as animals. They are only indirectly related, and subordinate to the Human co-creator.

You may, at any moment in your eternal continuum, reach within and therefore beyond the lower frequencies of self definitions into an arena of infinite possibilities beyond the limited creations of earth, giving you freedom from any circumstance of limitation and freedom towards the attainment of any desired dream of fulfillment. The only prerequisite for these desires is that they be eventually balanced in the total life equation.

Use any system of knowledge to which you feel led, but know that it is not necessary for your ultimate fulfillment. All "aspects" for your ultimate fulfillment are within each of you from the beginning, regardless of your birthday.

It is time to cease judging yourself through the crude definitions of the altered-ego. Know that the grand systems of knowledge have been diluted into fragmented partial life equations, which fall under the powers of entropy and decay. It is your responsibility to reassemble all of these unbalanced, partial truths through the Seed of God-Mind within your Hearts of Hearts.

When you reconstruct the Original Pattern of thought-forms reflecting the absolute truth that you are a Divine Emanation existing as a standing wave form, your "chart" will be but potter's clay forming as you shape it into a perfected model of now/future.

Accept and love who you are NOW and the tools for rebuilding a perfect life will multiply, enabling you to create ever greater changes in your lives. By accepting and loving who you are, you will project the thought-forms of your perfect origins. No power can thwart your efforts, if thus directed. No limitation can resist the powers of the Original program within the Heart of Hearts in recreating those walls of the altered-ego into bridges over the waters of partial existence.

These are not philosophic and metaphysical musings. We do not have the precious life-force to devote to opiated words of delusion. You have been exposed to enough of these, and these have clouded your awareness with lower frequencies of partial equations from the limitations of the altered-ego. Seek not merely a truth, for all is a truth. Seek rather the limitless Universal Truth of LOVE-LIGHT/GOD-MIND. For that is the only Truth that shall free you from the limited descriptions of your lives, offered by so many fragmented teachings.

I-dentify with the Causative frequencies of existence within the Heart of Hearts, and you shall be freed from the reactionary circumstances of the life drama – not through death, but through Light! You may experience, if you choose, freedom towards your true heritage as a Co-Creator in the causative manifestations of unlimited life in the Mansion worlds of THE ONE.

THE DIVINE CAPACITOR

"TAKING CHARGE"

> "Your task is not only to increase your energy,
> but to increase the capacity
> to hold light."

Questioner: Is it more energy that we need to raise our frequencies to the Genius Frequency, or is it more the overcoming of the altered-ego?

MaYaRa: Your query reflects many angles of thought. Let us methodically contemplate its parts as Divine scientists seeking the origin of its source.

First of all, the limitations that you become aware of by the altered-ego are all imagined. We are sure that you tire of hearing that life is an illusion. Life is not an illusion. Life on earth is an illusion, though it is a real illusion. It is more accurate to state that there is much more to life than you "normally" perceive within the narrow frequencies of awareness. Relative to the complete reality of existence, your perceptions are incomplete illusions.

As to your "either/or" framework, the answer is both. Any query or statement that is structured to encompass only one polarity of your inherent duality upon earth reflects third dimensional thinking. Therefore, it is necessary to increase your frequency, as well as to overcome the limited beliefs of the altered-ego, although one will automatically produce the other. Thus, increasing the frequency of the bio-computer diminishes the altered-ego's tenacious hold upon the awareness of the entity (as to its limitations). Learning higher frequency teachings, beyond what the altered-ego allows, raises the overall frequency of the bio-computer. Frequency and energy are synonymous.

Now, what gives the altered-ego the "I" of its identity is the organization of the many specialized life forms exuding awareness of their environment through a collective, sensory frequency. This provides communication within its physical system for the purpose of maintaining the balance of electrochemical structures necessary for its maintenance within the ever-changing matrix of energies within the earth's biosphere.

This awesome, mechanistic creation of harmonic resonances traps energetic thought-forms within its electromagnetic structure in the exact manner as the earth body. Further, it assembles pre-organized and random thought-forms according to natural and artificial magnetic lines of flux, just as the earth does.

You may liken the body to a capacitor as it performs the function of storing energy, and you may liken it to a transducer as it converts energy fields into thought-forms. These two processes are actually one, as the expansion and contraction of the heart-pulse are one. However, since your language lends itself to analysis rather than synthesis, it will serve a more useful purpose toward understanding your true nature if these two concepts are contemplated separately, at the onset.

First, it may be useful to understand the nature of matter as an energy construct. As you may remember from the preceding material (Chapter 6), we described the membrane tension formed around each cell, collection of cells comprising the entire body – and how this forms a large, complex, feeling/memory cell. This membrane tension is created by two opposing energy waves, intersecting at 180 degree values from infinite "points" streaming in and out of the center. Without this coming and going of an energy wave through itself, a standing wave form could not exist for any appreciable length of time. It could not exist at all as material creation.

If this "coming and going" is not clear to you, think of it as an action like "pulling taffy" made of light, whereby tenuous matter begins to form as it is folded in upon itself and stretched again, until textures begin to form. All of these textures are composed of the various patterns associated with the frequency of that particular light geometry.

A more accurate representation would be a hologram, from which a three dimensional form manifests from two one dimensional forms by doubling the image upon itself from another angle and two other points. If you use an infinite number of projectors and mirrors, adding a spinning motion to the whole affair, an object of matter "in time" in a membrane of tension would materialize to the senses when the frequency of the object matched that of the sensory frequency.

This is not so theoretical or esoteric as it might seem. Let us contemplate an obvious example, in physical terms, of a membrane of tension – the forming of a membrane of tension by the opposing water/blood and air pressures in earth environment. A state of equilibrium is achieved due to the laws of compression and expansion of fluids or hydraulics. The body is constantly expanding, radiating against the atmospheric pressures that compress it by the weight of the air that surrounds it. Thus, if the organism rises in altitude, it will eventually explode. Conversely, if the organism is plunged into the ocean depths, it will be crushed by the excess weight of the water.

This law applies to energy, as well as matter. For it is now known that energy and matter are interchangeable. This coming and going of light-forming-matter creates and maintains the universe of matter worlds. A partial equation of this process of creation is perceived by astronomers who perpetually gaze into the past of creation, perceiving the universe as receding from them or expanding into the void. Very soon, however, they will be made aware of the second part of this equation, revealing a universe moving toward them at an alarming rate. They shall be doubly awestruck to realize that this has always been so, and universes pass through each other with collision a virtual impossibility due to synchronous resonance of high energy fields, unless otherwise directed by intelligent beings working with THE ONE.

Now, frequencies of light passing near each other create a charge. As they pass through each other, they create membranes of tension or standing wave forms. As the numbers of intersections increase, more angles or sub-harmonics are created exponentially. Thus, thought-forms of increasing complexity are created which eventually organize into denser forms of matter to reflect in material existence that thought-form.

Your body, then, is a standing wave form of geometric light harmonics built of thought-forms, which compose the nodal points or building blocks of energy frequencies. As a capacitor, your body follows the laws of any individual cell, in that it traps various light frequencies within a membrane of tension created by the expansion of light from an omnipresent center or still point against the onrushing currents of light that compress it. Thus, a wall of equalized energy is maintained. This is referred to, by the Masters, as a "veil of light" or the auric field.

The only difference between you and the Masters is that they operate continually on the Genius Frequency – the Light-frequency of consciousness-awareness that is always in a perfect state of balance in any dimension. The higher frequency of you resides as the Heart Of Hearts, in which you may either enjoy the eternal moment of creation by stopping the illusion of time or continue to move through present energy constructs of past/future events. Perhaps you may see the futility of judging these seemingly opposing forces as good and evil.

FALLACIES OF DEATH AND AGING

In general, your body is actually a bubble of compressed light expressing a very unique thought-form in "time." This bubble acts as a capacitor, storing a charge of energy which expands and contracts in a perfect equilibrium with the forces of light that "cross" themselves in the process. In other words, when a physical body is dying, as you term it, the capacitor loses its ability to expand against the compressing light, causing the auric field as well as the other energy bodies to compress back into the center, stillpoint of its source as God-Mind. This explains the tunnel effect experienced in the so-called afterlife experiences.

What you term as old age, is typically the compression of lower light frequencies into their mineral states, as the higher frequency of the seed consciousness escapes into itself. If the higher frequencies of consciousness, known as the Spirit, cannot transmute the elements to an equivalent frequency, it must eventually withdraw into the still mind of THE ONE for recharging. Given that all matter is gravitationally trapped light, the seemingly "dead" body is never actually dead, even though its bones are scattered as dust. This explains the powerful, primal urge that even materialistically-minded entities have when they take such great pains to preserve or ritualistically dispose of the "dead" body. It also explains the claims of The Christ, who promised that the dead shall live again in perfected form.

Conversely, by directing the organized, as well as random, energy fields within and around the body from the command center of the Heart-mind, the frequency of the energy-bodies are increased. This retains a greater charge of light, and expands the membrane wall of tension. The individual cells of the body radiate a higher frequency of light, reversing the process of aging in the body. The lower frequencies are those that power the altered-ego and forms the gravitational magnetism of earth vibrations. Thus, the altered-ego only accesses thought-forms of the lower frequencies of gravity. In relationship to the surface of earth, these lower frequencies are horizontal. When sleeping, some of the energy-bodies of each entity are freed, to some extent, due to a relaxing of the gravitational forces that relentlessly reclaim the earth elements of identical frequencies. You may experiment with this reality by aligning the sleeping body with the polar axis or solar axis and note the effect.

The pure soul-ego, operating in and born of a higher order of light in the electromagnetic spectrum, can perform some multi-dimensional activities due to the ease in which the particle and the wave can interchange at this higher operating frequency. However, during its embodiment, if the entity chooses to operate through the gravitational frequencies of earth giving dominance to the altered-ego, the soul-ego is relatively inoperative, save in sleeping when it enjoys a brief respite of freedom.

The potential for the human body is unlimited when the entity chooses to resonate with the higher frequencies of Light from which it was created before its incarnation on earth. In this scenario, the body is used as an earth capacitor to store star energy as quantum energy packets of light. This intelligent star energy can then be transduced to perform interdimensional activities in full waking consciousness to instill consciousness-awareness in the elements of earth body.

As a transducer, the body may use selective frequencies of light quanta to transmute lower frequencies or to simply "link up" to other universal subsets of frequencies. For example, the Light quanta, that drive the heart, can be tuned to resonate and communicate with all identical frequency patterns of all hearts simultaneously.

In addition, the body as bio-transducer, resonating with the vertical rays of light of the Genius Frequency, can actually capture and transmute discordant, destructive thought-form harmonics (through meditation for instance) into higher orders of light by adding or subtracting frequencies of harmonics to match the Original Template of creation. All healing is accomplished by this process. The result is the ability to enter the causative arena of creation where the entity may exalt any life form or thought-form, generating healing powers from the etheric dimensions of cellular life. This can be applied to individual organs, as well as to the entire earth body!

Questioner: Why do the lucid, inspired moments in my life come and go? It seems that moments of clarity begin to get fuzzy and even confusing, and I am my "old" self again.

MaYaRa: You engaged or, shall we say, indulged in your analytical thinking processes (altered-ego-intellect). Attempting to analyze your lucid or inspired moments without losing them, requires great discipline and flexibility.

The fatigue that you experienced is due to the intellectual function of the altered-ego short circuiting the energy reservoir of your capacitor. Thus, the transducer function of the auric field "lost" its capacity to translate energy patterns that we send into the appropriate resonating syntax. When the intellect is faced with new material of a higher frequency, its immediate tendency is to short circuit its own energy for the purpose of blocking it. The nature of the altered-ego is to accept only that with which it is already familiar, because it cannot operate on a frequency higher than that of its own operating frequency, for it is composed only of those lower frequencies.

Permit us to digress here, but this a perfect opportunity to make a point that may help you. For the above reasons, your educational system follows linear paths of futility. It can only teach what it knows. It can only know what it teaches. It cannot learn what it does not know, etc., etc. Futile is an apt expression here, for the altered-ego consumes a vast and disproportionate amount of energy as it tracks itself, chasing its tail, protecting what it knows at the expense of learning what it does not know.

Only in the spirit of "not knowing" can one begin to know and this is no different for a system of education. You see, the altered-ego heartily engages in fear of the unknown. It is comfortable with what it knows within its limited frequency and is aggressively defensive against knowledge of a higher order or frequency of light. Each entity must create the space of sky into which the Eagle of wisdom may spread its wings and take flight into higher adventures in the LIGHT of THE ONE.

Now, the Siamese functions of capacitor/transducer require the precision balancing of all mind-centers within the body. Together they complete the circuitry necessary to resonate with the Genius Frequency. However, since the bio-computer is formed from elemental matter, there exists an earth-circuitry running horizontally through the body. The elemental body is thus bonded to the layers or banding of elemental frequencies in the earth's auric field.

Three dimensional awareness tunes into the horizontal frequencies of earth, forming sphere within spheres. There are many degrees of this banding within the lower frequencies. This explains how a third dimensional technology, such as that upon earth at this time, appears to be evolving as "progress," but in reality, it is only expanding through a minute, horizontal band of energy awareness.

All three dimensional thinking exists within the gravitational bands or spheres and the altered-ego can only draw from this subset of frequencies. The first three brain-mind centers of the sexual, digestive and solar plexus are firmly rooted in this energy domain. Three dimensional consciousness, then, is a form of gravity that eventually collapses under its own weight or compression. Thus, three dimensional technology must, by its very nature, devolve at the same rate as it evolves, continually canceling its efforts. Where it discovers a cure, it creates another disease. Where it educates, it creates ignorance. Where it dominates and abuses earth-nature, earth-nature must dominate and abuse in return. When will man understand?

We use examples of the larger social pictures so you can comprehend more clearly the nature of consciousness. However, the most important issue is each individual entity. This is where change must begin. As a microcosm, as a replica of the universe, each must personally begin the work. For the entity to attack the system is only a mask over its own personal inadequacies.

Now, the lower three mind-centers act as receivers only, pulling in frequencies that form the horizontal banding of earth. These mind-centers cannot function as transmitters. Thus, all actions, seemingly created by these mind-centers, manifest through a process of pushing and pulling people and circumstances toward or away from each other. In other words, any life dramas pertaining to sex, food, dominance, or territorial defense are horizontal movements that only pull entities around the spinning sphere of earth, creating the illusion of progress with no actual difference in frequency – all is earth bound! Thus, even the so-called "flight-fight" syndrome is merely this pushing or pulling action in two directions: pulling towards is aggressive behavior; pushing from is the behavior of fright and retreat.

The dual nature of the receiver/transmitter begins in the fourth brain/mind-center of the Heart of Hearts. The remaining three mind-centers also have this dual ability. Thus, the mind-center of the throat, pituitary, pineal, and the crown act as step-up or step-down transformers or transducers, depending upon what frequency of thought-form the entity desires. Thus, the first three mind-centers are only capable of expression in the horizontal world of three dimensional reactions, whereas the next five mind-centers bridge the gap to the causative arena of co-creation in the fifth dimension.

Questioner: Are you saying that there are actually eight chakras or mind-centers rather than seven?

MaYaRa: There are 24 mind-centers operating in 24 dimensions within your local universe. We include the eighth here to eventually expound upon the five subtle energy bodies of the human creation that each of you may develop through the coordination with the eighth.

Questioner: In the Eastern teachings, it is claimed that cosmic energy enters the human system at the base of the brain. Can you explain this in relation to this material?

MaYaRa: This area of the so-called primitive brain is regulated by the pituitary mind-center, gland or energy portal. Although cosmic energy is received in this area and regulated by the pituitary as a life sustaining intelligence, the capacity of this entry point to sustain higher light frequencies is limited. If this energy portal or transducer did not step down these high frequencies, the nervous system would burn itself out. Since human consciousness uses the cellular organizations of the animal kingdom to embody itself within earth existence, the function of this distribution center is largely the same as in the animal world.

The animal kingdom operates exclusively on the horizontal, gravitational frequencies of earth. The result is that cosmic intelligence is transduced or stepped down to match those horizontal frequencies. The obvious clue here is that the spinal networks of the animal kingdom function optimally in a horizontal position relative to the earth, translating higher codings of light into instinctual patterns needed in its day-to-day living in one, two and three dimensional awareness.

Now, as we have stated, mankind did not evolve from the animal kingdom by "natural selection" or by any other means. The assemblage of cellular forms into more complex communities were created by projection of thought-forms and experimented with until the various "tools" of earth expressions of higher thought-forms were perfected. Then, final alterations were made by restructuring the perfected tools or organs to sustain the higher frequency light consciousness of Adamic Man.

This structural configuration was a bio-structure possessing a vertical spine parallel to the incoming vertical cosmic intelligent energy. The pattern for this spinal configuration was first developed in the plant kingdom where the tree became the ultimate expression of combining vertical frequencies with horizontal frequencies. This provided an unobstructed, "clear channel" for causal frequencies to manifest higher Light frequencies into earth-mind, so that co-creating entities of the Light could upgrade the planet. Thus, the material link with Higher Mind established upon earth provided for Divine Husbandry with the female energies of earth-mind. The specially constructed vertical spine serves the same purpose as rotating a radio antenna dish to receive static-free reception. Like a radio receiver, the strongest reception is achieved when in proper alignment with the source transmitter. It is from this aspect of earthly creation that the spiritual, Light-ego is symbolized by the upright spinal column as "I."

The structural integrity of animals does not allow them to endure the sudden input of pure cosmic waves pouring into their horizontally tuned nervous system. A transducer is needed to govern the high frequency cosmic energies. Thus, in the human realm, the pituitary gland reverted to a step-down transformer, rather than a step-up transducer. As the human creation began to sink deeper into the lower, horizontal fields of gravitational frequencies, the biochemical structures were altered accordingly; and the pituitary regulator began stepping down the frequencies to match what the human entities could physically contain.

Since most of you have been floundering for thousands of lifetimes in the horizontal frequencies of earth-mind, the pineal gland has fairly atrophied. However, it is by no means inactive. It is, as you term it, "out of shape." Therefore, to demand instant spiritual enlightenment is to invite possible destruction. It would be just as foolish to jump up and run 500 miles at top speed after smoking, drinking and sitting in a chair for 20 years. Thus, do not be discouraged because you cannot simply read about these realities and suddenly walk upon the water, though sudden transformations are indeed possible.

Each gland or energy portal prismatically divides the Rays of creation into subfrequencies that resonate with specific areas, organs and mind-centers for the maintenance of physical functions. The human bio-computer is designed to handle much greater quantities of a much higher frequency than is needed for this maintenance. This human quality of mind accounts for the clues that scientists interpret as the 9/10 of unused brain matter. As mentioned earlier, the brain is only a physical memory bank containing far greater stores of information than "normally" used. Thus, you can see that the brain is only part of the story.

When the extra capacity of all mind-centers, glands, etc. are combined, the total picture of 1/10 of the capacity of the total mind of the bio-computer results. It is the nonunified state of the seven mind-centers that blocks the ability of the human entity to access the galactic information stored in the brain, as well as access Higher Intelligence.

Without these transducers to divide the Rays of creation into subfrequencies and control the amplitude present within the membrane wall of tension throughout the cells of the bio-computer, a strictly three dimensional body would literally explode, with the force of an atomic bomb, without the consciousness frequency necessary to control and transmute the physical vibrations coherently into higher Light frequencies.

The earth's ancient and present Masters have demonstrated these facts, from time immemorial, in every conceivable manner of teaching. Yet many of you remain in doubt – wondering, at best, if it is possible. This infinite frequency of awesome power does not exist in some far off place, nor can it be evoked or resonated with through self-serving frequencies of the altered-ego. It is termed by many as cosmic energy. What do you imagine yourselves to be made of? Cosmic energy. The practical process and preparations for recovering this power – explained in so many teachings – have become so many empty rituals under the auspices of religious dogma supporting various institutions.

Yet by proper balancing of the thought-forms through consciousness training, the entire electromagnetic field of the human bio-computer can be transmuted into the more subtle and far more powerful Light spectra – the Genius Frequency. In this state of consciousness, the so-called "miracles" are commonplace.

In the final analysis, one cannot separate the dual functions of transducer/capacitor, for these operate simultaneously through alternating functions of the cosmic pulse. Each entity is an instrument that, when finely-tuned, resonates with the Genius Frequency, opening the doors to multidimensional perception as a co-creator in the Light of THE ONE.

We reiterate for clarity. Each of your seven mind-centers is designed to tune to a select bandwidth, using subfrequencies of the Rays of creation. Your task is to harness these mind-centers through the powers of the Heart of Hearts, creating first streams, then rivers, lakes, seas and oceans of Divine-Mind frequencies with which you may transmute the elemental structures of matter into light – Free yourselves into the Light.

Questioner: Then, in general, are the teachings about right-living connected with the ability to tune to the Genius Frequency?

MaYaRa: Most certainly, without a doubt. We are endeavoring to explain a higher level mechanics of the human bio-computer that consciousness is locked into at this time, in your time.

The purpose of this book is to appeal to the intellect in terms that might awaken the memory of your true nature. Again, it is of utmost importance to avoid the justifications of these "teachings" in terms of "morals." The concept of morality has been relegated to a mere category within the dictionary of partial life equations – supporting various institutions at the expense of the individual's freedom in the Light. The altered-ego defines morality, on a personal basis, as just another personality quirk in the random patterns of psychology, generated by an accidentally created system of nature that does not "appear" to have morals. In contemporary thinking, one entity may be moral and another immoral, just as one chooses to own a specific brand of auto vehicle rather than another. Even though this view is true within the frequency of mind that perceives it, time is growing short for such "hit and miss" meanderings of consciousness that is experiencing its Omega point – the end of this cycle of time.

In our observations, we recognize the need for those who rely on the intellect to gather voluminous amounts of high frequency information necessary to raise the frequency of their thought-forms beyond the limits of the altered-ego. Each of you is the custodian of your organic computers. Your purpose in the scheme of things has always been to maintain the optimum capacity of your transducer/capacitors as a consciousness body from Cosmic Origins. Each entity has the capacity to govern when, where and how the Divine Intelligence of God-Mind is to be dispensed for the purpose of evolving conscious awareness within planetary bodies and the resultant races indigenous to those primal creations. You are the light of the world and all life within it.

What other purpose would have meaning in such a transitory system of densities which your consciousness permeates at this juncture? Truth held only by the intellect is imprisoned in the cell of arrogance. Truth wielded only by will becomes dogma. Truth living in the Heart Of Hearts connects you with the pyramidal, primal Intelligent energy of every atom in the universe. Truth must be totally embraced by all the mind-centers in order to resonate with the Genius Frequency.

Questioner: Can you further explain the part that meditation plays, regarding the material in this chapter?

MaYaRa: We reiterate, then, that meditation is not the elimination of thought, as is popularly conceptualized. The substance of the universe is thought. Do you suppose that one eliminates the universe when one meditates?!

The plurality of your earth station requires that we always evenly consider both aspects of polarity to attain a truly "unified field theory" operating on the Genius Frequency. In the Genius Frequency, the interplay of field charges is inversely proportional to the lower frequencies of the altered-ego. As your conscious energy field shrinks, the altered-ego expands and vise versa. This is a law, as sure as gravity embraces its own densities.

This inverse proportion of free energy is limited in the use of the altered-ego and unlimited in the use of the Genius Frequency. This is because the altered-ego literally feeds from its own light and when it has consumed the last quanta of light, the bio-organism shrinks into a transition – what you term as death. When you allow the higher frequency Light to swallow the altered-ego in meditation, the walls-of-tension surrounding the bio-computer expand in life and Light, allowing the Genius Frequency to flood the cells with God-Mind from the Heart of Hearts. Indeed, your *capacity* increases.

It is a common misnomer, in the Western mind-set, to believe that the solution to most problems is to turn up the power. Thus certain philosophies emerge: expend more energy to be successful, expend more energy to be more popular, expend more energy to stay healthy, etc. These are suggestions from the altered-ego, which must consume the light charge of the capacitor in order to accomplish its task. This depletes the bio-system of its life source, causing nervous dysfunction and cellular breakdown. Infinite energy requirements cannot be produced by any means suggested within the frequency of the altered-ego. It will first consume all available energy, while blocking higher frequency energy needed to maintain the wall-of-tension of Light around the cells. When this energy is consumed, the remnant light frequencies from dying cells will be expended until the bio-system falls below the life sustaining balance.

Questioner: Can a proper diet increase the frequency of the body?

MaYaRa: It is true that each food category resonates on different frequencies. Air is light, but there are limits to the amount of air you can breath. Water is light, but you would drown if you attempted to drink your way to the Genius Frequency. Thus, energy cannot be increased by expending energy, nor can it be increased by consuming more material. The altered-ego will eventually lower the frequencies of whatever is ingested, just as it does with knowledge.

Frequency can be increased by expanding the capacity of the field of consciousness, in the bio-computer, by raising the frequency of thought surrounding it. There are thought-forms that give energy and light, and there are thought-forms that take energy and light. In meditation one instantly knows the difference because one can immediately sense the frequency drop in the body when a low frequency thought-form is drawing light from the consciousness field. Thus, only when the thought-forms of higher Light resonate in the body can proper use be made of the higher frequencies that fruits and vegetables resonate with.

Awareness must be charged with high frequency consciousness, as well as the body. During sleep the physical body is repaired, to some extent, and the soul body is recharged. The entity recuperates from the onslaughts of the altered-ego as it is recharged with light during the sleep cycle. Waking consciousness is an organ of light perception and without recharging, this too, will dissipate and shrink into the elements. In meditation, one also charges the light-organ of waking consciousness-awareness. It is interesting to note the popular anecdote, "sleep on it."

The crucial point in this understanding is this: When the frequency of thought-forms is increased, the system's capacity to receive and hold a charge is also increased. On the other hand, it makes no difference if one dips a thimble into a bucket or into the ocean, because the capacity to hold the energy is the same. Your task, then, is not only to increase your energy, but to increase the capacity to hold light. Intelligent Cosmic Energy of God-Mind is like the ocean and you, as a capacitor, need only increase the capacity to contain it.

Thus, the capacitor function of your bio-computer is designed to expand to include vast energy fields of God-Mind so that your transducer may facilitate genius by transmuting the unlimited cosmic energy into intelligent consciousness awareness. In other words, expand the container and the light floods the cells, rejuvenating them and raising the over-all frequency of the bio-computer to match the higher intelligence working with THE ONE. Thus, the higher the frequency, the higher the capacitance. Light, like water, seeks its own level.

Meditating is an active function that opens and expands the consciousness capacity of the bio-computer to take the charge of cosmic energy and contain it in its awareness, transmuting it into consciousness. In this process, the altered-ego shrinks as the aggressive act of meditating expands the charge – the capacitance – of higher frequency light. This increases the boundaries marked by the walls-of-tension that form spheres of intelligent energy around each cell and around the body as a total cell. Simultaneously, the transducer function of the pineal gland is stimulated by the higher frequencies of God-Mind. With the light of the Genius Frequency "on tap," the pineal gland also enlarges its capacity. This channels healing frequencies into areas of the organism in need of conscious-light repair. The surplus transmutes the total vibratory resonance of the bio-computer, creating a unified field of conscious awareness of all the mind-centers.

Meditation is not used to block out life in any way. Meditating upon nothing results in attaining exactly nothing. The altered-ego is a shifty fear-ridden part of your self that tries to hide from the unknown. The altered-ego must acquiesce to the will of the higher frequency directives from the entity's "higher self." In the background, the altered-ego will tap an impatient foot, waiting for its chance to resume what it considers the more serious matters of fear and survival.

Proper meditation upon a goal conceived in the womb of wisdom and knowledge yields outstanding results. Wisdom is the arch enemy of the altered-ego – for when true wisdom expands in the light of the pure ego of soul, the altered-ego shrinks and Genius Frequency becomes available to consciousness awareness. Eventually, a true rebirth, a reawakening, recalls the Original Program of universal being. This universal being has access to the solutions for every conceivable problem. This, of course, renders the altered-ego an insignificant thorn to be plucked from your being as you merge into the totality of self.

Although we have stated that the capacity of the bio-computer is increased, this does not indicate that the intelligence quotient can be increased quantitatively by feeding it more information. This expansion is accomplished qualitatively by increasing the frequency of awareness, which in turn increases the capacity for true intelligence within the bio-computer. We know of many case histories of illiterate and so-called unintelligent entities that achieved superconsciousness through the Genius Frequency. All the "cramming" and studying of a lifetime cannot produce this genius, as can the persistent expansion of the walls-of-tension that form the auric field of the mind.

Questioner: When this expansion of consciousness takes place, doesn't the personal identity of the individual shrink as well?

MaYaRa: This is yet another misnomer born of the altered-ego's fear-ridden philosophy. It is only the altered-ego and all of its limiting functions that shrink and it, of course, fears that also. Your true identity has nothing whatsoever to do with the altered-ego. When the capacitor expands, taking the charge of Cosmic Intelligence, it expands into the God of self, which has its center in everything. With the passionate persistence of love, every entity will experience this, if they choose, and then they shall "know."

In summary, then, it is the increase in frequency of consciousness that expands the reservoir of the capacitor function of the bio-computer. The altered-ego claims that the entity shall lose its identity when, in fact, the I-dentity expands to include everything and every entity. *The entity becomes all-realized.* Through the process of meditation, the energy portals, glands or brain/mind-centers are bathed in the higher frequency light of God-Mind, which rejuvenates the bio-computer and increases the capacity for true intelligence.

UNIVERSAL CENTER POINT
"INSIDE ATOM'S HEART"

> *"The entire local universe*
> *is being offered*
> *into the reign of Christ Consciousness;*
> *and the Genius Frequency is made available to all*
> *who choose to be a part of its glory."*

Questioner: I still cannot grasp how increasing the frequency of the body can increase its capacity to take a cosmic charge. Can you explain the relationship of frequency to physical matter?

MaYaRa: To properly understand this super-reality, a conscious awareness of the unified field of consciousness should be contemplated. This field utilizes what we shall term the Universal Epicenter. To increase the frequency of thought-forms is to draw upon infinite supplies of consciousness awareness from the center of being. To draw consciousness from the center of one's being is to draw it from the center of all beings. Meditate upon that, beloved. Your meditations will reap a wondrous harvest of Light and healing. The frequency of consciousness awareness that accesses the Universal Epicenter is the Genius Frequency. This super-reality is the superconsciousness that awaits you – your right and heritage. We must, perforce, examine the very nature of the atom. For in understanding its structure and the nature of consciousness and Light, we shall reveal the epicenter of intelligence within the atom that we term the Universal Center Point. Indeed, this the Heart of the atom as well as the Heart of THE ONE.

Before we launch into this understanding of this angle of reality, know that in order to own knowledge as wisdom, one must experience it with all the mind-centers in synchronous resonance with the Genius Frequency. Therefore, in a strictly intellectual study, contradictions will continually plague the student due to the polarized nature of the intellect as a function of the altered-ego. We speak through these word/symbols to those of you who have chosen the way of knowledge back to THE ONE. We make this distinction because there are many ways to return. Once addicted to the altered-ego's intellect, few revelations may be experienced without the need for an explanations in sensory terms. Although the way of knowledge can be tedious and full of traps, it is a great joy to tremble under a waterfall of intellectual revelations, as a first step into the so-called unknown.

There is not a single grand truth that cannot be experienced by you in present earth plane existence. Also, there are many attributes of high frequency Light which must be experienced while embodied in an earth garment – not after you die. For if the entity cannot acquire the discipline and love enough to be a responsible co-creator in the earth frequency, it cannot be acquired it in the higher dimensions.

Know that there is no time like the present to effectively change your life, using whatever "tools" of consciousness you have acquired to date. For in the consciousness of God-Mind, there is no time but eternity in which to experience THE ONE. You have more tools than for which you may give yourself credit. Consider that the imagination is real! The raw material of imagination is the same substance and structure as the astral and etheric dimensions. IMAGINATION IS REALITY! Thus, there is no reason to deny yourselves the splendid anticipation of the inevitable by studying a two or three dimensional picture which eventually will transmute into a fourth and fifth dimensional experience. Be patient, all will be revealed.

Knowledge can be transmuted into wisdom in two ways. One is to reflect on previous (higher) experiences. In this case, fragments of knowledge can fall into place to explain the experience from a broader base of knowledge. The other, more indirect way, is to use knowledge to recall a forgotten experience. Knowledge is one key to wisdom. Wisdom is not simply a collection of facts, it is the experience of a fact. In any case, experience may be transmuted into wisdom by a fuller understanding of an event, regardless of its frequency. Conversely, knowledge may be transmuted into wisdom by an ensuing experience. Knowledge and wisdom originates and manifests in and through the imagination, which is in the fourth dimension.

With that in mind, open your imagination to that wonderful thought-form known as the space/time continuum. It should be clear, at this juncture, that Einstein received information about this concept through the Genius Frequency.

The concept of space/time continuum is a fourth dimensional awareness perception. "Relativity" is a contingency of space /time that Einstein elucidated. As always, from your perspective, there are two ways of viewing this concept. Most scholars only speak in terms of the above concept, space/time. However, we will now add its complimentary opposite: time/space. Thus, there is space through which time travels or moves (space/time), and time through which space travels or moves (time/space). In other words, whether you go to the mountain or the mountain comes to you, these are "sides of the same coin" seen from your time-frame and our space-frame respectively. These seeming dichotomies are unified by the action and illusion of motion within what appears to you as curved space. But the so-called theory of relativity is nothing more than a polarized relationship within a unified field of consciousness.

All so-called "discoveries" are actually rediscoveries of ancient truths and teachings from another angle of perception. A cursory study in Eastern or Egyptian philosophies, for example, reveals concepts identical with modern theory, albeit in a much more eloquent and poetic description. A brief study in the recent, intellectual history of man, reveals how the altered-ego can take control of a high frequency thought-form and drag it down to its own frequency in three dimensional consciousness.

The discovery of particle/wave physics is an example of a fourth dimensional reality fragmented by the same restrictions suffered by the altered-ego. These debilitating setbacks are a result of attempting to use low frequency thought-forms to interpret the higher, fourth dimensional thought-forms. Once again, the altered-ego's inability to comprehend high frequency revelation is evidenced by the speed and depths to which that revelation can be a divided issue among those representing one polarity or another of earth-mind.

What the altered-ego can comprehend is that a true revelation can "set the people free." It is acutely aware of this due to its propensity to dominate and sacrifice others for its own gain. With few exceptions, contemporary scientific thought has hacked Divine Revelation to bits by the analytical, linear-functioning intellect. The fragmented remains of the original equation is scattered and thrown to the "public" with great fanfare and confused excitement as to the progressive nature of the methods of the altered-ego and with false hopes for a better "future" for all – a future which never seems to come.

The above scenario is quite common and has plagued the true evolution of man on a social level. However, none of these "social" reasons is an excuse for the individual to shirk its private responsibility toward creation, on any level. We urge you, beloved entities, to think for yourselves. The Western mind has chosen the way of sensory knowledge to find the ultimate truth – all roads lead to THE ONE. However, you cannot wait for others to interpret this information for you. Begin now to study and draw your own conclusions in the Light of your Heart of Hearts.

Revelation, through science, is deliberately confused due to the myriad technical languages that are isolated and specialized for each interest group in order that their – private and institutional – positions be protected. However, all of you are geniuses, child prodigies of THE ONE; and genius is a frequency of thought available to all.

THE PARTICLE/WAVE THEORY

Now, the particle/wave revelation was not welcomed by the scientific hierarchy. Like all revelations, it shook the foundations of the established domain of the altered-ego and suggested many shocking inadequacies inherent in the previously held beliefs, fought for through bitter struggles within low frequency, polarized thinking.

The particle/wave theory suggested that the atom contains much less substantial matter than the dearly held beliefs that intellectual history claims. In fact, the evidence became more shocking as it was revealed that matter – as defined by modern science – can indeed be created and destroyed. This included the imminent possibility that there may not be any true particles within the atom to begin with! Thus, with great trepidation, the "break-through" was announced and heralded as a "triumph" of science, while an already confused public was told that they should now believe that the atom is composed of "mostly space." In the mean time, the particle accelerators revealed pictures of particles disappearing and reappearing in waves of energy, masquerading as other types of particles – another belief shattered.

Thus, even to the layman, this theory evoked serious and profound questions regarding the nature of reality and what this meant to each entity, personally as well as cosmically. Previous to that shocking news, the layman was grappling with the last "breakthrough," which reported the "fact" that their entire existence was composed of tiny, solid particles that ceaselessly spun around each other at speeds so fast that the world only appeared solid; thus, defending the validity of material reality by claiming that the particles were still "real." They were only smaller and faster than at first supposed.

We are not saying that all of the allegations of Western science are completely false. However, the above scenarios conclude that it is a question of comprehending higher frequency dimensions while using the lower frequency, third dimensional altered-ego that divides all revelation against itself in polarized consciousness. This occurs because of the inherent limitation of the altered-ego to comprehend or resonate with frequencies of higher consciousness. This polarized thinking, on a global scale of mass-mind, requires that each of you, personally, begins to integrate the religious concepts of the ancients and scientific concepts of Western mind.

For the fulcrum of all understanding is based upon the rather simple cause and effect axioms: Thought creates Light, Light creates consciousness-awareness; therefore, consciousness is Light. Thought creates form, the material worlds are form; therefore, material worlds and consciousness are Light. These simple Divine truths would, if consciously understood, unite every discipline and every study from nuclear physics to astronomy, medicine, business, religion, political science, psychology, etc. These axioms do not suggest the end of science or even the end of a particular discipline within science. It is the common foundation upon which all apparent differences are unified in God-Mind. However, the altered-ego is not predicated toward unifying anything, including itself. The altered-ego must, by its very nature, consume itself by creating its opposite and ultimately canceling itself in what many psychiatrists term as "ego death."

Questioner: If the true nature of the atom is space, and the apparent particles are waves of energy, how can it maintain its structure?

MaYaRa: The true nature of the atom is MIND and its substance is that of Light.

In the previous material (Chapter 6), we touched upon the concept of the brain as a galactic hologram. This is also true for all material worlds within the Mind of THE ONE. All is truth, by degree. Thus, truth is only useful to the degree that it captures and accurately represents the true Process of creation, i.e., the true nature of THE ONE. At this juncture, then, the hologram will suffice as a reference point in our studies. You see, the truth about your selves is the truth about THE ONE. How could it be otherwise? Therefore, THE ONE creates with the same functions and processes of mind of which each of you are capable.

Now, we shall examine the funda-"mental" nature of thought that gives the atom its structural integrity, indeed, its reality – therefore your reality. We shall expand upon the general axiom: form follows function. Since the function of thought in its pure form of God-Mind is an unfathomable mystery, we must start at a point in creation where Principles of THE ONE began to manifest as Light within MIND.

The first expression of Infinite Mind is geometrical energy constructs or thought-forms inherent in Light. The Twenty and Two funda-"mental" attributes of THE ONE are expressed in thought-forms known in ancient teachings as "Fire Letters" of creation. Understand that these are not primitive alphabets given to man so that he might eventually write books. These are Living, Holographic Emanations thrust forth into the infinity of God-Mind. With these Twenty and Two Living expressions of the attributes of THE ONE Eternal Mind, the plan for the universes are conceived. Understand also, that each of the Twenty and Two expresses the pure essence of numerical, geometric value. Each is a living Intelligence projecting a Geometric-Personality-Construct of THE ONE into the space of ITS own Mind.

The geometric energy-construct expressing the unification of the Twenty and Two Attributes is the pyramid. The inherent value and expression of this projected thought-form in motion is the foundation for the continuity and integrity of atomic structure. Your query is far more profound than you realize, for structure is the only reality of the atom. Various properties of Light function within that structure, giving the atom the appearance of being composed of particles. What appears as particles are actually intersections of Light waves as points in time within the pyramidal frequency of an energy structure in motion.

This pyramidal energy-construct perfectly expresses the unification of all seeming material diversity within the Mind of THE ONE. All expression of matter, forces of energy, universes and frequencies are unified by and through the pyramidal energy-construct. These light geometries of various pyramidal forms intercommunicate with all dimensions of consciousness Light and matter – gravitationally trapped Light – and occur outside the parameters of time, as it is understood by three dimensional awareness. Through this principle, then, all dimensions of consciousness, indeed, entire universes can and do exist within each other in simultaneous, eternal moments.

Questioner: Does this information apply to and explain many of the enigmas of the Great Pyramid in Egypt?

MaYaRa: Indeed. The numerical values expressed in the Giza pyramid are master codes for every other geometry, including – and in earth terms especially – the sphere and spherical relationships within a solar system, as well as its relationship to cubic functions connecting material universes to Light universes. As far as it is related to this material, its form follows the functions of the pyramidal energy-construct.

Now, since the first reduction in the frequency of pure thought resulted in the Light emanations characterized by straight lines, the infinite matrix of these lines or waves of Light, yielded the first atomic reality as infinite wave forms intersected at infinite points in the succeeding reduction of the Original Light Frequency. Therefore, the great Twenty and Two attributes of THE ONE emphasized, formed and gave power to the perfect tool of creation: the pyramidal energy-construct. For our immediate purposes, the pyramid, composed of straight lines, was not only perfectly suited to the characteristics of light, but the function of the values of the pyramid created the geometric and mathematical perfection needed to create spheres. Thus, a sphere is a pyramidal geometry projected as motion in time.

Questioner: Why is the sphere the predominant shape in the universe?

MaYaRa: Suffice it to say that the three dimensional cubing of the sphere has been one of the most sought after calculations in all intellectual history, and represents one of the most elegant formulas representing the GEMATRIA – sacred number system – in the material world.

But to develop fourth dimensional thought-forms that elevate the frequencies of your bio-computers, we should rather concentrate upon those qualities of the sphere that accomplished said purpose.

Thus, one gazes into the heavens and perceives infinite numbers of spheres and one gazes into the microcosm of the molecular worlds and behold, there are also infinite numbers of spheres bound in cubic functions – angular relationships. The universe did not, in one moment, accidentally explode or haphazardly produce a homogeneous cosmos of identical geometries. The sphere was designed and chosen because of its inherent nature to create curved space, without which a true time continuum could not function in the matter worlds. The perfect marriage of the pyramid to the sphere is the "Golden Mean."

Now, the energy-construct of the pyramid is the primal thought-form-principle used to structure the atom and to link each atom to another through its power to expand, yet focus in many dimensions simultaneously. Therefore, each atom has a Heart of Hearts pulsating the twin beams of the creation Ray from its center. Meditate upon this concept. Picture it and feel the beauty and wisdom of this unifying principle within all diversity. As you do this, you will begin to resonate with fourth dimensional frequencies. Therein lies the key to understanding what we term the Universal Center Point connecting every center of every atom to every other atom in a timeless tapestry of at-onement in the ONE MIND containing all creation.

Questioner: Would this explain the concepts of omniscience and omnipresence?

MaYaRa: This is an excellent query.

You have found these antiquated word/symbols sprinkled throughout the many religious teachings. They are very apt expressions of grand truths as regards the nature of atomic structure. We would continue to utilize them in this examination except that, like so many other word/symbols, the power and depth of their meanings have been tainted by the altered-ego, relegating them to poetic myth which the Western mind tolerates as historic anomalies in the ongoing perfection of the ape. Therefore, we use other word/symbols to bring fresh insights into eternal truths.

When science and religion are freed from the fetters of third dimensional altered-ego, these must, perforce, meet in a unified mind of THE ONE. Only in a fourth dimensional understanding can this point converge. Our purpose, in this book, is to augment this merging of science and religion. For what is truth for one and not the other can only be a partial truth, a partial life equation. Thus, reread the above and understand this as God-Technology. Then contemplate what is stated below as we contemplate this same God-Technology from the more religious approach. Truth in ALL is universal Truth, is it not?

Now, if THE ONE is everywhere, as stressed so often in religions documents, how can you not be? All major religions of the world teach that God is either in everything, or is everywhere, or both. Although, it is quite incredible that many who profess such a belief can deny that THE ONE is in you. At any rate, it is "logical" to conclude that you are also in everything and everything is in you. However, it is the predilection of the Western mind to ask "how" this is possible and "how" does it work. All that separates science from religion is terminology – confusion of tongues – and vested interests. Otherwise, Truth stands unified across all boundaries of thought and time. Truth has no opposite in the Mind of THE ONE.

Questioner: If civilizations in all of our recorded history have not succeeded in this realization of unified Truth, and considering the state of our present civilizations, how could it be accomplished now?

MaYaRa: The frequency of your solar system has increased due to its spiraling through its Omega point – the Biblical reference to

220 THE GENIUS FREQUENCY

the "end of time" – into a higher dimension within the Central Intelligence of the Galactic-Mind. Thus, the frequencies that were, heretofore, blocked are now opened by degrees and the possibility is immanent for unified Truth to reign in the new order and Dominion of The Christ Light. The entire local universe is being offered into the reign of Christ Consciousness and, therefore, must be cleansed, and the Genius Frequency made available to all who choose to be a part of its Glory. What you have not understood before can be grasped with greater ease as the frequency increases.

All of this is arranged by the Higher Intelligence working with the Master Plan of THE ONE. Therefore, you need only to continue your studies of high frequency thought-forms and adjust your lives accordingly. You shall understand what you have been unable to understand. You shall be what you have not been for 'er so long in your time.

We await ALL to personally share in the glory, NOW. You are no longer required to relive the past to understand it. You may not have had the capacity to "see" your true natures yesterday, but you may "see" it now! The Genius Frequency increases by degrees every moment in your time. Do not stand idle, watching the potential of all lifetimes drift past. Prove these Truths to yourself and turn these words-on-paper into rich and fertile soil of knowledge, from which wisdom sprouts into a mighty tree of life in the original garden of Light that shelters and feeds the children with eternal life.

That you are one with everything and everyone, and everyone and everything is one with you is no mere metaphor. From whence did such a thought-form originate (such a lofty concept)? It came from the facts and truths about the very nature and structure of the universe, from the revelations of God-Technology taught by the Masters of Light. These revelations were and are separated by the duality of thought through the altered-ego into science and religion, good and evil, heaven and hell, and all the dichotomies of earth. In the beginning there was no such duality in the heart and mind of the first, Adamic Man – not in the world, the solar system, the galaxy or in the universe. The dualities of the "fallen" thought-forms were allowed to run their full circle and now, in the fullness of that circle, the old order of the altered-ego must end.

Now, when consciousness enters the center point in the Heart of Hearts – when desire summons the conscious awareness trapped in the "veils of light," surrounding the atomic structure of your physical being, then, in the totality of your true natures, you experience the causative arena of no-time existence. In that point of consciousness, one escapes the curvature of space forming time. This is the state described as omnipresence and omniscience. It is the Divine Unicenter or Center Point or still point that applies, not only to THE ONE, but to your very natures as products of THE ONE.

We have briefly described this subject in somewhat religious terms. However, many "knowledge-mongers" are not moved by so-called religious poetry, regardless that it may be eloquent and moving as truth. The Western mind-set craves to know the "how" of it all. Yet the intellect continues to operate on the lower frequencies of the altered-ego. Let us resume, then, our contemplations of God-Technology, suspending the belief systems of the altered-ego long enough for the frequency of your consciousness to be raised by your true desires of God-Mind.

A frequency is a wave form, generated by thought within the space of mind, which is the substance of potentiality termed ether or æther. This is the substance of thought-idea/form – without which nothing could exist. Just as the medium of air or water makes it possible for sound to act as a carrier wave of frequencies that can span distance and time, so too, does the ether of so-called space provide the medium through which the higher frequencies of light and thought may move and have its being. We are aware that scientific thought has attempted to destroy this so-called "theory of the ethers" with their most powerful intellectual artillery. It has yet to be truly discounted. For even modern scientific thought has relied upon this concept to explain creation, albeit in rather fluffy terminology such as universal "foam," "string theories," and so forth. Why not indulge in some fluffy theories of your own?

In the space of God-Mind, various frequencies generate different shapes, just as various sound waves generate different patterns which "appear" when said wave resonates with another malleable medium. Therefore, every frequency resonating with a medium is associated with and synonymous with a particular shape or structure within the medium. Shapes are formed as angular relationships in the interaction of the wave form with itself and the medium through which it passes. Each form or shape has an inherent function that is used in the universal scheme of things.

The pyramidal energy-construct or frequency-shape possesses the inherent qualities to sustain the Unifying Principle of THE ONE throughout all dimensions of creation. Thus, the terms "frequency" and "energy-construct" can be used interchangeably, for these are one and the same. Differences are only "apparent" due to the medium in which the frequency resonates. When these frequency-shapes are pulsated, the electric nature of the universe is created. The frequency associated with the pyramid is universal because it contains all of the necessary geometric frequencies to create, sustain and transmute matter from one dimension to another and back again – from pyramid to cube to sphere to cube to pyramid.

It is important to remember, in your visualizations, that it matters not how many units of awareness are created. Every atom is a unit of pulsating awareness, alternating from the material realm to the etheric realm and back again, through the innate qualities of the pyramidal energy-construct. Thus, atoms exist as multi-dimensional units of consciousness. Since each of you consists of atoms, you may utilize the pyramidal energy-construct to do the same.

Regarding the particle/wave theory, when the frequency of a particle is accelerated or increased sufficiently, it ceases to exist in time and resumes its existence in another dimension. In doing so, its lower frequency energy collapses inward, spiraling through the pyramidal energy-construct. In that eternal moment, said unit of awareness, having exited through the point of one pyramidal energy-construct, enters into another, reversing its polarity and resuming its function as particle. Thus the atom's particle/wave properties are due to this pulsating geometry which creates the electromagnetic structures of the atom that "appear" to have permanent material structure within the frequencies of awareness within curved space.

Thus, the pyramidal energy-construct acts as a carrier frequency that creates the tapestry of interconnecting, pulsating geometries, providing interdimensional awareness and communication. Through this process, particles or energy do not "travel," for consciousness may exist in many dimensions simultaneously within and without a time continuum. Every atom of your being is permeated with and sustained by this frequency and its inherent geometry, giving you the innate potential to resonate with it. When your consciousness resonates with this frequency, you have conscious control of the very nature of the atom. This accounts for the many "miraculous" feats attributed to the Masters of Light, by witnesses to their "powers."

For those of you who struggle with this explanation we offer a simple analogy. If you were to fill your dwelling with stringed, musical instruments and play a note upon a flute, every instrument would resonate that note as each corresponding string resonates. That note exists, simultaneously, in many places through different instruments occupying different space/time coordinates. We have established that life-forms are resonant "nodal" membranes existing as tension created by opposing angles of light. Therefore, you are a "note" existing in a moment in time, yet, with the potential to exist in many places – dimensions – simultaneously. We shall return to the moment in creation when potential for atomic structure is manifested.

Questioner: I still do not understand how atoms are created. Could you explain this again?

MaYaRa: Only the altered-ego cannot understand. The other dimensions of yourself fully comprehend the nature of the atom because it "knows" of what and how it is made. Everyone possesses this innate knowledge. The process of learning is actually a process of remembering. If the atom consisted of particles of material, as you have been taught, each one would have to be created individually, as a seamstress might lay one stitch upon another to create a pattern of nature – an absurd notion. However, when you visualize the holographic nature of the universe as twin lights of creation passing through each other while spinning, it becomes easier to see the infinite points of intersection of these high frequency wave forms. Each intersection is a nodal point, a standing wave in time, that creates a particle/ wave. When you add the pulsating function of this spinning of the rays, it can be seen that the atom is a collection of these nodal points appearing and disappearing within the structure of the spinning pyramidal energy-construct.

In addition to the above contemplation, understand that every part of the pyramidal energy-construct contains the information to create every other part, making it indivisible by any value save itself which, of course, equals ONE. For this reason the truth of Omnipresence has its reality. Thus, Omniscience and Omnipresence, resting in the infinite potential of God-Mind, creates infinite atoms by the Divine law of Similitude anywhere and all times, forever. It is a grand Truth, is it not?

Perhaps the deceivingly simple statement, "center every-where, circumference nowhere," may begin to manifest as a reality in your consciousness awareness in light of the above contemplation. This statement is not a mere philosophical play on words. Contemplate this truth with the tools of knowledge we have set forth into your conscious awareness and you will expand the limitations imposed upon the totality of your being by the altered-ego. Think with your Heart, not your head.

Be assured that your true I-dentity will expand to include the limitless possibilities of manifestation as you realize the awakening of your world in a new cycle of enlightenment and freedom imminent upon the higher frequencies of event-horizons within creation. The Genius Frequency is no longer blocked and relegated to a dimly lit potential in the shadows of ignorance. Nor is it only accessible to a select few initiates as in earlier epochs in your time. It is accelerating into the very forefront of consciousness of every living entity within the earth plane. Do not fear these revelations, for these are the completions of your evolving God-Self from which you severed so long ago in your time. Embrace these, for these are your heritage. You are the revelations. They are *YOU REALIZED!*

Now, within every entity is planted one idealized, super-charged atom resonating directly with the frequency of God-Mind. This is your key to unlocking the door to the Genius Frequency: to Omniscience and Omnipresence. As we have previously stated, it resides in the Heart of Hearts. It is the primary resonating point for every other atom of your being. Therefore, it also has the capacity to govern and adjust the frequency of all other atoms through the power of the pyramidal energy-construct.

No other mind-center within the bio-computer has this continuous, Omniscient, open channel of life-giving energy to every other atom through interdimensional communication with higher Light Intelligence. For this reason, we have stated that all healing, all miracles, all superconsciousness is created through this God-Atom or Adamic Seed Crystal within you. Without this God-Atom, the other mind-centers would have no focus of a frequency high enough for self-realization. The physical heart is placed near this colossal life-giving power for obvious reasons. Thus to move your consciousness-awareness to its center is to tap consciously into the most awesome power and majesty of life.

This perfect God-Atom possesses the conscious ability to experience Omnipresence and Omniscience. Meditate again upon the previous contemplation regarding the exercise in Chapter 4. At some point in time, in your time, the pyramidal energy-construct will reveal itself to you.

Now, there are different configurations of the pyramidal geometries, i.e., three-sided, four-sided, etc. The configuration that functions in earth density creations is the four-sided version as re-presented by the Great Giza pyramid. You may behold this perfect idea-construct and realize that this four-sided, five-planed, five-angled, five-pointed energy-construct is the foundation for the pentagram existing in time. You may realize the significance of your five fingers, five toes, and five appendages of the body, and the five energy bodies of awareness accessible to you for high frequency communication.

Questioner: What is inside the pyramidal energy-construct, within the Heart of Hearts?

MaYaRa: Inside the pyramidal energy-construct is *Pure, Absolute, Pristine, Infinite, Omnipresent, Omniscient*, **LOVE-LIGHT/GOD-MIND** in the form of the Adamic Blueprint. For this reason, the mystical Eye of Horus is depicted within the pyramid in your ancient symbolic teachings. It represents the God-Presence within all and everywhere, in all dimensions at once for eternity.

This Divine Presence ignites and structures the continuous coming and going of Light forming all atoms of the universe. Therefore, when you enter that Presence, you are everything and everywhere at once in the ecstasy spoken of by those who have experienced it. In that dimension, your power as one with THE ONE dissolves all fears born of separatism, and the vista of eternal joy and love beyond description unfolds for you to share. That is what you are truly capable of, beloved. No words could exaggerate that truth.

The pyramidal energy-construct forms the DNA of cosmic consciousness in all dimensions. Through this geometric frequency of the Golden Mean spirals the double helix connecting all creation as ONE expression in the Mind of THE ONE. Just as the Omnipresence of DNA may be understood as omnipresent within all the cells of the body, so too may you understand the ALL pervasive Consciousness of God-Mind within every atom as it oscillates between particle and wave formations through the spiral staircase of "Jacob's Ladder." The frequency of God-Mind that creates the pyramidal energy-construct is the Genius Frequency. Therefore, the Genius Frequency may be found in everything simultaneously as a universal matrix of awareness.

Questioner: Is the Unifying Principle explained in this chapter the same as the earlier statements, regarding the LAW OF ONE?

MaYaRa: Indeed, what we have described is the God Technology serving the foundation for the LAW OF ONE where God-Mind has NO opposite in any dominion of creation.

It is important that you possess some understanding of the above principles so that those of you who seek the way of knowledge may open the door to the Genius Frequency. For the Genius Frequency is beyond the "apparent" duality of the material worlds. The concepts of good and evil, as well as all other dualities of thought, are illusions within the limited altered-ego of man.

However, your lives are not an illusion. The illusion lies in the I-dentification process of the altered-ego in the portrayal of the life-drama of earth as pitted against its own death. If you are unable to operate on the frequency of consciousness necessary to experience the LAW OF ONE, and you need to assign the polarities of good and evil to God and devil respectively, then at least redefine your choice of words, for all words are thought-forms of various frequencies.

Hasten your desire to realize self, beloved. For if you are to transcend, transmute and transfigure the totality of your being through the Genius Frequency, Living as the LAW OF ONE is the only truly liberating reality that can accomplish this ultimate goal. Know that the highest order of Intelligence working with THE ONE stands ready to assist those who choose to regain their true heritage. The outstretched hands of THE CHRIST await you. But not even God shall violate your free will – such is the Love radiated throughout creation.

Without the Genius Frequency emanating from the Universal Center Point in all center points, all that you term "good" and all that you term "evil" would forever remain so. There would not be the interfacing of polarities that create life. Centropy and pro-creation are the laws of manifestation when THE ONE contemplates SELF as infinite potential. Therefore, all manner of creation is sacred, regardless that a consciousness being chooses to I-dentify with one or the other of polarities. To "BE" at rest in the infinite potential is to resonate with LOVE-LIGHT/GOD-MIND, opening the Genius Frequency as eternal life.

Questioner: You have used terms such as: God-Atom, Primordial Seed Crystal, Adamic Blueprint, and Heart of Hearts. Are these all the same reality?

MaYaRa: *ALL IS ONE REALITY.*

Understand that if you existed before the creation of earth, there was, of course, no physical body as you know it to lower the frequency of your true I-dentities. All of the above conceptual aids are designed to help you remember the Divine YOU before the so-called "fall" of Adamic or perfect Man. Realize that these were grand beings of Light who shared, as co-creators, the joys and powers of THE ONE.

When first assigned to engage in the husbandry of the earth, Adamic Man, in this most splendid form "descended," as it were, into the realm of the co-creators responsible for creating earth. These co-creators did not desire Adamic Man, who did not directly sustain earth, to rule it in any way. The Adam and Eve story handed down to you, for all intents and purposes, will suffice for now. Realize that the "fall-of-man" suggests that mankind "fell" from presumably a "higher" place – more accurately, another dimension.

In your contemporary religions, there are little, if any, references to the state of mankind before the so-called fall. What we draw your attention to, then, through terms posed in the above query, is a function of and state of existence before the descent into the material planes where Adamic Man was summarily trapped. Consequently, man's light body was compressed by the laws described earlier in this document. The result was the Seed Crystal, God-Atom, Adamic Blueprint of the original Light-being, compressing as it was shrouded in layers upon layers of dense material elements of earth, blocking more and more of man's inherent Light body. By choice, then, Adamic Man became entrapped in the wheel or Zodiac of repetitive earth cycles.

Your task, then, is to recreate the necessary frequencies in an elemental body that shrouds the Seed Crystal or God-Atom so that it may expand to include the physical body once again and ultimately gain power over death and entropy and return to its original glory.

Questioner: Can you explain steps that can be taken to implement the process of becoming?

MaYaRa: We can simply list this process as four major steps.

> 1. *Use your intellect to organize and digest the words and thought-forms created to form a Divine Truth within self.*
>
> 2. *Use your imagination to visualize these truths.*
>
> 3. *Expand your sensory-data-processors (feeling/ emotions) so you may begin to comprehend what these truths feel like.*
>
> 4. *Internalize them in your Heart of Hearts so that you may merge with the true Center-Point of the totality of being, which will translate into Divine Action in your life.*

Questioner: Can you expand upon these four steps?

MaYaRa: Since each entity is unique in its place, time and conditioning, the following should be taken as a general outline. The answers are within self, and when enough high frequency information is assimilated and internalized, then the changes specifically suited to the individual are forthcoming. However, we feel a brief summary of the four qualities mentioned may be beneficial to some. They are as follows:

> <u>*INTELLECT:*</u> A function of the three dimensional altered-ego. It is an abstract sensory data processor designed to analyze and dissect earth-frequency material phenomenon and sort it into categories based upon observed, comparative relationships. Read and reread this material with a focus

on the "just possible," so as not to arouse polarized thinking. If the intellect is properly trained it may be used to describe, teach, and interpret high frequency thought-forms and experience.

IMAGINATION: A high frequency remnant of the "lost" faculty of true intelligence through communication with higher intelligence via the focusing and tuning mechanisms of the pineal gland. The altered-ego has subsequently taken control of this higher function of mind and relegated it to focusing upon sensory frequencies for the purposes of problem-solving in the day-to-day business of the food-chain-mentality. No creativity can be accomplished without this remnant faculty. However, since the faculty of imagination works in conjunction with intellect, one can effectively increase the frequency of perception and the entire bio-computer by visualizing high frequency, intellectual concepts. Therefore, it is extremely important to read and visualize higher frequency information to form a new model of your universe, regardless of how crude the model may be at first.

FEELING: The collective impact of large numbers of thought-forms focused upon by mind functions and awareness of the expansion or contraction of the membrane's light capacity. Thus, a good feeling ensues when the membrane expands with light, and a bad feeling ensues when the membrane contracts due to lowering of light frequencies into densification of elemental matter. This faculty of experiencing thought-forms chosen by the entity can be sensitized to a point where it can instantly detect what thought-forms are limiting and which thought-forms are expansive. Used with the imagination and high frequency thought-forms, ecstasy can result, creating a feedback so powerful that the bio-computer can be healed and experience contact with the Masters in a true revelation through experience.

INTERNALIZING: The sum total of thought-forms, modified and original, integrating themselves into the holographic light codings of the total bio-computer, forming the collective representation of all thought-forms, balanced and unbalanced, into a unique, personal preconditioning toward future events. In other words, the living body of the entity is an embodiment of the matrix of thought-forms it has cultivated through experience as past/present/future probabilities. You become the thought-forms that you focus upon and give life, and they become you.

The purpose of this is to understand the phases of Omniscience and Omnipresence. When you regard the entire bio-computer as mind within mind, the importance of internalizing information through the above processes and transmuting it into experiential realities, wisdom becomes paramount in true evolution of consciousness.

The difference between intellect and imagination is vision. The difference between imagination and experiential reality is feeling. Understand also the difference between feeling and emotion. Emotion is an accumulated, past-tense, cellular response to gravitationally trapped thought-forms. Emotion generally blocks the present tense of feeling, as it compares past events to a similar "now" moment in the illusion of time continuum. Feeling, as we define it, is a pure, present tense awareness of the immediate internal and external environment.

Suffice it to say that, through low frequency education, the altered-ego lords over all knowledge outside of its frequency of comprehension with the staff of criticism and fear-founded limitation. Therefore, it rules over the formation of collective belief systems installed on the cellular level of physical being on a third dimensional frequency. This accounts for the seeming difficulty of internalizing higher frequency knowledge – for any "new" information is first evaluated by the intellect that categorizes sensory data based on past, third dimensional experience. If the information does not fit, it is mindlessly discarded.

The purpose for the bio-organic computer is to learn to create and organize matter from thought in a dense plane in order to reflect the attributes of THE ONE in the physical worlds. For when you are again Master of that realm, you are Master of many as a co-creator in the Infinite Mind of eternal life.

To consciously practice directing your consciousness-awareness to the true center-point in the pyramidal energy-construct within the perfect Atom of your being is to expand the boundaries of membrane tension, forming the first "veil of light" around your being. The primary illusion in this consciousness maneuver is that the self, in this case the altered-ego, is dying. It will jerk and pull at your awareness with a death-grip of fear based upon the belief that to lose or confuse its identity is to succumb to annihilation.

Be persistent in your contemplations of this understanding through all four faculties of comprehension. Your energy fields of consciousness are immortal and these are born through the womb of the Perfect Atom. Think about it. Contemplate it. Meditate upon it until you begin to feel it. Then will you know it, for it will produce unspeakable joy within self.

Make the effort to expand into infinite God-Mind. We can assure you there is no death there. With these efforts, conscious contact will be made with beings of Light who stand patiently and lovingly, waiting to assist you in fulfilling your grandest expectations. In this expansion, there is no answer that cannot be obtained; no problem that cannot be solved; no invention that will remain locked in a prison of ignorance.

Do not surrender to the fear-based cynicism of the intellect, for there is vast confusion lurking in the shadows of partial life equations. Surrender instead to the primal, unceasing, nurturing, healing, pulse of life through the crystal frequency of Love centered within the Perfect Atom within the Heart of Hearts. This is where true genius resides – for that is where the unceasing perpetuation of life through LOVE-LIGHT/GOD-MIND dwells in the infinity of eternal life.

The Universal Center-Point is a function of the Infinity of eternal life, which has its circumference (time) nowhere and its Center (timelessness) everywhere. Through meditating and contemplating this information, seeds of knowledge will sprout in an experiential embrace of Wisdom, which you own forever.

Facts and figures, that are isolated and not resonating with the Perfect-Atom, become frozen in the wasteland of undeveloped potential to co-create. Partial truths of the altered-ego are incomplete equations, which when internalized wreak havoc upon the energy pathways supporting cellular integrity. Intellectual assessments block the life-support reciprocation from the Heart to the head and from the head to the Heart.

Think, beloved. If your physicists can demonstrate and accept the theory that the electron can exist as particle as well as wave simultaneously, and you have accepted the theory that you are composed of those same atoms – then.....WAKE UP! You worship scientific methods and results, yet when these reveal a grand truth you revert to fear and ignorance and continued research. The scientific mind is not something that certain scholars have and most others don't. Neither do spiritual qualities belong only to the initiated within a clergy.

The intellect can bear witness to the scientific revelation that each of you is a multidimensional being, yet it reacts with: "Gee, that's interesting. Perhaps, we should do further research." Why? Because the intellect has no Heart. Without the Heart of Hearts, facts and figures, regardless of how lofty or elegant, can never become Wisdom.

Why delegate your personal responsibility to those who have chosen the great burden of the altered-ego? The Whole Truth cannot be known by analyzing fragments of life equations out of context with the eternal moment. Your evolution is your responsibility. You have the intelligence, indeed, the right to question, analyze and draw conclusions about any form of science. You are the expert on your life. In regards to your true evolution, it is far better to have faith without intellect, than to have an intellect without faith.

Objective knowledge lies in science and simple faith lies in religion. Yet, if science "proved" beyond a shadow of a doubt that there is a God...then what? Would you be changed? All knowledge is subjective. The Mind of THE ONE even creates and permeates the test tubes into which more substance created by THE ONE is contained.

Thus, we put forth this book for those of you who are caught in the intellectual dilemma of "heartless" objectivity. Realize that you may ultimately prove to yourself the truth of THE ONE, if you but seek to answer your own questions through the awesome powers of the Heart of Hearts. The answers are forthcoming from the Heart of Hearts, not the intellect as it is presumed by third dimensional thinking. Ask in the spirit of Omni-"science" and Omni-"presence" within the Universal Point where the Divine Eye of Universal Consciousness "sees" in multi-dimensional powers of THE ONE. Discover the revelations within you – the genius within.

THE FOURTH DIMENSION
"NEW AGE TRANSITIONS & WAR"

> *"With the proper discipline on your part,
> you may enter the door through the space-time
> restrictions, which has prevented the majority of
> you from working directly with the
> Hierarchy of Light-Intelligence."*

Questioner: Is conscious realization of the fourth dimension a part of the "new age" phenomenon?

MaYaRa: Until now, we have endeavored to lay a foundation of understanding into your true natures and to elucidate that which has blocked that realization. We hope that we have served you and uplifted you thus far. We shall proceed into an examination of a greater vision of a greater magnitude encompassing the personal, solar and galactic changes occurring at this time, in your time.

All creation, everywhere, on all levels and dimensions, has pulses and cycles due to the nature of the pulsating, spinning, alternating nature of the twin primary Light Rays of creation. Thus, all levels of creation have breathing cycles. All significant religious teachings and even modern scientific data verifies the pulsating nature of the universe. We shall first examine the macro cycle of the solar system and galactic universe in which it has its being.

SOLAR AND GALACTIC CYCLES

The solar and galactic cycles may at first seem quite impersonal and abstract, but these have the most profound significance in the transitional period earth is now experiencing. This transitional period bears the signature of its ever-present influence upon the innate awareness level or frequency of consciousness permeating the very core of each layer of the atomic universe. The ascendancy of this phase of the cycle, termed "new age," is no mere shadow-play of technicalities upon the backdrop of inaccessible and impersonal solar systems and galaxies. It matters not that humans have not, as yet, invented machines to detect these high frequency changes, for the changes can be seen everywhere upon the planet.

The powerful alterations in the gravitational flux lines of earth reflect a "planetary personality" resulting in various tendencies in the behavior of entities who inhabit the earth at this time. Understand that the changes are in the resonant frequency of your planet, and the world events in the human drama are intimately connected. Understand, what science has deemed impersonal and abstract is vitally personal to every entity upon earth as the unfolding of the "end of time" is enacted as the final drama within the next decade in your time.

The overall increase in the frequency of atomic and subatomic structures, coded and accessed through the spiraling geometries of the pyramidal energy-construct, reveals a parallel universe of a higher dimensional order within the same space/time coordinates that you occupy. This parallel universe is an overlay, a superimposed superstructure made of high frequency Light; an extra-dimensional pattern of life that ultimately repatterns universal DNA for the purpose of absorbing the existing pattern of creation into the higher evolution of the greater, Master Plan of THE ONE. This is accomplished by a process of induction/resonance of extremely high light frequencies which will recharge a dying planet, catapulting it out of inertia and entropy before it slips into consciousness death.

This occurs in much the same manner every 12,000 years when the solar system reaches its ascending horizon, in relationship to its position in the galactic disc, as it spirals into a higher frequency of consciousness.

The pyramidal energy-construct is the medium and carrier frequency that facilitates this spectra-conversion of Light within material creation, supercharging the atomic structure. The result of this supercharging is that the multidimensional characteristics of atomic structure, i.e., particle/wave, manifest to conscious-awareness on a wholesale scale in the material worlds. In terms of physics, this is necessary to overcome the cubic function of negative mass in order to raise the atomic order to a fifth dimensional reality, which is not limited to cubic space.

From one perspective, this is like recharging or winding up the spring of an atomic clock. It operates as an ongoing interval of Cosmic Breath – without which, entropy factors such as gravitational forces created by the standing wave-forms would wind down intersecting Light oscillations. These would collapse consciousness bodies operating in the lower frequency wavelengths into themselves to balance energy/mass equations that are incomplete in the present state of existence.

SUPER COLLAPSE

This process of super collapse has been observed by scientists in the "discovery" of super dense bodies, such as those termed "black holes" and "white holes" and related phenomenon. This is a function of regeneration for purposes of creating new universes from solar/galactic systems that have completed one phase of consciousness programming, and are recalled into the spiral matrix of God-Mind.

These carefully controlled events are under the supervision of the Masters of Light, acting in concert with the Master Program of Redemption issued by THE ONE through the administrative powers of The Christ. Thus, new space/time foundations are laid by superimposing a new model of a higher frequency universe, necessary to sustain the Higher Light released from the central intelligence locus of each local galactic mind (Universe).

Thus, every atom is first surrounded by a new matrix of time/space events that eventually absorb the lower frequencies into the higher. Without this system of controlled transition of renewal or redemption, the expansive frequencies of Higher Light would implode decaying atomic material together with all consciousness beings resonating with the lower frequencies into the primal beginning of elemental matter – thereby destroying all the consciousness progressions so painstakingly nurtured during the previous 12,000 years of evolution.

Since all matter is Light, a condensation of thought frequencies emanating from the Mind of THE ONE, into lower frequency representations of Divine Thought-Forms, serves as the Energizing Principle, which is the foundation of the electron. Therefore, all matter is aware to the extent that rocks, water, air, fire and all life-form creations communicate through the electron, a multidimensional particle/wave unit of awareness. Degrees of consciousness are formed in the matter worlds when units of awareness (electrons) reach a critical mass of complexity in organic form. Thus, the organisms are a reflection of the intelligent entities that project the thought-forms of their creations.

The omniscient and omnipresent quality of the electron as a unit of awareness forms the backdrop for complexity-of-form through the projection of intersecting force fields within an intelligent matrix of matter/events. This is inherent in the condensation process of thought through the electron. Individualized consciousness is created as a result of this space/time, matter/event organization of awareness, which creates yet another expression (another facet) of THE CREATOR'S attributes.

All creation is unified through the function of the electron, forming spheres within spheres and dimensions within dimensions in continuous, simultaneous and unbroken communication between all universes of creation. In the material worlds, periodicity results in an Alpha and Omega cycle, or beginning and end of time. At this point all material creation that has attained a frequency high enough, through service to others, will spiral out of the entropic cycles into continuous consciousness-light, unbroken by the periodic interruptions and cyclic returns known as the birth/death, black /white, day/night, etc. – the cyclic nature of material creation.

Thus, the electron as a unit of awareness within material creation suffers the oscillations of polarities in the electromagnetic universe; while consciousness, the frequency from which the electron is created, is ongoing and eternal. When consciousness succeeds in raising awareness to its own level, the material creation representing the thought-form entity that created it ascends through the spiral of frequencies into the next higher dimension. This process is known as Jacon's Ladder.

In other words, conscious awareness (life) does not accidentally appear in the material worlds, as dictated by present earth theories of evolution. Awareness is created by consciousness compressed within the material worlds and is raised in frequency to consciousness – by expansion – whereby, the created and the creator merge as one to continue creation. A most eloquent program, is it not?

Questioner: Why are there so many people incarnating on earth at this time?

MaYaRa: The so-called population explosion upon earth at this time is due to the present completion of the Omega cycle. This phase of creation is referred to in your religious Book as "The Harvest."

All conscious entities, attached to their material creations – bodies, animals, etc. – are given the opportunity to incarnate at this phase of the galactic cycle for the purpose of achieving that which they have not accomplished heretofore. Each creates another body, which they may charge with consciousness, thereby raising the frequency of their material creations for the purpose of merging God-Mind with them and returning as one to the Kingdom of Light.

This phase of the creation cycle would be a pointless cacophony of suffering for the multitudes, if not for the pouring forth of the Light at the same time. However, pointless suffering is not the nature of THE ONE/I AM bearing gifts of Love, Light, counsel and assistance in this matter. Therefore, the frequency of consciousness is increased beyond that which is generated by the sleeping entities upon earth – for said entities to use as their vehicle of Light for the purpose of accomplishing their task if they so desire.

FREE AWARENESS

We shall term this great outpouring of Light "free aware-ness." For although it is a direct manifestation of Higher Con-sciousness, it remains as an overlay or superimposed structure of consciousness bodies until transmuted by the entity – so as not to violate the Law of Confusion or free will, as you term it. Thus, the power of your own redemptions lie within you, increasing in strength daily, waiting for your desire to transmute the electronic functions of your bio-computers to match that of the deathless Light. Through your own efforts you will OWN your Wisdom.

Great technological machines are not necessary to detect the presence of the initial surge of this free-awareness into the atomic structure of the earth body. One need only review recent history to realize the sudden amplification of consciousness as manifested in the recent "explosion" of the arts, science, techno-logy, etc. This is not a result of the current evolutionary theories of the food-chain-mentality – the perfection of the ape.

Contemplate this very simple fact. How is it that a species termed "human," supposedly evolving from primates, struggles for countless millennia under conditions far more adverse to its sur-vival than at present, with little "progress" to its credit, suddenly manifests such tremendous quantities of conscious-awareness within a mere heartbeat of a century? The boastful arrogance of the altered-ego, masquerading as science, cannot lay claim to this seemingly mysterious phenomenon. The so-called scientific mind may claim any accomplishment that it desires. But from whence does the scientific mind derive its consciousness?

By understanding the relationships between free awareness, free will and consciousness, one may dispose of fear-based arro-gance and begin to use these great gifts of Consciousness-Love for responsible acts of God-Mind. The key to understanding the gifts of this phase or creation cycle is in the universality of free-awareness as a nonpolarized, fourth dimensional supercharging of the electron – within a currently polarized electronic material field of positive and negative energy points – in a third dimensional frequency of existence.

It is to your ultimate redemption to know that THE ONE cannot manifest a biased emanation of the Genius Frequency. The ultimate powers of this LIGHT-LOVE/GOD-MIND are the ultimate gifts of freedom given to all. The choice of what to manifest with this incalculable energy is yours, as it has always been. But these powers are so great that the slightest misuse can bring dire consequences. Whatever thought-forms you embrace, create, incubate and release into your world, whether these be fearful or joyous, will be charged into manifestation with ever increasing speed, accuracy and intensity. Therefore, love of all life, discipline, caution, sensitivity to the environment and an ever watchful eye fixed upon the loftiest probable future is imperative, if you are to transmute free awareness into the consciousness of God-Mind and eternal life. For free awareness is just that – free. With this additional awareness energy, you may choose to accelerate your death or your life.

Questioner: How are the cosmic cycles working to bring about the changes of which you speak?

MaYaRa: As we examine the cyclic nature of the universe, it is wise to remember the oft' used axiom: "as above, so below." For one cannot be different from the other. Each is in the other. All magnitudes of matter are differentiated only by scale.

Due to the spherical domain of the electron, all condensed matter must revolve around itself, creating the space/time continuum. This is a law of material creation, from which no form within its third dimensional density is exempt. Very recently in your time, through the gift of free awareness, the Western mind has re-discovered the cyclical nature of the solar system, the microcosm of the atom, and the galactic wheels of creation.

Although the evidence for universal cycles is overwhelming on all fronts of modern thought, the fact that your solar logos (the sun) revolves around yet another, greater mind/ body complex is roundly denied – based upon the not too intelligent premise that scientists have not seen it yet. All third dimensional logic aside, there is a central mind/body complex around which your solar system (and all solar systems in your galaxy) also revolves. It is a star cluster termed by the ancients as the "Kolob." Hence, there are cosmic, galactic seasons.

Sufficient evidence is available for you to study regarding the ellipsoidal rotation characteristics of known solar systems and galaxies. Therefore, similar effects are produced on the galactic scale, such as your seasonal cycles resulting from ellipsoidal tracking, which causes various angular relationships to the central Kolob – spiritual sun. Thus, your solar system is crossing a dimensional threshold.

The awareness extremes experienced upon the earth plane typically range from what is termed by the Masters as "ages of darkness" and "ages of Light." The extremes of this pendulum of existence are due to your particular solar system residing on the fringe of the galactic disc. Due to the physical placement of your solar system, the high frequency forces exerted upon it are triggering catastrophic shifts. The very electromagnetic structure of these systems are changing.

Questioner: Are there systems of life within our galaxy that do not suffer these extreme changes?

MaYaRa: There are systems which inhabit other proximities to the central Kolob that do not experience these extreme, opposing swings of Alpha/Omega cycles. Neither do these systems experience day/night, hot/cold or positive/negative polarities. The entities who reside there do not suffer disease, pain, war, death, nor any form of entropy. They continually perfect and upgrade cities of Light Crystal architecture, and music of the spheres.

The earth is moving into the age of Light – a dimension into which those who choose will enter, never having to return to the black and white realities of a birth and death planet. The entity may also choose to return to a three dimensional system to teach and uplift another suffering humanity remaining from the previous "Harvest." If the age of Light were not a reality, your immediate century could not have generated an acceleration of awareness of the magnitude that earth is now experiencing. This is by no means the first time man has progressed to high technological and spiritual states. You have not yet begun to realize the power of God-Technology.

Crossing the threshold of the fourth dimensional barriers and approaching the fifth dimensional realities of the universe of God-Mind may be likened to what you term, breaking the sound barrier. In this case, however, it is more appropriate to state that your solar system is breaking the time barrier! For the acceleration earth is experiencing now is not a linear one, but a quantum acceleration of atomic frequency.

Thus, in certain galactic seasons, the angular relationships of your solar system to the Kolob results in winters of minimal free awareness and summers of maximum free awareness as the electron, the basic unit of awareness, is raised in frequency. In the winter of the galactic and solar double apogee, the so-called dark ages manifest as the entropic drag of atomic mass and the electron drops in its harmonic frequency or shell producing very dense veils or barriers between second, third and fourth dimensional awareness. For your solar system, this is cosmic winter. For humans, it is the night of the soul.

Questioner: What is free awareness?

MaYaRa: Free awareness is a qualitative reference to the electron as unit of awareness, the critical mass of which forms consciousness in varying degrees. In turn, the critical mass of consciousness is the point where the Genius Frequency becomes operative on a self-perpetuating basis.

Every condensation of thought into light and light into matter on any scale, be it an electron or a star, is composed of intelligent awareness. Therefore every star is a conscious intelligence, a sentient being with its own evolution of consciousness. From a third dimensional perception, your sun is dying; but from a fifth dimensional perspective, it is not. Many scientific observations have revealed conflicting data, such as an increase of solar radiation during a cycle in which it should be decreasing in intensity. This is due to the release of free awareness from the galactic center – all centers – of intelligence.

If the internal processes of your sun were continually in decay or entropy, this would not be feasible. You may apply this knowledge evenly in your personal life. For every atom in the universe is undergoing similar transformations, albeit in different dimensions. You see, the galaxy is also revolving around an intelligence source, along with all other known and unknown galaxies. But that is yet another teaching.

What is important for you to comprehend is that the very characteristics or properties of the electron are shifting into an innate capacity to act as wave rather than particle. The effects of the double helix of the organic blueprint is supercharged by free awareness as your sun and its Sun swing into double perigee in the spring of your cosmic cycle. Just as sun spots and solar flares have profound effects upon its planetary spheres, the influx of free awareness – as a quantum induction – profoundly effects the intelligent awareness and frequency of all matter.

The basis for electrochemical bonding is the value determined by the particular valency of the electron. When the frequency supporting the present particle/wave equilibrium becomes biased toward the ultraviolet wave spectrum, a fourth and fifth dimensional model of the existing electrochemical model is created, superimposed upon and existing simultaneously within same in the same space/time providing an interface for time/space orientation. In other words, *your light body becomes activated, bridging the gap between dimensions*. The frequency that generates the electron's shift from particle state to wave state is the Genius Frequency.

The Genius Frequency exists as a double, a fully-formed body of light within a body of denser light. This provides the immediate potential to resonate with that frequency through free choice so that one may merge with the Light in the radiant victory of God-Mind. Now is the time of times to embrace, without fear, the incalculable potential of your being during this most exiting and promising transition into an age of victory and joy. But you must choose to do so, beloved. No one, not even THE ONE, can do this for you.

With the proper discipline on your part, you may enter the door through the space/time restrictions, which has prevented the majority of you from working directly with the Hierarchy of Light Intelligence. In the age of darkness from which you have emerged, this feat was virtually impossible, save by the incarnated Masters who personally supervised the transformation of certain individuals and kept the candles of consciousness burning within earth-mind.

The nature of this grand opportunity is twofold, given the quantum mechanics of this galactic cycle. It is at once a mechanical, cyclical event in the Alpha/Omega cycle of lower frequency systems in need of recharging and an intelligent plan of consciousness graduation with the assistance of thousands of teachers and

Light workers of all dimensions and magnitudes. Thus, at every turn, messages, such as those described herein and others like them, are pouring into your consciousness for the express purpose of making the Genius Frequency available to all.

The intent of these teachings is to spark your tired faith and intellect into a new effort to prepare yourself for the magnificent changes that are manifesting within and without you in the next two decades. With this information – becoming knowledge, becoming wisdom, becoming Light – you may make more enlightened personal decisions concerning service to your fellow beings. There is, actually, no difference.

Questioner: Are the changes that you speak of the same as the Bible prophecies?

MaYaRa: Indeed, the prophesies regarding the "end of time" hinge upon the aforesaid knowledge of cosmic mechanisms. As far as those of the "second coming" are concerned, it is also true. Yet this must be understood as a fifth dimensional event that each entity must prepare for. In other words, when one begins to resonate with the Genius Frequency, one may partake of the Bread of Life with the Masters. This cannot be accomplished by merely subscribing to a particular dogma. It is a very personal, as well as a cosmic event.

Questioner: The "Law of One," as you have described it, recognizes no polarity, no good and evil. How are we to apply this truth if our lives are fraught with polarized decision-making?

MaYaRa: We welcome your confusion, beloved. By drawing your attention to the purest state of mind, indeed existence, as the primary attribute of Love-Light/God-Mind – to deliberate upon it, contemplate it, meditate in it – is to begin to raise the frequency of your bio-computer. The actions which prompt one to begin serving other-selves are spontaneously generated by that frequency.

To integrate this pure mind within the parameters of third dimensional perceptions to prepare you for the transition that is upon you is the purpose of this teaching and many other teachings of like and higher frequencies. Let us recapitulate the reality of unification, in polarized diversity, through fourth dimensional mind.

The LAW OF ONE states that behind and within all bipolar systems, all diversification and variations thereof, indeed within every atomic structure, exists the Genesis of its expression from THE ONE MIND. Therefore, the reconciliation and reintegration of all units of awareness, operating independently yet within THE SOURCE – every atom, race, religion, science, heart and mind – is assisted in returning through the Alpha/Omega programs of consciousness.

Questioner: Why can't the knowledge of good and evil ultimately free us from suffering and death?

MaYaRa: We shall attempt to clarify through fourth dimensional understandings this most difficult of truths for earth dwellers. We also wish to avoid argumentative queries seeking, for example, to justify why certain madmen should be proclaimed evil by those who judge them. Please refer to the segment of this book explaining the living thought-forms (Chapter 2). It may be seen that all share in the deeds of man. You see, one can never truly understand the nature of a fish bowl when one lives within it. Let us review, once again, the actions leading to the so-called "fall of man." This story is an analogue for a metaphysical process.

In the beginning, all co-creators I-dentified with THE ONE. The creation of all matter worlds required the use of negative mass and other polarized energy creations inherent in the laws of its very existence. In other words, there were no value judgments placed upon any elemental forces of intelligence necessary to create and maintain these material domains.

A group of co-creators chose to I-dentify with their creations when they refused to recognize the newly created Adamic Man who was deemed lord of those worlds and charged with the responsibility of evolving consciousness within the root races of life-forms created by the co-creators of those worlds. In order to prevent these fledgling Masters from gaining control of said worlds and domains, the "fallen" co-creators totally immersed their conscious powers within negative mass as they sought to maintain lordship over their creations. Thus, the split occurred and all the powers of the co-creators were used to diminish and negate the powers of the Adamic Lords. To this end, they were largely successful, although their reign could only last through the "end of time," which is upon you at this time, in your time.

To the three dimensional perception of the intellectual mind, the above scenario can be stated simply as: there is that which is temporarily deprived of the Genius Frequency resonating with THE ONE and that which is filled with the Genius Frequency reconnecting and I-dentifying with THE ONE as a co-creator.

It may seem incredible to many of you that such powerful entities such as the co-creators of worlds, given their powers by the Love of THE ONE, would even consider the cycle of third dimensional death to possess power in the illusion of autonomous kingship. Yet that is what you witness every earth day in your time. However, they controlled, but they could not incarnate!

Factors of entropy are not in themselves evil, for negative mass has an inherent function in manifesting material reality. Remember also, that the functions of negative mass are temporary factors, since the Omega Point or end of time recycles all negative mass. This causes all entities, who choose to remain in three dimensional limitations, to begin a consciousness evolution from primordial creation. There is no hell, except to lose the gifts of God-Mind and return to elemental awareness. Your solar system is now at the Omega Point. Such is the urgency of our message.

The bias toward, what you term, positive action and thought is a precarious, confusing, judgmental and dangerous three dimensional reality – a reality relative to the values placed upon negative functions leading to the condemnation of half of your world, half of yourself. You may term your perceptions as positive, if you so choose. However, inherent in and implied by this frequency of thought is the condemnation of half of all creation in your realms as negative and evil. When you engage in this third dimensional, polarized mind, your frequency and your position in the evolutionary scheme of things drops dramatically. Unless you correct this imbalance through the unity of opposites in the frequency of God-Mind, you may positively degenerate.

Thus polarized consciousness, through I-dentification with one or the other of the dualities, forms a deadly trap. The nature of the trap is this: Entropy, the condensation of electron waves into lower frequencies of mass, influences consciousness to regard the dense, material plane as the epitome of existence, which must be defended from an imaginary enemy representing that which cancels the other charge, the expansive side of consciousness.

In all cases, the enemy is an oppositely charged self. Thus, one enemy will polarize the other through its thought-forms and the resultant acts of separatism from THE ONE. Each enemy polarizes the other and each values itself as doing what is necessary or what is good. This, of course, is the basis for war on all levels of existence. Therefore, any entity or group that chooses to value the other as evil is destined for entrapment within the repetitive cycles of birth and death. In that bonding where each agrees to destroy the other, one is no better than the other. They have now become one in negative mass ruled by the co-creators who have their victims well in hand, for they are the rulers of three dimensional destruction.

It is of the utmost importance for you to understand that the polarity of consciousness is an artificial creation, a grand illusion, an atrocity perpetrated by the rebellious co-creators who elected to become one with the process of death and entropy. Thus, one may regard oneself and others as positive, providing that the value is not in opposition to itself.

Since each of you, as well as all creation, is sustained by THE ONE, you are indeed One. The world of polarized thought is an illusion because one cannot, in reality, be in opposition to oneself. Thus, it is not that the material worlds are an illusion, it is the "appearance" of the world that is an illusion.

In summation, the movement of your solar system in the grand cycle of the solar year, is moving into closer proximity to its source. It is thereby the recipient of Supercharging Light from the higher, fourth and fifth dimensions of reality. The carrier for this Super Charging Light of the Genius Frequency is within the function of the electron. Therefore, it is interlinked with and part of the very atomic structure of the universe.

Since this electron frequency permeates the very core of the atom, the evidence of its increase can be found in the day-to-day experiences of the planet and each individual entity upon it. This is reflected in the travel explosion, communication explosion, electronic age, etc. Consider that these circumstances instantly appeared upon the scene of consciousness when thousands of years before yielded sluggish results.

Those who choose to I-dentify with the self-protecting, self-serving, fear-cloaked densities of an artificially separate existence punctuated by death and wielded without love for all forms of life, must suffer alienation from the SOURCE of life by estrangement and death. This process is not a moral issue – not an issue of good versus evil to be avenged. This is the mechanical nature of consciousness when cut off from the eternal Light. It is not the willful retaliation of a vengeful god. Therefore, to judge your enemy, by your own righteousness, is to lock with those entities in a deadly dance of your own design.

The incalculable increase of free awareness rushing in the Heart of every atom of your being may be used in any way you choose. However, the mechanics of consciousness may not be changed, for its roots reach into the very soil of creation to extract and reorganize consciousness of the higher frequencies of God-Mind.

Rejoice at this time, in your time, for the doors to the threshold of Light are thrown open for you to step through to realize the totality of your being as a pure reflection, individualization and realization of the Divine Source of THE ETERNAL ONE.

Use your greater powers of perception in the fourth dimension, which recognizes and easily comprehends the LAW OF ONE. Your lives shall be greatly simplified as the perpetual struggle with self as good and self as evil melts away into the "Peace that passeth all human understanding."

When you realize that so-called "evil" is a natural process of entropy in the lower frequency creation, your outrage will cease and the eternal Light of THE ONE will flood your being in an unimaginable rapture of healing, peace and Genius as a co-creator. What you forgot, you will now remember.

Contemplate this message in your Heart of Hearts and the intellect will cease to be outraged. For reason is a powerful tool that clarifies the workings of creation as an act of Love and not an accident born of violence. Stretch your minds to encompass fourth dimensional perceptions. For in a third dimensional understanding, one cannot comprehend the entrapment of the mind in polarities of dense frequencies.

Loving part of yourself and others who represent that part, and hating other parts of yourself and those who represent that which is hated will tear you apart. To truly co-create is to be ONE with self. We can only suggest that you leave the judgments of polarized mind and embrace the totality of life. When you do, you will transmute and transfigure the additional free awareness given at this time, in your time, into consciousness in the Genius Frequency.

FINE TUNING

"THE BIO-COMPUTER"

> *"You have become
> what you are
> through contemplating
> what you perceive yourself to be."*

Questioner: Could you explain, in more detail, what contemplation is and what it does?

MaYaRa: The mechanics and purpose of contemplation is a tool of consciousness and a key to unlock the Genius Frequency within. It is part and parcel of the consciousness-matrix, the flux, the ebb and flow of your beingness in this dimension. Let us look more deeply into this tool of manifestation.

All of you are organic transceivers existing as a nodal point of resonant tension within the energy-tapestry of matter/event continuity. The Genius Frequency manifests as free awareness possessing no polarity-charge. All matter/event energy-constructs known and unknown are precisely balanced divisions of the primary frequency of thought, which generates it. In other words, each of you exists as an organized, orchestrated, quanta-light-body of consciousness compressed into a time/event matter-energy-construct forming the human temple, a frequency-matrix to house the individual expressions of the Infinite Creator within a planet that is evolving into higher frequencies of consciousness.

We have reiterated the above definition in many and varied ways and will continue to do so. For if you are to use your intellect for any purpose, it would be wise to redefine your true natures again and again in order to loosen the dark grip of altered-ego and its limiting definitions, recycled through millennia of fallen thought-forms of ignorance.

The limited definitions of your true natures are propelled by the momentum of reverberation within cellular mass – echoes of past/present influences of false promises of power from a source other than THE ONE. Although, it can be truthfully stated that all of the many paths lead, eventually, to THE ONE, many are also fraught with fear, frustration and suffering, unnecessarily delaying their triumphant return. Moreover, since this is primarily an intellectual study – most studies are – we shall concentrate our information in the area of contemplation/meditation – two sides of a very powerful tool to aid in your understanding, such as wisdom and knowledge, of a broader spectrum of your true colors.

Review carefully the steps to assimilation and internalization in order to grasp the processes involved in an intellectual contemplation. We specify "intellectual" here for various reasons. One is that there are many types of contemplation. For example, one may venture forth into the wilderness or even one's flower garden and experience through contemplation the overwhelming awe of nature's creative majesty. In this example, the intellect is instantly bypassed and awareness takes over as the bio-computer registers vast quantities of organized beauty in the present/present continuum. This type of contemplation would be located primarily in the Heart-mind.

Generally, an intellectual entity will stroll through the garden labeling, rather than apprehending, the reality of the moment. In lieu of the experience of the flower, the intellectual views it by suspending most of the feelings of connection with the total bio-computer as the intellect asserts itself: "Lo, it is a flower – spelled f.l.o.w.e.r. – named rose of the genus Rosa, having thorny stems and producing variously colored petals, composed of...etc...etc." You must ask WHO is describing your world for you. Is it you?

In this case, if the intellectual possessed the discipline to instantly relax the energy blocks and open the total bio-computer to identify with the rose by becoming it, the type of contemplative exercises given here would not be applicable. However, this is not the case for most of you, locked in the webwork of the altered-ego. When deeply entrenched in the altered-ego and what it purports to "know," the intellectual may, perforce, use more of the same for the purpose of overfeeding the altered-ego until it fairly bursts at the seems, allowing the total bio-computer to process the overflow. When this occurs you have pried open the doors to true consciousness-awareness on the threshold of the Genius Frequency. That is what we are attempting to do, beloved.

For the intellectual, then, contemplation is a very useful tool. Do not forget, however, that the intellect is a function of the altered-ego. Therefore, it possesses a voracious appetite and the tenacity of competitiveness. The intellect is an arrogant, self-centered creature competitive in its training to "win" by "knowing" more than the next entity. Yet it is fickle, and will turn upon you, shutting down your awareness mechanism when it perceives that another entity "knows" more.

Contemplation will work for you only when you delve deeply into your studies of high frequency information. You may begin with the basic tools of the scientific intellect such as cross-referencing, analyzing, computing, comparing, theorizing and speculating. But you must go further to overcome the altered-ego. You must synthesize information with your intuition with an eye toward how everything is the same, not different.

Filter all information, even in your mundane experiences, through the ancient Hermetic axiom: "As above, so below." Then you will begin to realize that every conceivable pattern discovered or observed, regardless of how remote it may seem from you, is actually found somewhere inside of you in its exact form. The vegetable kingdom is within you. The animal kingdom is within you. The mineral kingdom is within you. The galactic kingdom is within you. The whole of the atomic universes are within you. Therefore, whatever you may study, know that you can only study self. And most importantly, whenever a profound "breakthrough" surfaces, know that it must apply to you. Thus, one can describe a rose and fill a thousand books, but one will never know the rose until one becomes it through realizing that the patterns, life force, colors, processes, aromas, cycles and the very soul of the rose are within you completely.

Yet there are those of you who have not known by what "name" to call the rose for lack of an "education," but have known it far more intimately and truthfully. Through contemplation, Masters, such as you are, may know the rose by the sound of its voice, its atomic vibration, rather than by abstract symbol. You may know anything in the universe as an artist knows the creation that he/she labored to create. For, indeed, you have created the rose and do not as yet remember.

To contemplate, truly contemplate is to step beyond the boundaries of altered-ego's inherent system of closure. It is a matter of removing the polarities of assimilation. In other words, why question the intellect? Why search the intellect for what it knows? Regardless of its educational prowess, it will run out of information and the rose shall still not be truly known. Rather, ask the flower within to teach the intellect and the rose shall be known by resonance with its beingness. That is true learning. That is true contemplation.

Contemplation is asking the questions for which the answers are endless, for that is the nature of life. Life is not a closed system. You may frame it, but you may never contain it. However, you may resonate with all of life and therefore become it. You may contemplate the infinite flow of frequencies through the matrices of matter/event time-constructs that, in themselves, are constantly changing, constantly engaged in the flux of becoming infinite. Infinite is ALL that you can become.

So where is the finality the intellect craves? Nowhere! When may even the greatest intellects claim to know? Never! All matter, all energy, all frequencies flow and interact through all creation as codified, open-ended holographic matrices of thought-forms expanding and compressing into eternity. Since you are a replica of everything-there-is in the universe, what is it that you cannot know, beloved? Nothing! You see, to truly contemplate is to go beyond what you know intellectually, for the purpose of becoming who you truly are.

So in the case of humans at this juncture, contemplation is intellectual knowing coupled with the visioning of imagination and resonance of feeling, which assimilates the frequency of those functions that create true knowledge of being. Therefore, it is the action-polarity of the transmitter part of you that merges with the rest-polarity of the receiver part of you to create the timeless, infinite present/now.

True contemplation, then, is to use what you know by formulating a vision, overlaying this template or vision upon the reality in question with an open mind to accept modification in the name of the highest truth. This is actually the philosophy of pure scientific thought, but it has been long forgotten through the corruption of the altered-ego. If you are predicated toward reading linear space/time documentation of symbolic codification of reality (books, documents, etc.), then by all means read. But read higher frequency documents than you at first understand and sense the feeling response from the Heart-mind. Read the highest, loftiest truth you are able to digest and go beyond into becoming.

True contemplation in any area of focus or subject yields truth which is free of judgment – truth which is relatively free of distortion of third dimensional mind, for true contemplation is open-ended. It accepts no finalities, for it is a function of the infinite dimensions of the Genius Frequency resonating with God-Mind in an infinite pulse of infinite life. You are a universe. what is it you do not know? Contemplate that, beloved.

A word of caution is in order at this juncture: *Contemplation is I-dentification*. Contemplation is a most powerful tool of becoming. Indeed, you are and will be what you contemplate. Why waste your precious life in contemplation of any subject less than the grand truth that you are. You have become what you are through contemplating what you perceive yourself to be. Contemplation is a sacred process of God-Being manifesting desire through thought-forms into life processes of becoming. All creation is contemplated into existence. You have become everything that you have ever contemplated, for it is the essence of the desire to know and one cannot know until one becomes.

Contemplation is an active frequency-coupling of the seer with the seen, including what is imagined. It is the petri dish, the incubator which provides the space for free awareness to transmute and transform into life forms in various dimensions. It is the all-pervading, omniscient catalyst and sustainer of life and cause of all creation. All creations are contemplated into existence by THE ONE. Divine Contemplation finds resolve and forgiveness in every problem and seeming atrocity through the LAW OF ONE. It is a responsibility which you may use as you wish. But it is a weapon in the hands and minds of the spiritually immature upon your planet that can only be corrected by contemplating the highest truth without end.

Thus, if you contemplate limitations and death and self-serving power over life, you will find that you have relegated your being to a mere interloper of your own evolution and a harbinger of suffering. All who contemplate the same life scenario perpetrated by the altered-ego, regardless that they be the "haves" or "have-nots," share in the illusion accepted as the reality of death. Therefore, the appearance of good and evil and life and death is an illusion shared by those who contemplate it, giving it a personal reality, not a universal truth.

The contemplation of fear and death and the lust for manipulating others is a closed system, which constitutes only the exercise in free choice by those too ignorant to know other choices. *That which gives all life to all life cannot, nor will ever contemplate such a system.* Therefore, those that do, starve themselves of themselves from the Light of THE ONE in the Mind of THE ONE. Yet even they shall never die. They gradually but surely lose their life force as they feed upon each other, consuming themselves until they eventually cry out, reaching out to the Light that gave them life. That time, in your time, is now.

To contemplate the death technologies and the death philosophies is to hack yourselves to bits upon the scientific and religious alters of ignorance only to find that you did not die, you only contemplated the fear and suffering – and suffer all the more in the misery of knowing that you were loved at every moment into being and the illusion of death is all that you had to offer in return. Even then, all is ultimately forgiven.

Just as contemplation is the active polarity of the transmitter function of consciousness within the bio-computer, meditation is the passive polarity of the receiver function of same. Understand that we exaggerate the division between the two. In reality they work simultaneously to bridge the gap to higher frequencies of consciousness for the eventual realization of your true natures as co-creators with THE ONE.

Contemplation is the active principle in visualizing a truth until it is assimilated by the organic, as well as the other energy bodies comprising multidimensional beings such as yourselves. In this process, the visualization is continually modified through the fine-tuning of meditation within the contemplated thought-form. In other words, contemplation keys you into a specific frequency of thought-form and meditating receives that frequency through an unobstructed, clear, unbiased channel throughout the seven mind-centers forming the bio-computer.

Thus, it is important to first "key in" to the desired channel or frequency through proper contemplation, before receiving information through the meditative gateways forming the space/time anomalies that permit you to gain knowledge through experience. Because knowledge without experience is an empty vessel.

Questioner: Then, are the teachings, that describe meditation as the absence of thought, partial truths?

MaYaRa: This is very accurate.

The notion of meditation as the erasure of thought is not only a partial truth, but it is a dangerous practice without the contemplative function as a guidance principle. That is, it suggests that the entity should open itself to any random thought-form which will resonate with it, giving it access to the life force stream of consciousness that the entity is responsible for. One would not deem it wise to abandon the body temple any more than one would deem it wise to abandon one's home and belongings. Neither would one randomly spin the radio dial expecting any channel to fulfill your exacting desires. You can see how a hit and miss approach may yield satisfactory results, yet it may also yield disturbing results.

Take note also, that once a frequency is keyed into, you are in a passive state of reception. The results are similar to dream triggering in that the very last thought-form contemplated before crossing into the fourth dimension is the first to be manifested as a reality. Therefore, if one relinquishes conscious guidance into the fourth dimension any number of peculiar manifestations may result. Contemplation through the transmitter and meditation through the receiver are continually interactive in the interest of the desired communication and reality. This occurs regardless of whether the entity is aware of the trigger.

Once the entity has searched for and locked into the Genius Frequency through contemplation, the open channel, through the meditative constant, allows free awareness to pour into the bio-computer. This floods the mind-centers with virgin Light Spectra (free awareness) which may be freshly programmed through further contemplation of a specific thought-form to ultimately manifest that thought-form as part and parcel of its being. When you begin to feel what is contemplated, it becomes experience, and manifests physically in third dimensional body through resonance with the elemental environment.

This interplay of functions of consciousness-awareness is subject to certain seemingly random interference patterns. These are byproducts of thought-form equations that are incomplete in the ultimate life scenario of eternality. The "ship at sea" analogy is useful here. Your third dimensional body and fourth dimensional light body may be understood as a vessel or ship, a sampling of earth, kept on course – i.e., cellular integrity – by the helmsman or conscious-resonator.

At any given moment, there are constant, varying forces in flux, such as geomagnetic and solar electromagnetic "storms" modified by angular pulls and pulses from the arrangements of solar bodies or planets. Many of these subsets of resonance or winds of mind are harmonic, healing, consciousness-raising angular momentums which may be resonated with and contemplated in their own right.

However, some of these subsets of angular momentum, i.e. the anguish and suffering of earth and children of earth, will prove to be disruptive deviations from the course of resonance in higher frequencies and dimensions. These deviations must be balanced by the frequencies of God-Mind through the conscious and deliberate intent of the contemplator/helmsman. Proper meditation, then, is not merely abandoning the house or vessel of consciousness. It is providing the clear sky by which to navigate.

To accomplish this, it is necessary to summon the original contemplation "template" in the same way that the helmsman corrects for compass direction and star coordinates. When these are not accessible, the helmsman uses sheer "gut instinct" and projects the template/star-scape within his mind through the cloud cover. For this reason, there shall be moments more difficult than others to maintain the higher frequency.

In ancient times, great navigators of consciousness used astronomy and astrology expressly for the wisdom gained by knowing the cross-currents and prevailing/shifting cosmic winds of collective consciousness balancing. In any case, without the conscious intent of contemplation upon a high frequency template of creation, vast amounts of time may be given to correcting imbalances or rediscovering the same faulty course.

If you find yourself swayed by thought-forms disruptive to the course of integrity, simply relax and set up the contemplative template until it stabilizes or is centered within the Heart of Hearts, and continue to receive a clear channel within the frequency of the template.

Questioner: Would you expand more on the "contemplative template?"

MaYaRa: Recall an example of the nature of your I-dentity, as given in previous chapters, of the starscape and how its intelligence is alive in you as you are a microcosm of that galaxy.

Does this explanation evokes some fragment of vision? To whatever degree that it does, that is your contemplative template. If you contemplate the similarities of the tree to your biological infrastructure, you are cognizant to some greater extent of a visual realization/feeling/experience. This is your contemplative template. It may be a pictograph, geometry/symbol of archetypal intelligence structures, symbols or the words themselves. Indeed, any and every thought-form is alive and can serve as a contemplative template because each has a unique electromagnetic and geometric signature.

However, we heartily suggest that you contemplate only those that connect you directly to the Source of the Genius Frequency. For it is most beneficial to contemplate your genius in the LOVE/LIGHT-GOD/MIND of THE ONE. For a true contemplative template should be a map to freedom.

We stress once again the responsibility born of maturity, wisdom and child-like innocence. The above explanations of a contemplative template are simple yet produce profound and far-reaching results. We ask that you take stock of the recklessness in which you presently engage your powers of contemplation.

Contemplation is not something to be acquired. It is a function of daily living, the very creative processes of life. Contem lation creates and incubates thought-forms. *EVERY THOUGHT-FORM YOU DELIBERATE UPON IS A CONTEMPLATION.* This includes contemplating what you like as well as what you hate. Therefore, you will, indeed, become what you like as well as what you hate. Perhaps now you can see why the perception of the Law of One is critical to your survival in terms of consciousness and eternal Light.

Now, when your contemplative template locks into the desired frequency, thus stabilizing the receiver, you are ready to meditate. In this phase of the consciousness switching, concentration upon the template is gradually relaxed and the unobstructed channel to free awareness begins to flow as light into the body through the template. Since free awareness is virginal – without charge/polarity – it is not magnetized or contaminated by any preconceived thought-forms. Therefore, its transforming power has infinite potential.

As feeling, you may recognize this state as a very gentle, humming resonance. It is always a soothing, healing, peaceful feeling ranging to ecstasy. You may feel like you are floating, drifting, moving, falling, balancing as well as feeling security and love. Also tingling sensations, rippling energy effects and euphoric sensations move about the biostructure leading to unconditional Love/Light. Surrender to that feeling only. We can assure you it is not difficult to do. Let it engulf you, saturate you with its archetypal purity.

Until you learn to sail, as it were, you may drift in and out of this feeling. Reset. Check and recheck the biostructure. Scan for tension in every muscle and organ. Then relax, and very quickly recall the contemplative template. At this point, your experience will deepen. Strive for this "second wind." It is said that "love is sweeter the second time around." Give in to your intellect occasionally and use it to scan memory banks to add facts and details to enhance the template. Then, slip into the resonant humming, pulse and feelings of peace and healing.

Recapitulate this sequence several times, noticing that each cycle produces a more profound experience. When you are familiar with the rhythm, you will know how long the next cycle will be. At this point you may insert a secondary contemplative template.

The secondary template may be one that is more intimately connected with your immediate, mundane activities, such as problems that need to be solved. It may take the thought-form of a question or an attribute that you desire to enhance, such as what your highest purpose is or to acquire greater healing powers. Keep this secondary template simple like a pictograph or word or feeling to be empowered. Now hold this secondary template as the sun holds its planets and pours light into them. Do not manipulate the template. Let it stabilize so that it does not change in that moment. Then, let the resonant humming/pulsing of euphoria saturate it with Light of free awareness until what you feel indicates that it is alive and radiant within you. Let it become part of your infrastructure of the primary template until it melts into the totality of your being. At this point you may slip into a meditative state of reception of free awareness once again. It will flow into the thought-forms that you contemplated.

When you are ready, gently recall the primary template and sense the ever deepening significance that it holds for you – the ever deepening reality, which it is becoming for you. Very gently, not suddenly, begin to awaken bio-sensual contact with environment. Be sure to give a few minutes to your duplicate light-body, now charged with free awareness, to synchronize with the lower frequency of the organic body. Do this by visualizing your duplicate light-body, which is slightly larger than the elemental one, centering perfectly and in sync with it. When you feel that it is totally aligned and centered, linger a few minutes, contemplating the light-body saturating the ele-"mental" one. Thus, you have completed a powerful contemplative/meditative cycle of transformation.

Questioner: Is this realignment process due to the light-body being elsewhere?

MaYaRa: It would be misleading to state that the light-body is "elsewhere." The focus may be elsewhere. A light-body, as consciousness-form, may be everywhere and nowhere.

You may conceptualize it as existing in a greatly expanded state, radiating evenly from the center point of the Perfect Atom/Adam in the Heart of Hearts.

We suggest the aforementioned procedure of "grounding" due to the various psycho-organic imbalances which electromagnetic and geomagnetic disturbances may present to the light-body at the moment it condenses from higher dimensions into lower ones. For this reason, you may experience some distress or moodiness after meditations, especially after a sudden jolt into the elements causing an uncentered light-body, for a period of time. It is not especially dangerous. It is merely uncomfortable and diminishes the feeling/connection to the bio-computer and the heightened awareness/consciousness that you previously generated.

Questioner: Is it always necessary to use this procedure in the order that you have given, that is, contemplation first and then meditation?

MaYaRa: You may, of course, just sit and begin meditating. But the chances of opening the channels of free awareness, again, become a hit and miss situation.

Without proper contemplation upon a high order frequency thought-form, it is quite possible to enter into a meditative reception of a low order of frequency thought-forms. Therefore, to gain some assurance of the highest quality feedback, some forethought should be exercised.

You may note that the original, pure, ritualized procedures of the ancients, or what you term "primitive" cultures, were designed to provide the most expedient course to true realization within an otherwise, seemingly random event/matrix of human tendencies.

In contemplation, the entity tunes to the channel desired and in meditation, it is received through the stabilization of the bio-capacitor to receive, store and resonate through the resonator/glands/chakras. These, in turn, radiate said frequency thought-forms to cells – and environment – as per the template via the unlimited free-awareness that permeates the universe.

The medium of free-awareness is simultaneously available to every dimension of creation. Thus, of itself, it is extremely potent and efficient, as is the transceiver medium connecting all scales, macro and micro into ONE WHOLE thought-form. Only a medium that is not inherently a polarized energy can fulfill such a cosmic requirement.

It is important to reiterate what we have stated in many different ways. That is, the overview of your existence is an interwoven tapestry of positive and negative energy matrices – positive and negative energy is merely energy changing directions – permeated and supported by a frequency of thought common to all polarities, known to you in this understanding as the Genius Frequency. No energy polarity is even possible without this frequency of unified, free awareness. Therefore, tuning into this frequency of thought enables you to operate from the Universal Point of consciousness: UNI, meaning one; VERSE, meaning word/song. Thus, ALL IS ONE/WORD/SONG/LIGHT/LOVE. Therefore, Love is a frequency, a physical/cosmic, tangible, measurable force/glue in the tapestry of creation.

All interdimensional communication that you term "channeling," takes place in, of, and by this frequency of thought, since this frequency is the fielding function of THE ONE MIND. It enables everyone who contemplates its awesome scope, in the knowledge of their true natures as God-Beings, to bridge gaps that form the membrane walls-of-tension between one dimension and another.

As we have stated, one of the attributes of the Genius Frequency is its omnipresence. Due to its primary function of UNI-VERSAL matrix interfacing and its UNIVERSAL resonant fielding capacity, its harmonic pattern exists in a time/space epicenter of awareness. Because it is timeless, the procedures for resonating with this UNI-VERSAL resonant field are fairly obvious. Therefore, ALL time is within your space of being.

Just as the spherical nature of creation manifests and supports the cyclic nature of time, so too, does the relative motion of bodies manifest and support polarity of charges in time. Thus, bipolar charges are inherent in motion, as singularity is inherent in stillness. One thus begets two.

You are so ensnared by this motion/time cycle/event duality that you literally "knock yourselves out" in what you term "sleep." A far more accurate word for this process is resonate. Since you have separated consciousness from primal awareness, one can only resonate with the Genius Frequency during subconscious states in the absence of third dimensional stimuli, only to consciously destroy that resonance during the so-called "waking" of stimulated emissions.

Questioner: If the Genius Frequency can only be "locked in" through meditation, then how can one preserve it?

MaYaRa: Through contemplation. Contemplation is a function of your so-called "waking" consciousness that you can use simultaneously as an adjunct to the intellect, thereby gaining control of the reactionary altered-ego.

Fine-tuning the transceiver is consciously achieving a non-polarized energy field matrix of conscious-awareness. Once this frequency is locked into the very geometry of mind, it may be used as an adjunct to daily active awareness modes, albeit in a slightly more conscious manner. That is, you do not have to be in a trance. A true Master IS always in the present awareness of being.

Moreover, there is a cumulative effect in direct proportion to the depth and quality of your contemplative/meditative experience. There is a profound physiological change in resonance that lingers long after a state of free awareness has been realized. During even the briefest moments, the bio-computer exhibits a shift to wave behavior as light quanta packets. At this moment, an alignment of psychic/cellular mass occurs, resonating with its pure state as true crystalline wave length, opening you to true connection with the Cosmic Intelligent Matrix of which you are part and parcel.

Questioner: Can you explain in more detail what the "Cosmic Intelligence Matrix" is and how we are a part of it?

MaYaRa: The Cosmic Intelligent Matrix is inherent as the infrastructure of free awareness as a living touchstone to the Genius Frequency. It is codification of quanta light emanations imbued with undeviating mathematical angular velocities, and stabilized through further manifestations of crystalline thought-forms. It allows for infinite variations through its spiral DNA blueprinting via its ability to simultaneously move in and out of all dimensions.

The Cosmic Intelligent Matrix resonates the exact coordinates of geometric proportion found in the Great Pyramid. Through the pyramidal-energy-construct, the Cosmic Intelligence Matrix produces infinite variations of its higher Light Correlate. Thus, the veils of confusion upon your plane become translucent by the realization of free awareness in self organizing matter. Thus, THE ONE creates an infinitude of manifested and potential creations and universes, which may only return to THE ONE in its pure state of ONENESS.

This Matrix is a tool by which geophysical models of crystalline fields as galaxies and as microscopic infrastructure are woven within the tapestry of free awareness. Thus, the Cosmic Intelligent Matrix appears built and carved in stone as pyramids, ancient art forms and teachings, which act as, and indeed are, resonators for continued connection between earth and other galactic Intelligence – regardless that humanity may be in darkness. Therefore, the channels into earth are at least always open. The form and function of the Intelligent Matrix organizes the patterns re-discovered in, what is termed, fractal geometry. Therefore it is simultaneous throughout scale.

Fine-tuning your bio-computer through contemplation/ meditation forms angular resonant fields, linking electromagnetic field frequencies with those living models of Cosmic Intelligence Matrix – all operating on the Genius Frequency as a thought-form within your sphere of awareness. With every effort, regardless of how minute, another block of your pyramidal energy construct is set into mathematical/geometric angular perfection within the CHRIST-LIGHT/Frequency.

The only guidelines you need are those that mirror the creative process in its true wave form: the oscillatory configuration of creative wave harmonics. Pour your knowledge and exercises into this Sacred Wave Form of contemplation/meditation for accelerated effect in receiving higher thought-forms directly and with minimum distortion.

In summary: To "contemplate" is to set up communication and resonance with the Cosmic Intelligent Matrix by willful intent and some degree of vision with open-ended parameters – as a flow-form adapts to form and function in the eloquent efficiency of hydrodynamics. Thus, in contemplation, one sets up the specific architecture in which the Genius Frequency is found.

To meditate is to receive, into the total bio-computer, resonant frequencies that are synonymous with the frequencies that support (and constitute) the contextual reference as defined by the contemplation. Therefore, meditating upon "nothing" – self canceling – usually results in a blockage prohibiting higher communication. Since there is no frequency that supports "nothing," its contextual reference can serve, at best, a form of relaxation and respite from the relentless din of the altered-ego. However, it is certainly not a guarantee for enlightenment, any more than is driving down a street in a trance. Thus, purposeful meditation has far greater benefits as it is used with its natural adjunct, contemplation.

Contemplation/meditation is a looping process that is self clarifying and self perpetuating. However, inherent in every thought-form is a resonant frequency. Messages are received on that wave length only. Therefore, carefully selecting the highest frequency thought-form will generate messages on that frequency of consciousness-awareness, creating a feedback loop resonating within you, circulating peaceful, healing Light-filled solutions and resolutions to any problems or goals that one may encounter or desire, commensurate with the Plan of Light of THE ONE.

Any attempt to manipulate others in the sacred process of life opens a system of entropic values of partial truths, which may entrap one in a disintegrating spiral that siphons energy from the vital body. Again, this is not a moral issue! For the mechanics of consciousness are set forth clearly within strict mathematical/ geometric codes of angular resonance. Cellular integrity disintegrates when out of phase-synchronization with the Original Frequency of the Template of God-Mind.

The important question is what to contemplate? Therein lies the responsibility. Therefore, we suggest that you contemplate the highest thought-forms of Light that you are capable of at any given moment in time. This will virtually guarantee the appropriate resolution and inspiration needed to raise the frequency of your bio-computer.

Many do not as yet "know" – on a conscious level – exactly what is needed to fulfill their true and highest destiny. However, as you progress in consciousness evolution, the awareness of Higher goals will fill the seeming void allowing you to directly cognize your immediate needs to facilitate each step taken into Light. For you will ultimately realize that the needs of the many are the needs of THE ONE and the needs of THE ONE are the needs of the MANY. That is the law of unity, weaving tapestries of universes within universes in coherence within LOVE/LIGHT-GOD/MIND, your heritage.

This Divine Tapestry is sensitive to the slightest thought-form contemplated by any being. Disruptive and disintegrating thought-forms are felt throughout the universe through the web-work of free awareness. For these reasons, we can only heartily suggest that you contemplate the Genius of self as a microcosm of Divine Laws and the healing of the planet and all life rather than "wishing for things" that may inherently retain factors of entropy. Project your beauty into life and it will surely reflect it to you a thousand fold.

1. As you practice the art-form of contemplation/ meditation, you will become aware of the natural rhythm or oscillation inherent in the frequency of the process. This process speeds up as you become more adept at merging space/time and time/space in a continuum of Infinite Mind until a synergistic resonance manifests higher communication. In other words, you will no longer expend energy and long time spans in "tuning" to the Genius Frequency. You will become the Genius Frequency. In that transformation, death will no longer loom before you, casting shadows of fear across the threshold of your eternal God-Self.

2. Take responsibility and act as a cocreator. Use your powers of Infinite Mind to project peace and healing to the suffering and oppressed in the earth plane and beyond. You may contemplate and visualize the healing of specific locations on and within earth. Through contemplation, you may connect with all Sacred Coordinates connecting earth to Higher Realms of Intelligence.

3. Be a beacon of Divine Light/Order. Pulsate with the oscillations of planetary heartbeat while contemplating love for all life upon and within it, in all kingdoms. Receive, in your meditations, feedback from these contemplations strengthened by the Cosmic Intelligence Matrix of supreme ordering of chaos in the lower realms.

Questioner: Can an individual really make a difference in the planetary situation?

MaYaRa: Since the principle of free awareness is omnipresent and omniscient, it cannot be separated from any other part or parcel of life without grave consequences. Therefore, every individual's responsibility remains, as always, a shared one, as well as a personal one.

What you think are your inner-most secrets are not secrets at all. For every thought-form contemplated affects every other thought-form, as it adds to and compounds the holographic energy-constructs that form the reality, in toto, on all levels of life. Know also that you are not alone in this most exiting and promising of times, in your time. In the Omega Point, there is the Alpha and the graduation from the life/death cycle that has enslaved you for so long in your time. Each of you is an unfolding, flowering Light that will uplift, heal and fulfill ancient prophesy of Light beyond the solar logos.

To fine-tune your bio-computers to the Genius Frequency is to prepare the foundation for living in fifth dimensional Light. However, it is first necessary that you master the fourth dimension of thought-form. Begin NOW! If you have begun, increase your efforts, for the time is at hand. In preparing this way, you will not be shocked as the blinders are removed revealing the other dimensions. And they will most assuredly be removed as your solar system shifts into new spectral-awareness/consciousness levels of higher frequency star power.

With each passing moment, in your time, your thought-forms are magnified by this quantum shift in electron valence and atomic bonding. With each passing moment, your thought-forms register greater and greater impact on world-reality. There is a Light beyond lights that sustains you through this process of ascension. The Masters of Light await your invitation into your Heart of Hearts. Reach out to them as a co-creator in service to Light/Life. You shall not be abandoned. No, you shall never be abandoned. You shall be embraced in a Love that cannot be described. It is your responsibility to reach for it. Ask for it. Become it. You are all in All, one in ONE. Contemplate this and you shall BE/I AM.

BEYOND CHANNELING
"CONSCIOUS LIGHT RESONATORS"

> *"You will bypass*
> *intellectual frigidity,*
> *and a resonance with the related*
> *thought-forms of revelation will uplift you as you*
> *realize how miraculous you are."*

Questioner: If the Genius Frequency is always and everywhere present around and within us, then why must we work so hard to utilize it?

MaYaRa: If to live and act in profound feelings of Love, contemplate the glories of the creation and experience peaceful meditations is "hard work," then you have a difficult journey to traverse. The proper perspective here is not to "utilize" anything. It is resonating with the presence of God-Mind. Although every entity exists in a perpetual state of free-awareness, not all entities resonate with it. Unless you maintain that resonance through your own, personal consciousness, the fruits of the Genius Frequency remain dormant.

The vast majority of earth-dwellers eat from the "tree of knowledge," or "good and evil." Therefore, reasons are needed to perform the slightest task. Your educational system is designed to provide the reasons explaining third dimensional reality as it appears to the altered-ego. When the appearances change, as they are wont to do, more reasons are added to the last ones – all-in-all portrayed in a linear tracking of the appearance of time. Thus, third dimensional education attempts to develop skills rather than consciousness, cunning rather than true intelligence – not understanding that skills are acquired automatically in proportion to the frequency of consciousness.

Thus, education through manipulating historical thought-forms to suit a temporary need within a specific environment is the source of the tragic limitations placed upon the ignorant and educated alike. All of this requires an exaggerated amount of time in the race to death, leaving little time to contact higher intelligence through higher frequencies of consciousness. In the food-chain-mentality of present thought-forms, time is viewed as "time invested" and the logic of this travesty resounds with partial equations such as: "One has very limited time;" "Life is short;" "One must have power over something or someone – regardless that it be accomplished in the most difficult and time-consuming manner possible – and then you die."

MIRRORING

When you properly understand the true processes of creation and the true order in which these occur in the universe, as well as within you, you begin to understand that the altered-ego attempts to accomplish its partial equations of life in a backward fashion. This is due to the reflective nature of your existence upon earth-plane. That is, the earth-plane mirrors the creative process back to the Source and, therefore, appears to manifest in reverse order. That which you see is the inside out, as it were.

We endeavor to instruct you in the proper and efficient techniques, attitudes and knowledge to ignite a resonance with the higher frequencies of your innate natures, so that you may truly emanate, once again, the processes of THE ONE and accomplish far more in a fraction of the time-span than you experience at presence. From your personal perspective, you may have enough time to accomplish your missions. But from a universal perspective, the Omega point is at hand. There are opportunities for quantum leaps in your personal evolution that will not be repeated for hundreds of thousands of years by your counting. From the latter perspective, time is running out, beloved.

The proper order of creation is from the "top-down" as you term space/time events. You are not crawling up from the primordial ooze, shedding your scales, spitting water from your lungs for the purpose of destroying life on earth. You are projected *into* earth for the purpose of elevating its consciousness, as well as your own.

This is not an either/or situation. Only in the ignorance of a polarized altered-ego will one be tempted to begin arguing for/ against, top/down versus bottom/up theories. Contemplate the true significance of the Law of One and you will begin to visualize the wave-form harmonics of creation pouring into and out of earth, producing standing wave forms that the altered-ego recognizes as objects. All is going BOTH ways simultaneously.

When you emulate the Divine Creative Process, you resonate with the Genius Frequency, supercharging the capacitive/ transformative qualities of the bio-computer. When you begin putting this into practice, education in any field can be quantized. In other words, if you desire to articulate Divine Creation through music and you are resonating with the Genius Frequency, you simply create the instrument of your choice and voicing, and play with virtuosity. The same would be true for any field of study. Indeed, that is how it once was and shall be again, if you choose.

Questioner: There are many in our time who engage in what we term "channeling," that is, communicating with disincarnate entities. Could you comment on the "trance channels" that seem to enjoy absolute verifications regarding this phenomenon?

MaYaRa: Your line of questioning is pertinent and the following information regarding it may help in furthering the understanding of the Genius Frequency.

At this juncture, you should not be surprised if we redefine your term "channeling." Your planet is plagued with the confusion of tongues and it is most beneficial to redefine word/symbols often, as they are organic in nature. In the not too distant future, one language will again be universal upon earth. It shall not be English as you know it.

The term "channeling," although an apt expression up to a point, results in ambiguities when applied to higher truths. We shall refer to this phenomenon as light-resonators. We shall further qualify this term with the following prefixes: Conscious, subconscious, voluntary, and involuntary. Since everyone is a light-resonator, this term serves us well to further define the degrees and processes that manifest from the inherent function of Light.

Suffice it to say that Light-Resonators is a term with sufficient clarity to permit the exploration of the many "psychic phenomenon" occurring on your plane of existence in ever increasing numbers. By using this term, you may perceive how a primary modality of thought transference may occur on many different levels of consciousness. The understanding of a light-resonator will give a broader base from which to include the many levels and processes that transpire in telekinesis, telepathy and transference through various spectrum densities, such as electromagnetic and gravitational fields.

Just as you may touch or bring a vibrating tuning fork in proximity to an object to witness the sympathetic vibrations induced by the source tone, so too, does your physical biocomputer resonate with given spectrum emanations or thought-forms connecting each manifestation to the other. However, the beat-note or tone emanating from the tuning fork manifests different results when applied to substances of different densities. Applying the source frequency to metal will not give the same results as that of a wooden instrument. And though some will reproduce the tone with different overtones than others, the beat-note is always present in the harmonic. Even when one active tuning fork drives another of the same pitch, standing waves develop producing harmonics in addition to the pure tone.

The purpose of the contemplation/meditation exercises in the preceding segment of this book was to gain control of the resonant gates of the bio-computer unlocking the fourth dimension. When that is accomplished, a resonant memory factor is retained (remembered) for the reception and transmission of cosmic resonances and overtones produced by the Divine Source, the Divine Tuning Fork, if you will, of THE ONE. It is simply a matter of resonating with the harmonics of a thought-form frequency in the particular octave and beat-note to which your bio-computer is presently tuned.

As you work on these exercises, quantum changes in the driving frequency of the bio-computer may be realized and progressively higher frequency thought-forms can resonate with and therefore produce higher frequencies of information. Further, certain access codes, similar to those you use in computer language – albeit in a geometric construct – guarantee that entities vibrating with destructive low frequencies of entropy cannot contaminate the purity of the higher dimensions of LOVE-LIGHT/GOD-MIND sustaining the universes as a whole.

Occasionally, such low frequency entities may acquire certain knowledge (i.e., magic, sorcery etc.), which they use to manipulate others who are of like vibration or frequency, for that is the guarantee of freedom of the Law of Confusion under the LAW OF ONE. However, they are powerless to affect or influence in any way those entities vibrating on a higher beat-note frequency in resonance with the sacred harmonics of THE ONE. Those who refuse to make the physical and mental adjustments necessary to resonate with the Genius Frequency cannot receive the "keys" to freedom. Without this access frequency, no entity may penetrate the veils of the higher dimensions, regardless of their cunning or power. Fortunately for you, it is a fail-safe system which guarantees infinite life in the Light, and universes and dimensions of joy beyond counting.

SUBCONSCIOUS LIGHT-RESONATORS - SLR's

Now, let us examine the more extreme cases of light-resonators which you term, "trance channels." These entities can be categorized as subconscious light-resonators and for the purpose of brevity, we shall use the nomenclature of SLR's. The chances of an accidental SLR is about one billion to one. So for all intents and purposes, the SLR is an entity, who by karmic strengthening of the energy bodies through using one or more life cycles in service to others, has developed a bio-computer that resonates with entities of higher dimensions (or other dimensions) through previous agreements and light-work.

Some SLR's incarnate into life scenarios which are so different from the previous ones that recapitulation of patterns in the formative years of a present life/body cycle – stored as access codes for cellular memory – are not easily triggered by anything in the present one. As we shall see, these are usually the most shocking or unusual cases, since so-called psychic talent is suddenly exhibited seemingly without any "background." In contrast, many of these entities have similar life scenarios which trigger strong urges in the formative years. In conventional terms, these are recognized as talents or strong, early goal-forming. In almost every case, these "early talents" and interests are recapitulations of former patterns. Thus, a musician in a former life cycle, in many cases will exhibit musical tendencies in the present which manifest as high probabilities of continued application of an area of awareness.

In the former case, although the capabilities were previously established, the life scenario is so completely different that the entity experiences profound confusion as to what is its life purpose. Thus, the SLR builds tension within the mem-brain of consciousness until one moment, in a seemingly unrelated life circumstance, the entity begins to resonate with the frequencies of another dimension. In these cases, the first impulse is to entertain notions of insanity. This limitation is usually overpowered by the strength of the subconscious recognition of other dimensions. However, the resistance of the altered-ego is usually so intense that the conscious activity of the bio-computer breaks the circuit of sensory awareness, shifting into what you term as a trance.

The SLR's are those that seem the most sensational. These are contrasted to those who are "geniuses in their field" or child prodigies who – although gaining information through trance – are considered acceptable because they are simply engrossed in their work in some obsessive way or another.

Those who choose a life scenario that has no previous patterning in cellular memory are generally those who through various stress or trauma trigger the resonance connection or contact with other dimensions. We have found this method to serve well in the reverse psychology of credibility – as most on your plane would not have the preconceived intellectual ammunition to effect a successful assault upon one who operates entirely outside their immediate historical background. For example, a house wife suddenly enters a trance state resonating profound truth and prophesy.

Once the initial contact has manifested, the entity making subconscious contact must arrange for a conscious decision on the part of the SLR for continued contact. If the decision on the part of the SLR is one of denial, the contact is terminated for that life cycle or a future time in this one. Thus, the Law of Confusion or free will is respected. If the entity decides affirmatively, then a series of instructions shall be forthcoming explaining a technique for re-entry or rendezvous. Thus, even though the moment of "meeting," contact or resonance with another dimension is prearranged by the entity before its incarnation, the momentary conscious verification and acceptance of continued contact or resonance is the "signature" binding the agreement for further work. This contract, as it were, may be canceled at any time. Note also, NEVER will any higher source of Intelligence force its will upon an entity for any reason.

Although the numbers of entities who perform this service have increased dramatically in the last decade of your time, they continue to be a minority and shall continue to be. The reason for this is that they are the second stage or wave of communication from higher dimensions during this Omega point in the cycle of the universe. The third stage shall be grander in scope and involve millions of entities.

The first stage consisted of the prophets of old as documented in your Great Book. The second stage has been outlined above. The third stage is where the sub-harmonics of this wave first spreads to hundreds of thousands of entities upon your plane. In concert, fellow humans of every race and creed will expand the wave of Light to yet hundreds of thousands more.

CONSCIOUS LIGHT RESONATORS: CLR's

This latter group shall be termed conscious-light-resonators or CLR's. For the above reasons, these CLR's do not go into trance states but have the more demanding job of deciphering higher information from the everyday animal awareness, which presently is called the "real world."

CLR's, as indicated by the increasing numbers of those who choose to be involved, play an important role in the rapid, quantum evolution of consciousness by the experiential nature of reality in higher dimensions of existence manifesting upon your plane at this time. That is to say, it is not enough to see, hear or follow any established teaching. Neither is "believing" enough to make the transition into the fourth and fifth dimensions.

RESONATING WITH AND EXPERIENCING THE LIGHT OF THE GENIUS FREQUENCY IS THE ONLY MEANS TO CRYSTALLIZING NEW PARADIGMS OF EXISTENCE IN THE DIMENSIONS INTO WHICH THE EARTH IS NOW MOVING.

How is this being accomplished? We shall begin this understanding by defining the term conscious-light-resonator, CLR. We will then apply this definition to your own situation and to others who shall be and are operating in many areas of earth-plane experience, all interconnected by the Light of Free-Awareness that shall manifest great changes upon earth and within each entity. We shall also explain how this third phase of resonance is available to ALL who seek the higher dimensions of reality and their true identities as children and workers of the Light. Your future is hear, NOW. Let us reiterate:

THIS THIRD PHASE OF CONTACT IS NOW AVAILABLE TO ALL WHO DESIRE TO WORK WITH THE HIGHER LIGHT.

While the above statement is not news – the Genius Frequency has always been available to all – the news is that you now have assistance on an unprecedented scale from Master Intelligence from other dimensions, working with the plans of THE ONE, patiently awaiting your decision to serve in this exodus of humanity, indeed the earth, to its origins in higher Light realms of creation (we are not speaking of space-gods with fancy hardware).

Now, the primary difference between SLR's and CLR's is that the latter may or may not have a prearrangement from previous cycles. That is to say, in this third phase of the Omega cycle of "harvest," you may consciously decide to resonate the Light through the Genius Frequency, regardless of prior life circumstances, regardless that you were not a direct descendant in a lineage of priests, prophets, seers, gurus or geniuses. The time involved in reaching some viable degree of conscious contact is in direct proportion to your depth of desire. Thus, some of you possessing a rather dubious past may indeed quicken your spirit even before those who may possess a comparatively fruitful past-life experience, if the latter are blasé, jaded, self righteous or perhaps, lazy. Wherever you stand in the scheme of things, NOW is the time to quadruple your efforts, for the results are rather long term – FOREVER.

If you do not recall the preceding segment of this book, we heartily suggest that you review it. For the proper contemplation/meditation upon the infinite beauty of creation manifested by LOVE/LIGHT-GOD/MIND will permeate and indeed cause it to manifest by resonating with your bio-computer. It may begin to trickle through the infrastructure of your thought-forms or it may explode into a rapture that will change your life in an instant. Either way, the rapture is forthcoming, if you so desire. Remember, you have assistance from many Masters in other dimensions of Light. The time, in your time, is short indeed.

Now, we will use the author as an example of the mechanics involved in the process of conscious light resonating. As a CLR, you do not enjoy a definitive verification of contact with any outside intelligence. We shall attempt to put your ongoing doubts to rest and in doing so we are hopeful that many others, confronted with similar doubts, shall find comfort and encouragement in these insights.

It would be advantageous to recall or review the opening segments of this book where we stress that the faculty of genius can be and is manifested by entities in every walk of life – that all of you have at various event/moments in your present life/body cycles contacted other energy dimensions of intelligence, regardless that you remember it at this time. Of course, there is the ongoing contact that occurs to everyone in what you term as the sleep cycle. You are, in fact, multi-dimensional beings.

Since Free-Awareness frequencies are omnipresent and neutral in their relative charge and, therefore, function without time or space limitations, you can indeed create space/time within time/space to manifest the necessary simultaneous overlap of consciousness with other dimensions. Each entity should carry on their own personal research into this for each will ultimately experience the benefits, serving others with their acquired gifts on a very personal level.

It is a most difficult task to search for missing "links" from without when the links are within. Regardless that verifications of your abilities are witnessed by your peers, it is not suggested that you wait and see what the so-called experts have to say about all this. There may literally not be enough "time" for that. Experience the Genius Frequency for yourselves and receive the Light which you seek and are a part. We shall digress for a few moments in a contemplation.

The concept of space in its true proportions are relative to you as a bio-computer. Your science has established that you are composed almost entirely of space. It has calculated that if the spaces were removed from your material structure, you could fly through the eye of a needle, as a bird through the arc of a rainbow. Contemplate that. Although your scientific formalities generally block higher knowledge on many levels, on occasion it reveals a grand truth and you casually reply that it is merely "interesting." Seize upon these revelations! Contemplate them. Stretch your mental bodies. The altered-ego will resist the new thought-forms in this information. But if you persist, you will bypass intellectual frigidity and a resonance with the related thought-forms of revelation will uplift you as you realize how miraculous you are.

In light of this scientific revelation, you might ask yourself: If this is true – if I am composed mostly of space – how can I function? What am I? What is the coherent force that gives my illusion of mass its tremendous, trillion-fold organizational patterns? What holds all of this in place as a living being? How can this similitude and function be so reliable through thousands of generations and yet create another image, once again? Contemplate these ideas and questions.

Contemplate these types of questions so that the intellect can be primed to probe higher frequency knowledge rather than defending what little it knows. One should reserve judgment about ideas that seem impossible, unbelievable or contrary to what has been taught. Explore these ideas innocently, exuberantly, like the child in nature that you are. Before we move on to further explanations pertaining directly to the subject of this segment, let us contemplate again this universe of space that you are.

For in the vast space within you, the hyperspace of the Genius Frequency, there exists living blueprints, Intelligent Conscious Beings whose responsibility is to maintain these Blueprints throughout the flux of the universe. There are whole Light Beings existing in dimensions of Light beyond light, outside of space/time limitations that now restrict you.

There are Spectra Beings who shall appear to millions in the days that rush toward you in the final transition of earth consciousness – in the Omega point. These Beings are commissioned by THE ONE to embody the matrix of thought-forms that engineer the genesis on all levels of creation and becoming. They are the Masters who maintain the stability of form that you sense as matter. They maintain the stability of DNA as it provides regenesis of cellular integrity throughout the powerful magnetic, cosmic flux and entropy. They exist eternally to project the thought-forms of THE ONE into Divine Tapestries of angular light geometries that create standing wave-forms of light, motion and matter. They help you and wait for you to join them in the glory of creation, of eternal life. They teach the depths of joy in a centered being who emanates from a Source beyond and before there were worlds.

Why is this seeming digression so important to our examination of "channeling?" Because as CLR's, you must seek a more accurate vision, a personal vision of life in other dimensions within you. To the altered-ego, the intellect, regardless of its degree of aptitude, is its prized possession. The intellect is used to defend the belief systems created in its ignorance. Therefore, since everyone is inherently a Light-Resonator by nature and everyone channels information continually, it is a matter of what information, what higher truth is permitted entry into your consciousawareness. Therefore, the "salvation" of every entity is based upon personal work, personal merit and personal responsibility for all of life. Thus, belonging to a political, religious or scientific organization will not guarantee anything, unless personal effort is exerted to understand your true natures as responsible co-creators with THE ONE. The world can only be changed one entity at a time. You must change!

Each of you personally must, through your own efforts, become aware of and convinced of your highest natures and the responsibilities that come with that inherent nature. When sufficient resonance is established through the proper understanding of who and what you are, your capacitor/ mem-"brain" is charged and expanded, and the synaptic firings of your biocomputer begin to form super-holographs of geometry that sync-lock with the dimensions of the Spectra Beings. In other words, you establish access codes that resonate organically to connect you physically to the Genius Frequency.

When this occurs, you will sense that you know more than you know. You will ask questions and truly inspired answers will emanate from inside your being, and those answers will ring and resound with truth. Your intellect will always have its doubts as it has been trained to do so well. Yet the totality of your mindcenters will register its truth.

Now, you may have experienced many contemplation/ meditations and have increased your knowledge gained through books, experience, cellular memory, and most importantly, through the burning desire to know the truth of the higher nature of your existence. After an entity discovers and embraces these, the actual chemistry of the bio-computer is changed and the resonance patterns of thought-forms generated from you into earth and cosmos through the transceiver functions of mind are reflected back to the Super-Luminal dimensions as a pure state of inductive inspiration that uplifts you to greater visions. Again, as your thoughtforms change, so too, will the physical body as it is respacialized and filled with Eternal Light, unlocking and dissolving the gates and blocks to your true liberation.

Conscious-Light-Resonance is not something that is limited to a space/time/event in a church or at a computer. As you begin to expand your resonant potential, your entire life will change. You will be "channeling," as it were, on a continuous basis the Higher Light in all moment/events, even in the mundane affairs of your lives. You will make new and more appropriate decisions. You will be guided to meet other individuals who are experiencing the same changes and your sense of family will expand as you begin to help, assist, guide and serve others, so that they in turn will uplift others. Until you begin to feel this frequency of Light, you shall be entrapped in the partial equations of third dimensional entropy and death.

Thus a CLR is a far more comprehensive and practical modality of consciousness that benefits the individual and the world in most diverse and unexpected ways. It may appear that this is not as dramatic, entertaining or mysterious as what you term "trance channeling," but we assure you that the need for "trance" is diminishing in its role to awaken humanity. For the true awakening lies not in the mere witness to the phenomenon of others, but in the EXPERIENCE of knowing the creative processes of THE ONE. The Cosmic Winds are blowing, beloved. Set sail.

Although the author has never written text of this nature in this current body/life/cycle, the impulse to undertake such an ambitious project came upon him rather suddenly. A closer examination reveals that unbeknownst to him, he followed the above scenarios in this text quite closely. In a previous document, not of the nature of this work (a sci-fi screenplay), he stumbled upon a vibratory/sound/matrix (name) that suited what he considered an imaginary being who would fulfill the role of emissary and keeper of wisdom to be revealed to a world of chaos and destruction. The vibratory/sound/matrix that appealed to his sense of playful intuition was "Mayara." This is more accurately inscribed as MA-YA-RA for this sound/shape resonates with three levels of being. So he dreamed a being who could answer his questions. Him-self!

The combination of this vibration/sound/shape, Ma-Ya-Ra, became for him a "household word" as it were. This coupled with his innate sense of responsibility for the creation of a story that was uplifting and spiritually sound established the initial access codes or resonance with higher purpose. The initial "contact" with the Genius Frequency was at first obscure and as he merged this effort with wake/sleep cycles, the ideas began to pour into his mind.

After finishing the document (the screenplay), some time elapsed before he began an intensive effort to open the blocks to his innate knowing. During this time, many experiments were implemented producing cleansing effects in all five of his energy bodies. It was after this that he intuitively began to approach his quest with deep contemplation/meditation upon a higher meaning of life and a growing desire to be of service.

It was during this period that he cultivated and resonated with the frequencies necessary to begin supercharging the biocomputer with sufficient quantum energy thought-forms in the fourth dimension. It was also during this period of time that he received or "felt" the impulse to begin this work, much to the protest of his altered-ego. This impulse, translated into a word/ symbol, would be equivalent to the somewhat ineloquent statement: "You write a book."

In this case, the results were gradual, yet steady, with indications of resonant contact produced only in the early stages of the sleep/wake cycle and only on infrequent occasions at first. We use this case to demonstrate that there may not be fireworks, trances or overwhelmed friends, yet the work speaks for itself. For the entity acting as a CLR must struggle with the altered-ego that provides the denial, self-criticism and doubt. Yet persistence and constant attention to the intuitive rather than the preconceived yielded results beyond his expectations.

A true CLR, then, is inspired by Higher Intelligence. At no time is the personality and waking consciousness/awareness vacated from the bio-computer. In a manner of speaking, we meet halfway in the effort. When blockages occur, we give inspiring advise through spatial pictograms in the auric field of mind. These pictograms cannot be apprehended by the seeker without constant vigilance and focus of attention. When an energy block is too intense to break through and the seeker maintains desire, we guide the entity through complicated maneuvers of synchronicity, such as a series of "chance" meetings of entities who might, for example, suggest a place to visit where an insight may be realized, which in turn reveals another insight, triggering another set of thought-form geometries, which may result in another line or paragraph of this book.

The entity is encouraged to use his/her own resources before offering additional information. When the entity experiences lucid contemplations and resonance is sync-locked with the Genius Frequency, many pages – using the example of writing – are written in short periods of time, in your time. At times, resistance is applied to the entity's lower frequency thought-forms so that through-put becomes virtually impossible due to extreme fatigue or interruptions, etc. This preserves the integrity and high frequency content of the message. Yet at no time is the entity controlled in any way. For every idea, suggestion, or solution to a problem must be earned by the seeker. And that, beloved, is a great reward. It is also a great beginning.

Understand that the Genius Frequency is by no means limited to writing. In a manner of speaking, the Genius Frequency is a carrier wave of free awareness given in unlimited quantities by the Love of THE ONE to all who seek to return to the Light of ITS knowing. Once you begin to resonate with this frequency, amazing results will manifest. You suddenly realize that you know far more than you knew before in any field you choose to explore in the Name of THE ONE.

Each of you has one or more guides that work with you during your sleep cycle. But so much is lost in the transition between conscious/subconscious modalities, that progress can be painfully slow. By Consciously Resonating with Higher Intelligence through the deep desire for Higher Truth in contemplative/ meditative efforts, the bio-computer is chemically reorganized and the very tissue increases in voltaic charge. These chemical shifts result in an overall frequency shift utilizing new holographic geometries, which resonate with Higher Intelligence through the language of Light.

You may believe in any number of concepts, but you cannot speak the language of Light by operating from a relative position of polarized thinking. Each of you is unique, therefore, each of you will begin contact in a unique manner. It may be more or less direct, miraculous or mundane, earth-shaking or serene, but it is only you who can make the decision to change, to rise to your true potentials – and make the effort NOW to do so.

Do not be discouraged if you seem to have many blocks to higher frequencies of thought. Only through a burning desire to know the Light will the blocks dissolve. Begin a new wave-pattern of contemplation/meditation. Relax into it, knowing that the results are forthcoming. Do not resonate with thought-forms of fear, prejudiced, anger, self-pity, greed, lust, revenge, limitation or manipulation. There is no opposite of LOVE/LIGHT-GOD/MIND. Resonate with the Frequency that creates, drives, and sustains universes.

Do not waste your precious time waiting for angels to knock upon your skulls with lightening bolts, for they are not permitted to interfere with free will. Although it is possible to trigger visitations from extremely high energy entities, the bio-computer must be prepared and cleansed to absorb that kind of Light frequency without profound damage to the biological structure. Thus, each of you will be met halfway. The degree of each effort is met with yet another, higher one. In your Great Book, it is plainly stated: "Seek ye first the Kingdom of GOD and all things shall be given unto you." Purposefully set forth on the quest for contact with your personal guide or higher Master, not in worship but as friends, to assist you from the other dimensions. They are part of what is termed "higher self."

All Masters and Guides wait eagerly to embrace you, to assist you in these final days of this phase of evolution into the Higher Dimensions of Light. You shall accomplish in weeks what you could not accomplish in lifetimes before. The frequencies of Free-Awareness are pouring into your earth in quantum proportions. Take advantage of the cosmic winds at your backs and choose to sail into the eternal Light as you lift other beings along the way from the waters of suffering and fear. Be your own ship of freedom and Light. Be the Conscious-Light-Resonators of this Golden Age of Light promised by the Masters and given freely at this time.

As this scribe learned by his efforts, do not only ask questions, but answer them yourselves. Trust in your Genius. Cease your relentless searching for someone else to provide the answers that exclude you from knowing. Have the faith of a child of the Light in Knowing that you can live forever, if you so choose. Be open to change for the Truth is never static, it always returns to THE ONE.

The Truth is not a possession, it is a process of THE ONE. If at first you falter, prop yourselves with the works of great beings and Masters, but do not stop there for that is not your knowledge/experience. But do contemplate inspiring works and meditate to receive your own contact and inspirations.

Go into the blueprints within the Heart of Hearts and seek the greatness that you are as a co-creator, and take the responsibility as a partner and friend of the Christ Master, Jesus. Then go into the Peace of THE ONE and behold the secrets of yourself in THE ONE. You need only to desire and try. No priest, scientist or guru can do this for you.

ALLOW – *ALLOW* – *ALLOW* your Genius to blossom in the morning of your awakening.

SUPERLIGHT

"THE LIGHT OF GENIUS"

> *"SuperLight*
> *IS the binding force*
> *behind, within, and beyond*
> *all manifestation in all dimentional universes."*

Questioner: It seems that the Genius Frequency encompasses all areas of life and this frequency is inherent in our daily functions, as well as the more usual manifestations of extra-sensory perception and channeling. You have stated that the Genius Frequency is more or less synonymous with "free awareness," which helps in my understanding. But could you elaborate more explicitly upon what type of frequency it is? Is this frequency an intelligence or a type of carrier wave?

MaYaRa: The short of it is this: There is no difference between the Intelligence and the Carrier of free awareness of which you speak. What else could "carry" the scope of all creation but intelligence, and how could it be separate from that which creates and sustains it? For in the space-between-the-spaces of ALL-THERE-IS is a dimension of existence of which we speak. This dimension, the domain of the Hierarchy, is synonymous with the Beings that reside there. Since free awareness is omnipresent, their ability to manifest influence, as well as embodiments, may be achieved multi-dimensionally and simultaneously without space/time parameters and restrictions.

Questioner: Does your intelligence-energy reside there?

MaYaRa: To comprehensively answer this query is far beyond the scope of this book. We are not the Hierarchy. However, we have access parameters which permit us to communicate and work in concert with them. We humbly serve as intermediaries between your third dimensional plane of existence and the fifth. Our purpose is to usher your plane into a fourth and fifth dimensional understanding and to act as a contact point, resonant point or access code to the higher dimensions.

What is important to your understanding at this juncture of your evolution is to realize that it is possible to resonate with these dimensions through awareness mechanisms of your bio-computers. These already contain said dimensions and Divine Programs for the purpose of evolving into them. Further, to consider these ultra-dimensions in three dimensional terms of existing in "another" time and space, that is, other than your own, is to fall prey to the black-and-white, polarized limitations of the altered-ego and its attending intellect. Thus, as we have stated, it is not enough to merely "believe," it is not even enough to know. It IS essential to your evolution that you BE the realization of these dimensions. To accomplish this is to resonate with the Genius Frequency, a latent gift which all of you possess.

Now, to articulate more precisely what the Genius Frequency is would entail that you experience it. That is, to fully answer your query is to articulate, in your quite limited syntax, the cosmology of an opened-ended universe and the infinitude of The Master plans regarding it. The scope of this book does not permit such a task and a linear, intellectual analysis would diminish the time more effectively used to resonate with the experience.

However, it is beneficial to examine a facet or aspect of the Genius Frequency that we have touched upon in the previous study, i.e., the frequency of light on which this is based. We shall examine, then, a concept that explains not only functions of the Genius Frequency, but the basis of many higher dimensions. We have used terms such as Light beyond light and Superluminal Light in order to open your intellects to a dimension of Light that you cannot perceive in third dimensional awareness. In our contemplations, we have asked you to visualize all the spaces between the spaces, be it day or night, as being "solid" or filled with another type of Light-energy. We shall term this most wondrous and beautiful foundation of creation as SuperLight.

SUPERLIGHT

SuperLight is important to your understanding because it concerns how the various energy transference, externalizations and manifestations of Light-Information move and have their being through the free awareness medium of pure consciousness. It is important to gain and utilize some knowledge possessed by your contemporary scientists and, also, of the Ancient Masters who gave forth the thought-forms of science in the beginning of this, your present cycle. It is important to understand where the schism began, which, perpetrated by the lords of the altered-ego, separated the ancient Wisdom into the common knowledge of the church of myth and religion and the science of the "state" of government of nations. It is time, beloved, to resonate once again with the SuperLight which marries the "Bride" and "Groom" of present/future humanity with its ancient heritage as a direct extension of THE ONE.

It is important for you to comprehend SuperLight so that you may answer your own questions regarding the so-called miracles and paranormal, in more scientific terms, of future understandings. Do not think that you must wait for mass media to "headline" these revelations for you, for you have learned to mistrust them, spawning large numbers of entities engaged in helpless cynicism. Science, however, serves a purpose in the unfolding of creation as a natural balance to the corrupted dogma of organized religions, seeking to give a semblance of inspiration and knowledge, from which wisdom may crystallize into actual REALIZATION of your god-natures.

SuperLight is Light beyond light: Beyond Light, here, does not refer to Light which is distanced or far away. It is a causative factor in the initial formation of subspectrum Lights as you perceive these on your narrow wave-length band of awareness. That is why the ancient Masters taught of the Light within or beyond the darkness. For the light that is obvious to you is that wavelength which participates in the matter/antimatter universe, producing the illusion of a black and white reality as perceived by you in your night sky, giving false credence to the base logic of the altered-ego proclaiming that, "There is something, then there is nothing, for I see in the light and I do not see in the darkness."

Your scientists presently are rediscovering through subquantum physics that beyond all relative matter/values there is a continuum of energy dynamics that endures. Indeed, it is a binding force that interacts with and yet supports quantum light relativities, but is separated from it. It is a value, a quality that transcends, supercedes and violates every known law of relativity in matter-values, going beyond all verifiable laws within their third dimensional reality. They struggle with the understanding of a Super-

Light and attempt to mathematically formulate and theorize, without upsetting the "carts" of historic continuity; and ask that you wait hundreds of years in your time, if need be, until "they" and only they may offer proof of something else, on their own terms. Do not wait for them, beloved.

Yet proof is offered on a daily basis upon your plane of experience. Miracles abound, profound happenings are being experienced by tens of thousands. Millions tell their stories of how they witnessed visions, prophetic dreams, bending of metal, the U.F.O. phenomenon, the out-of-body experiences, miraculous healings, channeled entities from other dimensions of existence, etc. Are they ALL to be declared insane or merely victims of very mundane aberrations, which cannot be fully explained? Skeptical scientific intellects, operating as a subset of the altered-ego, peer coldly into the eyes of a miracle, arrogantly protesting that these are all fraud or happenstance occurrences of extreme chance. But what, pray tell, beloved, is a miracle, if not a higher function of SuperLight, a causative matrix/event of higher thought-forms, altering that which it has created unto an even greater creation?

Your questions cannot be answered unless you begin to remove the limited logic of the altered-ego. It may be easier to set your conditioned intellect aside, rather than struggle against artificial and limited belief systems composed of third dimensional thought-forms. Why continue to rely on the so-called objective reality of the intellect that cannot hope to explain or encompass the miraculous nature of life? It will obviously require a SuperLogic to fully comprehend the SuperLight of which we speak. Thus, let us examine this subject with the Mind of the Heart of Hearts. Only from that mind-center within your beings and within your bio-computers can you begin to grasp the awesome reality of your true natures.

Measurement of light values upon your sphere, through the intellect of scientific pursuit, have, indeed, yielded fair mathematical representations of what is witnessed by mundane, sensory-logic of the bio-computer. These measurements have verified and coincided with the key measurements as set in stone by the Masters of Light in the geophysical model of third dimensional space/time/matter – the Great Pyramid of Giza. These measurements have yielded an understanding of light within the parameters of certain velocities, setting the third dimensional light limits – the limits of the threshold of space/time.

Now, this notable and praiseworthy feat of science notwithstanding, it is only the beginning of (or perhaps better said, the end of) an understanding of properties of a certain type of light which behaves as particle-wave rather than wave-wave; though, in reality, it is both. The numbers involved in this calculation, limiting light to 186,000 miles per second in your counting, at first, were so overwhelming that the questioning stopped and so did the understanding of the interdimensional relativity of light. It seemed quite enough to deal with that staggering figure, yet it fit quite nicely into the equations of the day, conveniently rendering the concept of infinity impractical and unnecessary. To add to the confusion, it was postulated that light only traveled in straight lines, adding a rather insurmountable paradox to a universe obviously constructed from spheres in orbit.

This slightly enhanced, three dimensional model proved so inadequate that the hopes for space travel over long distances, which this new "breakthrough" was supposed to augment, confounded the problem beyond comprehension once again – so one limitation merely boxed in another. The new calculations revealed such useless information as a particular star existing at some point 1.2 billion light years away.

At this point, the Einsteinian calculations were revealed, approaching the concept from another angle, further confounding the realities of the day. Einstein proposed that by measuring light relative to space (that which you consider formlessness and void), it could be proven that space is indeed curved. Therefore, light must travel through a curved space. You may guess that the complexities of this theory were enormous, for the true nature of light is, indeed, a straight line. His theory upheld the ancient teachings of the "ethers" by demonstrating that what appeared to be empty space was, rather, a sea of magnetic forces that possessed the power to bend light through a curved "void."

This modern confirmation of ancient teachings was overshadowed by the implications regarding subquantum physics. The revelations of Einstein, as well as other eminent thinkers of the time, were pilfered by the government with the cooperation of science. The result? Hiroshima and Nagasaki – a classic example of reality, as defined by the altered-ego. What was missed at that critical and propitious moment would have provided a far better alternative than the wholesale annihilation of the innocent. Had the same effort been put forth in the teaching, given in its entirety, as was given to pursuing the bomb, a great solution to your national dilemma would have developed and an unprecedented communication with the Masters, through the Genius Frequency, on a national scale would have established peace in a karmic-free victory. Again, death was chosen over life.

But if you ask the question, "What does the nature of light and nuclear power have in common?" some interesting deductions may be revealed. The first generalization is that the splitting or fusing of the atom releases quantum energy packets producing the elemental properties of light and heat in one instantaneous expansion from subquantum atomic bonding to the speed of light in a timeless instant.

Now, let us reason with superlogic. If the so-called particles of a nucleus are in fact frequencies of SuperLight, then a fuller understanding of SuperLight may be realized. The theories of gravitational attraction fall apart when applied to the staggering numbers involved in the nuclear bonding process. It can never be answered nor understood in those terms. For matter, as it has been conceptualized on earth plane, does not exist. There is only energy and energy bundles, packets or nodal points which quantify into density as energy moves from infinite potential into finite dormancy and back again.

Energy potentia in a dormant or semi-dormant state gives the illusion of matter or mass. The energy of all creation is in fact LIGHT/light – that is, SuperLight and common light. All is LIGHT, super-holographically organized into patterns producing harmonics of itself in the form of electromagnetism and gravity. Together these produce the so-called curves of space. Space itself is electromagnetic/gravitic, causing light to turn in upon itself. This produces a finite dormancy, a space/time continuum, a suspended animation, if you will, that is temporarily entrapped in the dimension of matter/anti-matter as a dense thought-form, which you have come to perceive as "your world."

Now, beloved, contemplate this nuclear business again. What does this have to do with you? EVERYTHING! You are composed of atoms. Therefore, the same laws apply to you, and the ancient axiom, "Know Thyself," should begin to take on a new meaning. It would be wise to reject all limitations imposed upon you by the altered-ego, as it is dictated by the intellect and attending administrators who have elected, with your permission, to block your god-natures.

You contain the same awesome amounts of dormant Light that we have been speaking of – *You are ALL LIGHT!* As we proceed in our examination, apply this knowledge to YOURSELF. This knowledge and the genius inherent in you, is not the responsibility of your scientists, government, or church. It is your responsibility!

Now, as we have stated, the key to understanding Super-Light is in the mysterious and incomprehensible power of the bonding process, which creates the energy bundles or packets known to you as atoms. Much has been learned by your scientists since that tragic moment of conception, which eventually gave birth to the tree of death or anti-life. The primary reason we use this example is that most of your learning regarding this subject was severely hampered by the post-war trauma. The negative effects of this power technology of death was, to an extent, glorified, for it was given credit for producing a very tenuous illusion of peace. IT (war) was justified, beloved, to honor the death of innocence!

What remains to be seen and proven by you, not only your scientists, governments and religions, is: *THAT WHICH PRODUCES THE COMMON LIGHT OF YOUR SOLAR LOGOS IS THE SUPERLIGHT OF THE ONE CREATOR*. Again, beloved, remember that what is above is also below and what is outside is also inside.

Let us return to the fragmented teaching of Light – not of so-called ancient myth and folklore, for mankind has long been lost to those particular thought-forms, but of so-called facts revealed by scientific verification. The latter not only facilitates the "here and now" of contemporary word/memory syntax, but is the most effective means of feeding higher thought-forms into the mind-bodies via the intellect.

SUBQUANTUM PHYSICS

Let us explore now what has been termed subquantum physics. This branch of knowledge is designed by the altered-ego to exclude the general populace. However, subquantum physics is covered extensively in ancient teachings, which evokes the excitement and confidence in knowing that the TRUTH has not changed, nor shall it ever. It may, however, be rediscovered in the various fragmented thought-forms currently popular. Thus, all roads lead to The Source.

Subquantum physics is a fragmented, superficial mathematical rendering of the mysterious energy-bonding process containing vast amounts of power. We shall omit the tedious, complex mathematical extrapolations of the private language of science and continue to examine this subject, using terms now familiar to you as set forth in the preceding chapters of this book.

The nodal points comprising the membrane sphere of tension within the nucleus of an atom are actually bound by Super-Light. That is, the binding energy and the subquantum energy packets are composed of the same SuperLuminal forces, the same "glue" that binds all energy-forms, be it your sun or your bio-computer. The energy packets termed protons, neutrons, etc., are holographic resonant points of the pyramidal-energy-constructs of SuperLight.

Through conscious Intelligence and SuperLight, which is also consciousness, common light is polarized and suspended into subquantum energy packets through sacred geometries of sound. The result of this polarization is the superquantum electromagnetic field which provides the parameters of the "space" or mind for the electron to orbit, creating valencies, shells or spheres within spheres, which accept and "marry" other orbital shells of like vibration or of harmonic compliments forming in turn, molecules, which form variations upon that theme, i.e., your periodic chart.

SuperLight is the force of LOVE-LIGHT/GOD-MIND binding ALL matter worlds. It is the subquantum force of atomic and the superquantum force of universal coherency and integrity of creation. SuperLight is also the universal cosmic constant – a Divine Medium of free awareness, through which all so-called miracles manifest upon your plane. This is the Mind-Stuff of THE ONE and the Spectra Beings of Light Who step down this SuperLight to form matter-worlds. These Beings live and have their Beingness in this SuperLight, therefore, they have access to all domains and all dimensions of existence, simultaneously.

Reflect upon this. Contemplate it. For the Masters have explained this reality of Eternal Light through simple parables often laced with cryptic terms. Not because they were master myth builders, but rather, because they spoke to entities who had different word/memory complexes on many intelligence levels within differing historical moments.

But those days are gone. You may now rediscover these truths using your scientific mental processes, techniques and knowledge. However, this cannot be fully accomplished until your science of dogma is transformed into a Sacred Science of liberation for all who are in union with THE INFINITE ONE. The Masters taught of the Light within the darkness. Who among you earth-bound humans are arrogant enough to believe that these Masters were not teaching subquantum physics?

Every atom comprising your bio-computer is bound by the quantized frequencies of SuperLight, serving as an awareness that organizes the key programs of intelligent life forms upon matter-spheres, which act as electrons orbiting their nucleic suns in multi-colored spectrum systems of matter-creation and beyond.

Questioner: Then why is it such a deep mystery? Why is it so difficult to understand?

MaYaRa: The Mystery of which you speak has its depths in the fundamental nature of your physical existence upon a third dimensional plane. It is only your perception, intellect and language that has polarized SuperLight. For SuperLight permeates your beingness, and each of you has a total energy-body composed entirely of SuperLight – should you desire to resonate and I-dentify with it.

Throughout this book, we have made references to different types and levels of light, i.e., "light," "Light," and "SuperLight." We have deliberately avoided defining these differentiations in terminology for two reasons. The first is simply that the altered-ego is irritated by the unannounced changes in syntax. This subtly stirs an inner knowing to awaken. The second is that this "inner knowing" already knows what is being taught. Suffice it to say, there are different kinds, levels and dimensions of light. It is not in the scope of this work to define these levels in detail. However, we leave clues for you to contemplate. The most important thing to understand at this juncture is that there are different orders of light. The following are three major orders of light:

<u>light</u> = common, visible, _<u>Spectrum</u>_

<u>Light</u> = infrared, ultraviolet, invisible, _<u>Spectra</u>_

<u>SuperLight</u> = universal, multidimensional, _<u>Specter</u>_

In order to create material worlds, SuperLight must be converted, which results in SuperLight turning Itself inside out, so to speak. It is also "stepped down" in frequency through Spectra to Spectrum conversions that subquantify a Superquantum Intelligence Source. This is accomplished through the double pyramidal-energy-construct, causing double spirals of codified energy to spiral into polarities of matter/antimatter as SuperLight is reduced to common light, which is gravitationally trapped into a vortex of space/time that you experience as physical life. Without this process, there would be no universe or no creation as you know it. Divide the Light and it will "fall."

Questioner: If there are so many other dimensions of Intelligence, and we have originated in those dimensions, then why is this process (our life experience) necessary?

MaYaRa: In the dimensions of the SuperLight, there is infinite life organized within many dimensional universes, each glorious and perfect unto itself.

However, there is no need to minimize the matter worlds. To do so is a limitation of the Creative Spirit of THE ONE. It is also a limitation constructed by the altered-ego which occupies only the perishable boundaries of entropy and anti-matter. Using your higher logic, it does not seem so preposterous to presume the existence of many matter worlds, which have achieved a splendid and ideal expression of THE ONE. It is not wise to generalize the current predicament of your earth body with the whole of third-dimensional universes.

There is no need to recapitulate the intent of the lower intelligences who have elected to isolate your particular experimental quadrant of the immediate galaxy. They are temporarily enjoying the ability to manipulate others into worshipping them, their thought-forms and emotions. They assist in supplying the "proofs" used to lock the intellect in a limited frequency range that resonates primarily with your yellow, single sun system and an extreme few of the lower, "constellations." These limited systems, when isolated from the source of SuperLight, suffer the extremely limited latitudes of energy thresholds in the orbit-cycles indigenous to these types of sun systems. Know this, beloved: that your earth shall not remain locked within these extreme cycles much longer. A new place is being prepared even as your Great Book states: "There shall be a new *heavens*"– PLURAL – and "a new earth!"

Most importantly, recognize the uniqueness of the earth station. Only through embodiment of the flesh, tempered by trial, error and ultimate victory, may the soul advance as a complete individuality in unification with THE ONE in the worlds of splendor as a Co-Creator with THE ONE in the infinite creations of Light! Do not be distracted by the other, lesser experiments upon your plane. These exist for you to learn and to remember, so you do not make those mistakes when again your moment arrives to create life-forms, planets and sun systems. We shall move now from this splendid digression to our examination of SuperLight. We did not intend to shift focus here. However, we sensed the embers of fatalism smoldering beneath the query.

Now, you may equate SuperLight with SuperQuantum energy packets that bind all atomic and therefore all matter as building blocks of light. The final shape of the thought-form as common light-matter-form manifests as specific polarized magnetic and graviton fields of a given planetary solar system. Part of these magnetic and graviton fields form negative mass and serve as a reversal of the blueprint or the mold into which atomic matter is assembled into physical dimensions.

Questioner: Does SuperLight exist as positive mass or as negative mass?

MaYaRa: Neither. For this reason it is so important to grasp the Law of One. For that is the Law of SuperLight. From SuperLight, all negative mass and common light issue forth. Therefore, Super-Light, the Light of THE ONE, is beyond all polarities. It is omniscient and omnipresent, and sustains ALL matter and anti-matter through the frequency of LIGHT-LOVE/GOD-MIND. But it is not dependent upon the fluctuations of centropy and entropy. It IS, always was and ever shall be, just as the Masters have taught for 'er so long.

Perhaps you can understand, now, that there is NO opposite to THE ONE. It is the fondest hope of the fallen ones and the largest hoax ever perpetrated upon mankind, that there is a force that is equal and opposite to THE ONE. This crippling illusion is the "abomination and desolation,"as stated in your great book of codes. It is the analogue of a false hierarchy.

Questioner: Then negative mass does not have the "negative" connotation that has been attributed to it through common language.

MaYaRa: Absolutely correct, beloved. Without the creation of negative mass, SuperLight cannot translate into three dimensional matter.

You may say that the universes of negative mass are the "lower heavens." They are simply the next dimension or fourth dimension of creation. Generally, the masses witness this dimension only after the death of the physical body. Many have witnessed this dimension while transcending the physical bio-computer and have returned with beautiful as well as horrifying news. What they report is their own minds.

For this reason, there is much confusion upon your plane of awareness regarding the so-called spirits and the overall environment there. The reason for this is that few are able to move beyond the threshold of the fourth dimension into the fifth dimension where the threshold of infinite peace and joy reign supreme as a great ark upon the galactic, crystalline sea of SuperLight, which the prophets of revelation have tried to describe to you. Perhaps we should clarify this point further.

THE FOURTH DIMENSION

The fourth dimension is a mirror image of your earth plane. It is the astral body of the earth and all life upon it, faithful in every detail, to the last atom, only on a much larger scale and a much faster time-frame of existence. Thus, every life-form/thought-form has its counterpart, its mirror image in the astral realm or fourth dimension. Therefore, good and evil, as you know it, exists there as well as a product of free will for the purpose of teach/learning the responsibilities of co-creation.

This also explains the ancient stories describing various cosmic wars. For when the Masters entered the astral body of earth, vibrating in the frequency of SuperLight, they "cast down" lower frequency thought-form entities who elected to block direct passage from earth plane into higher dimensions, through the fourth dimension or astral dimension because they took refuge there. It may interest you to know that this is occurring even NOW according to the prophesies from the Masters of Light.

Further, it may interest you to note that, for the above reasons, physical death of the bio-computer and release of the remaining individual energy fields into the astral world does not guarantee salvation, as many a false prophet, guru and self-appointed priest has claimed. One must master life in a flesh embodiment before one can master the fourth dimension to access the fifth. The reason for this is that in the fourth dimension one experiences the instant manifestation of thought-forms and the instantaneous attraction to similar thought-forms that attach themselves to each other. Thus, it becomes clear as to why endless incarnations ensue. For an entity quickly discovers that it is easier to work out destructive tendencies in the slow motion world of flesh. The Masters have correctly taught you that life in the third dimension, when properly conducted, will resonate a Light-Body formed entirely of the Genius Frequency. Then the Gates to the "Higher Heavens" of the fifth dimension shall be opened without fail – where a "peace which passeth all human understanding" shall prevail eternally.

Therefore, each of you is composed of a body of Super-Light which remains dormant until the proper steps are taken to ignite the resonance needed to bind it to the individual soul experience. Yet the collective image and similitude of the archetypal blueprint of your true origins exists as a living intelligence entity emanating from the realms of SuperLight.

Contemplate this, beloved: the Light within the darkness equates to the Tree of Life within the sea of negative mass. Super-Light is the missing capstone from your third dimensional pyramid. SuperLight cannot be forced upon you. The gates to forever are opened by your free choice, desire and intent to participate as a co-creator of Life in the forever ongoingness of the Infinite Plan to serve all creations of THE ONE.

The illusion perpetrated by these entities who block the gates is one of darkness, void, death, karma and return. Their lower logic says: "There is darkness which you cannot perceive; in that darkness is the end; when you close your eyes for the last, time you cease to exist for there is nothing in darkness that is of life." But you see, beloved, the universe could not exist in such a fragmented and partial equation.

Perhaps this understanding taxes your intellect and you feel despair at ever knowing the truth of creation. However, if you analyze this inertia of the intellect you find that it is only the altered-ego, a fragmented intelligence, that falters in the attempt. For the altered-ego is composed of limited and partial equations of life functions that factor into a spiral of entropy and a denial of the true heritage of eternal life.

Denial of the eternal nature of creation is the value judgment based on the perceived mechanical nature of matter worlds. It is simply a limited program designed to stop you from reaching your goal of freedom – a freedom that propels you out of the control of the lower intelligences who seek to maintain control of their minute portion of creation.

Think. This is the long and the short of it: To deny the infinite Life sustaining work of THE ONE is to terminate the resonance with the SuperLight of the Genius Frequency. It is so profound, yet so subtle. To be trapped into thought-forms that embody the vibration of "denial of life" is only to deny your own ongoing life. You will do well to remember always that every thought-form IS a frequency. Therefore, thought-forms of denial and hatred are asynchronous resonances which play out in the material worlds as annihilation.

SuperLight **IS** the binding force behind, within, and beyond all manifestation in all dimensional universes. It is a frequency of structured intelligence within free awareness that supports all thought-forms of creation. ITS frequency is that of LIGHT-LOVE/ GOD-MIND. SuperLight, through the sacred and universal geometries of the Pyramidal-Energy-Construct, can communicate through all dimensions continuously and simultaneously, providing the moments of contact directly with Light Beings working directly with THE ONE.

There is a hierarchy of creation due to the "step down" functions that must be implemented in order for the matter worlds to exist and evolve. Generally, throughout the lower realms of this hierarchy – i.e., the outer lip of your galaxy – there exists the choice of synchrosimilarity or asynchrosimilarity. These are not opposites. Meaning, in your terms, that you may choose to serve the self in the final statement of the death scenario or you may elect to serve others in the final scenario of ongoing life in the many dimensions.

Listen, beloved: You may use any term that suits your fancy, but the TRUTH shall exist unmolested, forever. Service to others and SuperLight are synchrosimilar frequencies. That is, you, as a third dimensional being, cannot quite transform your five mind/bodies into the SuperLight frequency. But you can resonate with SuperLight and open the channels and gates to the Genius Frequency, eventually being absorbed into it and becoming one with it.

How could the universe be sustained and the evolution of consciousness into Co-Creation be accomplished if the asynchro similar frequencies of service to self were used by all? If THE ONE served only THE ONE, the universes would instantly vaporize into nonexistence. The fact remains, beloved: THE ONE has created all life by serving that creation with the LOVE-LIGHT/ GOD-MIND of the SuperLight of ITS Being. To live and act in any manner unlike or without that Image and Similitude of THE ONE is simply to program annihilation. This holds true for every Co-Creator!

Contemplate this statement, beloved, whenever you become weary in the learning process of the higher sciences of Light. For the Great Master Jesus, revealed a profound teaching to open the same Gate to forever for all entities. You are the Original Ones, the Adamic Man, sent to seed the planet. HE came to give you the message that it was time to prepare to go home. Not a false samadhi of the fourth dimension, but of the true Co-Creation in the higher dimensions.

Without the understanding of the fundamental simplicity of HIS teaching, as reflected in the above statement, all the fragmented sciences of your world shall never bring you in resonance with SuperLight. For the higher Science, of which we speak, is a synchrosimilar vibration of truth, encompassing all religions, sciences and governments as one thought-form of SuperLight using the Genius Frequency as the access code for interdimensional communication.

Therefore, SuperLight serves all, is available to all and supports all. IT makes its appearances to mass consciousness on your plane in the form of great vehicles of Light which offer new program solutions into the earth in the NAME of THE ONE through the Genius Frequency. You may choose to resonate with it and benefit from the solutions on a personal and global scale, or you may choose to resonate with the lower, common light intelligences who compound the problems of life with the limitations of the altered-ego through its inherent destructive thought-form energies. It is always your choice.

SuperLight is locked in every atom as a function of the binding force and the potentiator of transformation into higher dimensions. Therefore, you are filled with it, as is every molecule and atom. SuperLight manifestations of Intelligent Beings will reveal themselves to you if you have worked to free yourselves from the death-grip of the altered-ego and thus free yourselves from the fear to go deeply into the seeming darkness of yourself to encounter the Light of the Genius Frequency. You must develop the discrimination to avoid thought-forms of self-serving death scenarios. For you may only resonate with SuperLight and manifest the results of the Genius Frequency if you can awaken the synchrosimilar thought-forms that resonate with THE ONE in the totality of your beingness. That is, you must go beyond the strictly intellectual functions of linear reasoning and use your entire bio-computer, not just your brain center to think.

To resonate with SuperLight, all six major mind-centers or chakras must be unified and unblocked so that the entire organism can serve as a bio-transducer and Divine capacitor which will expand the auric membrane to accommodate the relatively rarefied energy frequency of Genius.

Questioner: Are there any indications as to the early stages of SuperLight resonance and can you suggest any further exercises to enhance this process?

MaYaRa: In addition to the exercises already stated regarding contemplation/meditation, you may add the following:

> *Begin by directing your awareness to the lower extremities of the feet and legs. Isolate them in your feeling mind and pay attention first to any sensations, being careful not to judge them as good or bad, for if you do, the altered-ego will generate a complicated series of memory/complexes that will sidetrack your faculty for pure, free awareness. This applies to all the following areas of the bio-computer.*

> *Carefully and methodically move your awareness inch by inch upward, dwelling upon each mind-center or chakra for a period of time and move on.*

Each time that you contemplate a cycle, moving from the soles of the feet to the crown area of the skull, you begin again, increasing the speed of the cycle. Begin by using two complete cycles, that is from bottom to top and from top to bottom in a single breath. As you become more proficient you may double the awareness waves within each breath until you begin to feel waves of pure-awareness coursing through your bio-computer.

Take note of every nuance of energy transaction within your bio-computer from toe to crown, scanning and breathing until you sense the waves of Light, like a beacon or an ocean wave building from the center of the earth and breaking into a spray of Light at the shore of the skull's crown, continuing on into the center of your galaxy.

Again, there are as many combinations of the above described sensations as there are individuals experiencing them. The purpose of this exercise is to develop the necessary awareness sensitivity to subtle feedback signals indicating the initial resonance phase of SuperLight pouring into it. It is very important to note that these initial signals are subtle, yet very pleasant, ranging from a dim perception of the energy fields which surround you, which manifest as tingling sensations and slight quavers or rushes of energy in the musculature or any and all combinations of the above, to ecstatic revelations of connections with all creation and all life. Just become conscious of the Light that you are.

Perceptually, indications of initial contact with other dimensions may also manifest as lights moving in the peripheral field of vision and sudden shifts in orientation to dwelling places or resting surfaces, such that it may seem that the floors or walls seem to slip or move. You may also sense for a moment that you are falling or floating, or that you shift within yourself. Pay close attention to these phenomenon, beloved, for they happen more often than you normally allow yourself to be aware of.

It is also quite counterproductive to indulge in the distractions of the altered-ego, as it evokes limited rationale and judgments. That is, you may find yourself wasting a great deal of awareness energy trying to explain away various signals, such as a sudden and unexplainable gust of wind that sends you on a search to find an open window or door. You will minimize or extinguish your efforts by attempting to cram ultradimensional experiences into your third dimensional reasoning.

One general rule, however, is that all resonance with Super-Light is an uplifting experience. At no time, during a true experience, will the entity sense oppression, manipulation or a loss of vitality. Always, the entity feels more connected to all life and the ability to change a situation with the force of this Light. Thought-forms of a global magnitude shall suddenly seem possible. Solutions to perplexing problems will often reveal themselves without the entity having to ask, albeit in an indirect manner at first. Eventually, your power-point to truly live in the breath and scope of the eternal moment, transcending the cross of space/time into vast new possibilities of freedom and Co-Creation with Masters, will become a reality larger and grander than any you have ever dreamed. It is ALL there, inside you. Go within and find your peace.

We reiterate that this is not a "mind game." Your entire bio-computer is needed in this resonance process, since the blueprint for your entire beingness exists in the dimensions of Super-Light. Every atom of your being exists in the dimensions of Super-Light. Every atom of your being contains subquantum and super-quantum wave-length values. The sum of this atomic collection is greater than its parts, forming another body of SuperQuanta Light Packets beyond the parameters of the common light that you witness as third dimensional vehicles.

When these two dimensions of SuperLight merge, an ignition takes place wherein *you become the archetype of man in the individualized form*. All dimensions are accessible to this stage of energy beingness. Although, presently, it seems to you to be science fiction, the time is fast approaching when SuperLight will increase, according to your prophets, as the end or the **OMEGA POINT**, the end of a space/time cycle in your universe. You only need prepare yourself for the freedom of SuperLight through the Genius Frequency, your true inheritance. *But you must prepare!*

A DYING SUN

"THE ETERNAL LIGHT"

> "Through
> The Genius Frequency,
> you as co-creators are able to partake
> in this glorius plan to repair the life zones of
> third-dimentional creation."

Questioner: Can you explain in more detail the interrelationship between "common light" and "SuperLight"? Also, you have equated the sun in our solar system with this common light. Where does our local sun stand in relation to SuperLight?

MaYaRa: As you wish, we shall examine the nature of common light of your Solar Logos, which is so inextricably and intimately bound to the bio-chemistry and thought-forms of producing life on earth.

Let us define the term Solar Logos: Solar, obviously refers to your sun – a singular sun system, and Logos, which is the Living Word – a codified matrix of energy transmutation into a life/death, self-consuming point of awareness. The sun is an awareness transceiver just as you are, radiating energy frequencies as well as receiving electro-gravitational inputting.

The latter statement is particularly important in this understanding. For the definition of your sun is far more than an astrophysical description of a medium star that you happen to be locked in orbit. It is your Solar Logos. That is, an embodiment of the life/death attributes so stated, which define the physical transmutation of energy thought-forms that provide the infrastructure for chemical life transactions within its children – the children being the planets it supports. Thus, your Solar Logos is the prime programmer of your bio-computers, and jailer and warden of your souls in the relentless recycling of three dimensional karmic slavery. What dies in your sun, dies in you.

EVOLUTION AND DE-EVOLUTION

The attributes and functions of your sun's processes, whether scientifically or mythologically described, bear witness to the intimate workings of the cycle in which you are presently bound. Your sun, although a prime mover and life, giver is also a finite energy system of entropy and decay when cut off from the Source, SuperLight, which created it as a free entity. It was the so-called "fallen" lords of light, charged with the propriety of thought-form energy programming through the sun's radiant spectrum, which effectively severed the Higher Program that redeems and regenerates the sun. For in and of itself, the sun is a self-consuming entity, which eventually collapses upon itself into a decimal point forming a gate into another dimension. This cosmic "decimal point" can result in a positive or negative mass polarity, as evidenced by what is termed mini-white and mini-black holes.

What is true for your sun is also true for you. For each of you mimics the bio-chemical thought-forms produced by your Solar Logos, unless you take responsibility for your own self-perpetuation through resonating with SuperLight. You see, the original plan was designed to compensate for the entropy factors inherent in a single sun system on the lip of galactic creations.

The following is an overview of the general schema of creation of worlds: A sustaining sun system is created – usually more than one. At the proper moment of condensation of light, planets are consolidated into orbits according to predetermined sequences, environments and functions interrelated to the functioning of the whole. At the proper moment of planetary condensation, the blueprints for constructing the basic building blocks of life are projected into the chosen planetary environment, tailored to the harmonics of the chosen planet – in the case of earth, amino acids, etc. Actually, the planetary body chooses from cosmic DNA.

After the building blocks form a spectrum of self-perpetuating life forms, the root species of a planet are permitted to develop according to the predetermined laws of that particular Solar Logos – elemental, mineral, plant and animal kingdoms. Then, the Divine thought-form image of archetypal Adamic Man is projected into the planetary field where they manifest a physical form that, while resembling the already established root races, do not descend from their lineage. The purpose of this last phase is to provide the intelligent guidance by Masters who instruct and shepherd the root species until they can independently evolve consciousness in the name of THE ONE.

Thus, from the projection of Adamic Archetypal Man, a Seed-Being (Adam) is created from modified and perfected parts of the building blocks of the planet's kingdoms. These kingdoms were originally developed by the local creator-gods involved in the supervision of multiple species creation. Once this scenario is manifested, HU-man carries out the work sanctioned directly by

THE ONE, for the purpose of "redemption" or raising up of consciousness from a root specie to a co-creator status of Adamic Man.

Man's mission, then, in conjunction with the lords of light of a particular quadrant of the galaxy, was to establish a regenerating system of consciousness on the frequency of SuperLight, which would counter the effects of entropy inherent in third dimensional creations while raising the harmonics of light within the root species of a planet. It was at that point when the "fall" of Adamic Man occurred and the frequency of SuperLight was blocked through the influence of the rebellious lords of light.

Questioner: Why was SuperLight blocked?

MaYaRa: For the plan to be implemented, the lords of light would have to step aside, so to speak, surrendering "their" creation to the Adamic Lords – the forefathers of mankind – working directly with the Original Plan of THE ONE. These "fallen" lords of light rebelled, as they did not want to surrender control to a fledgling Master creation (Adamic Man) who would, in turn, raise even more masters from the root race creations of the original lords of light.

Thus, the fallen lords succeeded, temporarily, albeit millions of years in your time, by corrupting the somewhat naive creation of Adamic Man (Adam), rendering him to subservience to the "lower gods" of material creation. These lower gods promised, in return, the sovereign reign over kingdoms of the earth – which, of course, was already issued to them from THE ONE. The elemental intelligences kept certain functions of creations to themselves to maintain absolute control over their particular domains, knowing full well that the solar system would eventually die as it spiraled into entropy and death without the life support of SuperLight of THE ONE.

You see, beloved, rather than surrender to the plan of THE ONE, these lords of light chose the short-term power and control of their "personal" creation. They conspired to continue their reign by retaining control of all singular sun systems in varying stages of decay, thereby migrating from one dying sun to another in an attempt to remain one step ahead of death. The plan was instantly foiled and a quadrant of the galaxy sealed, denying access to the realms of splendor and joy until the necessary corrections were made.

Thus, lords of entropy, lords of death they became. They I-dentified with entropy, destruction, decay and death, for they had the freedom to choose. Perhaps now you may realize that entropy, decay of matter, is not evil in and of itself, for it is a natural function of third dimensional creation. The turning point then, is in the I-dentification process of free will or the Law of Confusion. When you I-dentify with death, you are a significator, participant and representative serving those who personify this limited third dimensional function of decay.

What happens when SuperLight is blocked from a third dimensional solar system is this: Not only is the rejuvenating energy of eternal life cut off from the sun's life cycle, but the life forms upon planets acting as receptors of the sun's energy intelligence must emulate the emanations of the parent logos. That is, all species creation upon the designated experimental planet must suffer the cyclic spiraling into negative mass and back again into elemental mass. This is due to the constant radiations which pour into the planet from its parent sun or solar logos. These life-giving/deadly radiations pour forth their birth/death, black/white, food-chain-mentality of survival that occupies the mind forming the altered-ego.

Soon your scientists will develop means to calculate radiation in terms of frequency, rather than particle collision. This revelation shall indicate a seemingly irreversible degeneration, a de-evolution which has spanned some 2.5 billion years in your time. This staggering revelation will mandate a new paradigm of life: That the sun may indeed continue to "burn" for some millions of years, but its ability to support life as you know it is approximately thirty years more!

The action of solar flares and sunspots in relation to atomic frequencies will open a new understanding of the true nature of thermodynamics and hydrodynamics, through which graviton radiations function. Suffice it to say that the destructive wave emissions from your sun have increased dramatically to their most dangerous levels. This action is directly reflected in the many plagues, diseases, wars, and planetary upheavals steadily increasing in the past 6,000 years, and at greater frequencies in the last 200 than ever before.

Many calculations have indicated a dramatic increase of ultraviolet radiation pouring into earth and much of this has been misconstrued to be a result of the depleted ozone layer in the lower astral body of earth. This appalling destruction, notwithstanding, the ozone layer, in the best of conditions, could not adequately screen the quantum increases in the solar destruction upon body earth. Moreover, unseen and, at present, unmeasurable quantities of anti-matter frequencies are contributing to the breaking down of DNA helix bonds which are manifesting destruction of the biological immune systems on cellular levels that have matching frequency harmonics: As the hydrogen bonds of nucleotides disintegrate, all cellular activity that remains in the lower frequencies must also disintegrate.

Those upon earth who erupt in acts of violence and destruction are those who unwittingly and consciously I-dentify with the destructive, self-consuming entropy of the parent logos. For they act as the mirrors for the reflections of the tides and storms of a disintegrating luminary. Thus, the chemistry of the bio-computer and its chemical constituency mimic the sun. As the frequencies change, the harmonics forming the chemistry change. Therefore, if one I-dentifies with the common light of the sun and its food-chain-mentality, one must suffer, by resonance factors, the disintegration of cellular integrity. The sudden eruption of individuals, with or without an unstable personal history, to commit heinous acts of violence and destruction are the most direct evidence of resonance with solar death.

So we see here, that your parent logos has been effectively cut off from the quantum regeneration of SuperLight by the lords of light who covet their creation despite its temporality. Since your sun is your primary central intelligence or collective mind of the solar system, the self-consuming phase of the solar logos is broadcast as thought-forms of destruction through energy waves pulsing through three dimensional frequencies of common light. This common light frequency is what establishes and powers the altered-ego in the human entrapment of consciousness. It develops and maintains philosophies of survival, manipulation and dominance via the ever-present threat of death and slavery. It is for the above reasons that the program, termed "redemption," is now operative on a mass consciousness level of understanding.

These are some of the reasons for the many pyramid structures built within and upon your planet. Thus, the Masters of Light working with the redemptive plan of THE ONE built the pyramids as cosmic antennas and transmitting devices designed to bypass the solar logos and tap the vital SuperLight indirectly. These devices were a temporary fix that injected precious Life Force into the earth body, so that the species would continue to receive the frequencies of Light necessary for release from the powerful, recurring cycles of entropy of that type of solar system.

Thus, the pyramids, among other functions, store charges of SuperLight in the crystalline interior of earth. In this manner, enough high frequency Light could be stored for use in consciousness evolution, albeit on a much smaller scale than can be produced when the solar logos is directly receiving the charge. So, with the parent not cooperating, the children must take up the work to keep earth from decay and destruction. The work became very difficult indeed, as you can see by the state of human affairs. Without this life giving SuperLight that the Masters of Light maintain, the earth would have perished long ago. It was the interception and manipulation of the sun's energy transmissions that caused the Original plan of THE ONE to be changed, and emergency steps to re-balance the systems were implemented.

Originally, your solar logos energy fields broadcasted and embodied archetypal resonance patterns on the Genius Frequency of SuperLight, giving the communications link to the third dimensional bio-computers manifested by the Adamic Projections into the planet's bio-system. However, the archetypal energy projections were tampered with and altered so that I-dentification with the powers of the solar logos wrought destruction. Thus, the need to bypass the solar energies and tune your transceiver mechanisms directly to the subtle, yet far more powerful SuperLight frequencies, is paramount to regaining your freedom. You cannot depend upon the great amplification station (your sun) to feed and channel the frequencies of SuperLight of Love-Light/God-Mind in true tele-thought communication with THE ONE.

Recently, societies of the earth have been given keys to great scientific understandings to compensate for the deterioration of the solar frequencies, so that the human children of Light could overcome the negative drag that propels life-forms upon your plane into negative spirals of recurring entropy. These gifts to humanity were seized by the scientific community and billed as "breakthroughs," and have been used instead to glorify various orders of corporate/scientific/governmental "high-priests" within the human kingdom. The foundation of this distortion of the altered-ego is the theory of evolution, which conveniently tracks the linear development of humans from the animal kingdom. Worse, these breakthroughs – in thinking patterns – have been used to attempt to prove that some humans were superior to others; thus, the bondage of the solar paradigm was renewed, merely transferred, from religious dogma and barbarism to scientific /military dogma and barbarism. It was those who resonated with the destructive principles of the sun that used this new wave of intelligence to produce the atom bomb that functions on the basis of solar destruction. This game has gone on for millenium, beloved.

You see, scientific keys to understanding have been given to many civilizations so that they could escape the tyranny of destructive thought-forms and energy harmonics issuing from the dying sun. Civilizations that have risen to much greater heights of power and intelligence than your own have also "fallen" due to the "temptations" or dominant thought-forms issuing from the parent logos – sun-god. Thought-forms of war and death issue from the solar logos and are mirrored on the earth – as warring and death by self-consumption.

Since the last phase of the Omega Point is upon you, these and other teachings are simultaneously being re-revealed to individuals, as well as scientific, religious and governmental groups upon earth. From this wave of SuperLight pouring into earth, at this time, the global communications network has exploded into more unified mass-consciousness. Soon you shall see even greater signs of this wisdom revealed directly from higher dimensions of Light as a mass revelation uniting the recognition of the coming changes that will bring those of like mind and heart into the SuperLight of the new world and new suns.

The previous scenarios of ancient civilizations, which shall be revealed in great detail as the records surface upon the earth, will reveal the reality of this grand cycle that is concluding now, in your time. The helping hand, as prophesied, is taking control of the destiny of the solar logos for the benefit of all life-forms now trapped within its jurisdiction. Those who choose the way of THE ONE shall be liberated into the original program of eternal Light.

The implementation of this program is being accelerated in geometric proportions due to the tremendously destructive frequencies emitted by the sun at this critical stage of its ability to support the subtle life-forms supporting higher consciousness. Your civilization, by and large, is using the new mind patterns of thought-forms to amplify rather than to counter the above mentioned effects of the sun's grip upon the planetary mind. Such catastrophic destruction of the earth body is now accelerated beyond what damage the sun may cause. You see, your third dimensional scientific war machine is aiding and abetting – actually mirroring – the destructive onslaught of your sun. There is little choice for the Masters of Light than to take rather drastic measures to heal and correct it. They need your help in this matter. They cannot save you from yourselves. They can only save the foundation of planetary life.

Many speak of healing the earth. Now we speak of healing the sun, indeed, the entire solar system. How is that accomplished? How is a solar system repaired? The details of this are to be revealed at a later time, in your time. Suffice it to say that healing any sun or planet is based upon the simple fact that anything intelligent that can transmit thought-forms can also receive them. Therefore, you can resonate with the SuperLight of eternal life and transmit thought-forms of SuperLight to the sun or any creation. That is your right and duty as a co-creator.

If you have trouble accepting this reasoning, realize that the altered-ego is shutting down the higher dimensions of your innate intelligence. The altered-ego inherently knows that within its third dimensional domain, it cannot repair a sun, a planet or even itself. Yet it displays boastful pride in manipulating the balance of nature out of balance. It wallows in its so-called accomplishments, which were originally given as gifts unto mankind by Masters, only to have those gifts maligned into partial equations of a death technology.

Do you suppose that this death technology can heal the earth? We draw your attention to these points so that you may realize that the repair, or what you term redemption, is already taking place on all levels of all dimensions in your local universe. Hear this message that you may align yourselves with the Divine Forces of SuperLight, that you may consciously be a healer of planets, solar systems and universes, and that you may reap the benefits of your own repairing and healing as co-creators in the ongoing triumph over entropy and death.

Hear this message and know that you are not alone, faced with an overwhelming task. Align the sextant of your Heart of Hearts with the coordinates of SuperLight pouring into earth from dimensions beyond that of the common light of your sun which provides the seemingly endless cycles of rebirth and death spiraling into negative mass as it winds down into ever greater magnetic bondage.

As we have described previously, you are not blinded, as it were, by veils of darkness. Your perceptions are distorted and obscured by the illusions of veils of common light: That is, of the common light of your solar logos based upon the primitive radiations of fission and fusion. There is LIGHT BEYOND light operating on frequencies far higher than that of your common light spectrum.

Through the Genius Frequency, you as co-creators are able to partake in this glorious plan to repair the life zones of third dimensional creation, in order that the higher frequencies of Super-Light may be quickened upon earth to heal not only life on earth but the solar system as a whole.

It is important to realize that life on earth mirrors the conditions of the parent logos when the awareness of the residing lifeforms cannot develop consciousness beyond that of the local intelligent-awareness. As your sun consumes itself, so do you. As your sun sinks deeper into energy debt, so do you. As you sun radiates deadly nuclear explosions that rip apart its body, so do you. The bondage of earth life-forms to solar processes and thought-forms are so interconnected that the altered-ego believes this to be the work of its own doing, as well as a universal scenario.

Yet this bondage is only a bio-chemically-based, third dimensional awareness. Therefore, all chemical groups in a given planetary ecosystem are composed of similar awareness-consciousness frequencies. It is fruitless, then, to attempt to manipulate third dimensional chemistry. It is the coherent field of SuperLight that heals and transforms common light chemistries into higher Light Chemistries. The integrity of all creation, whether it be a cell or a planet or a star, is dependent upon the sustenance of Super-Light. It is not dependent upon the chemical mutations that mankind believes will cure all ills. Those are the very codes that form the chemical constituents of all third dimensional creations that are spiraling into entropy. Introducing more of the same can hardly be termed healing or progress. Without the higher dimension of consciousness introduced into a solar system such as yours, every single chemical transaction is controlled by the sun. All is cured through Light frequencies.

In every Heart of Hearts there exists the Seed Atom. The LIGHT of that Seed Atom burns far brighter than the common light of your sun. It is the ultimate gift and it is powered by Super-Light. Therefore, each of you has the power to begin resonating with that frequency that draws upon unlimited power to heal. Yes, even the universe! We do not ask that anyone should believe this message. We only ask that you contemplate these concepts in your Heart of Hearts so that the truth shall be personally revealed to you. For it is our wish that when it is, you are sufficiently prepared to begin your true work in Light.

SuperLight is free from third dimensional chemical, gravitational, cyclical and other polarized, self-consuming factors of entropy. Therefore, SuperLight Beings are free from all bondage to three dimensional luminaries. This is also your heritage that you come back to remember time and again. You return because you must free yourself by reversing the manner in which you enslaved yourselves. The Masters of Light, working with the redemptive plan of THE ONE, are ever ready to help those who choose to work with the Light across the threshold of death into the "new heavens and new earth" – and a new sun. You do not have to die before this becomes a reality. You may do it now.

Until you change your third dimensional biochemistry through transformational thought-forms of SuperLight, you shall remain in the magnetic bondage of common light to experience solar disintegration. Although much of this important work is accomplished in the sleep cycle, without direct interference with the sun's chemistry, it is easily undone as you burn and consume yourselves during the day.

Perhaps you have wondered at this, too obvious, cycle of day and night recapitulating a birth/death cycle within a half-life of 12 segmented moments in time. Understand that in dimensions of SuperLight, day and night do not exist; dualities do not exist; entropy does not exist. Only infinite dimensions exist as a plurality in perfect unity with THE ONE.

Your temporal bondage to the solar logos is so obvious and so repetitive that it escapes detection. Your third dimensional chemical bodies are active during the interaction of the sun's actions and processes, and seemingly inactive during its absence. Moreover, if you try to remain in the so-called waking state for more than a few cycles (days), profound consequences to the body are the result. Without a recharge of SuperLight, the cells of the body, patterned after the solar system, must reflect the parent sun's self-consuming nature. Every solar upheaval is reflected in each cell; therefore, each cell suffers disintegration. Contemplate this.

During the sleep cycle your bio-chemical, as well as other energy bodies, are rejuvenated by SuperLight, without which you would quickly perish. It would be wise, then, to engage in more conscious sleep work. That is, remembering and keeping an account of your dreams, as well as contemplating a high frequency thought-form, without losing focus, up to the moment of sleep state transition. This takes great discipline and the rewards are also great. "Normally" as you awake, the veils of light descend. The frequencies of SuperLight are instantly restricted and filtered, leaving a conscious awareness of only the common light frequencies. Thus, the above exercises are invaluable in maintaining a higher degree of SuperLight influences during waking moments. Focus on the transition between dimensions.

Questioner: Can you explain in more detail how contemplations and dream-work can help in raising conscious awareness of Super-Light?

MaYaRa: By consciously holding a high frequency thought-form as you expand into sleep, slipping through the veils of consciousness limitation, the encoded thought-form matrix becomes the access code that opens certain pathways of intelligence in the fourth dimension, which is usually the dimension one operates in during the sleep cycle. As always, in the fourth dimension, each thought-form instantly creates a reality and can also instantly change as the thought-form changes. The access code or thought-form that you are last aware of before shifting into sleep is the triggering mechanism that determines what subject matter and experience you will have in the fourth dimension.

For the vast majority, what is considered waking consciousness is physical awareness and, strictly speaking, is not actually consciousness as we have defined the term. That is, you acknowledge only what the physical senses report through the first three chakras or mind-centers.

Thus, by connecting a high frequency thought-form at the moment of sleep transition or at the crossroads of consciousness, a resonant coupling is ignited, momentarily unifying the causative and reactive modes of consciousness. Each night that you succeed in this type of resonance, a truly waking moment is created that connects waking awareness with sleeping consciousness. The result is that when you awake, you pass into the veils of light with some connection with the previous state of consciousness. Each increment becomes a permanent addition to your overall conscious-awareness state of being until a critical mass triggers a truly waking experience, never to be forgotten. During daylight hours, in your time, resonance with the Genius Frequency is enhanced and strengthened so that your physical body will begin to remember its true origins, even in the midst of distractions of solar onslaughts that presently restricts consciousness in your waking cycle.

As a capacitor/transducer, the mind-center mem-"brains" expand and store quantum charges of SuperLight, which will begin to override the need to absorb and therefore partake in the lower, destructive light emanations of your solar logos. It is then that you can consciously begin to I-dentify with higher orders of intelligence beyond what the senses perceive as common light sensations. Therefore, SuperLight, at the critical moment, transforms the bio-computer into electromagnetic reality structures, raising the resonance of the body to Genius Frequency, even in the thick of the illusory veils of common light interference.

Questioner: Please explain the reasons for sun worshipping, in regards to the Egyptian and other civilizations.

MaYaRa: There are two distinctly different variations upon this theme. Regarding the Egyptians, in those times when the Masters of Light descended upon earth in vehicles of Light technology, their mission was to first re-awaken the consciousness-awareness of the connection with local creation and second, to re-awaken the connection with the many universes under the LAW OF ONE.

As universal archetype of the similitude of the Adamic race in the image of THE ONE, the sun was the primary solar transducer/capacitor of that which sustained the Divine Image as well as the localized root races, including plant kingdoms of earth as modulated by the assisting planetary domains within the solar system. Therefore, the sun was an accurate representative and participant in the Divine Plan of transformation of root races into the hierarchy of creation guided by Adamic Man.

These teachings were animated and enforced by the sun's condensing powers that magnetized the embodiment of Super-Light. Thus, it was demonstrated through those teachings that the sun was a step-down transformer for SuperLight pulsations of THE ONE Who desires that all creatures ascend into the Light through the shepherding influences of the Adamic race, projected into the planet for that purpose.

However, the teaching was misconstrued to mean that the sun was the one power of creation to which all owed their allegiance and very being. This latter misconception provided a convenient tool consisting of partial life equations, enabling the false priests to subjugate the race life-forms. Thus, in this action, an altered-ego was taught and developed, based upon proofs that the root races must sacrifice their I-dentities to the self-consuming aspect of the lower spectrum emanations, with the promise that they would be reformed as a more powerful animal capable of eventual earth domination.

The second variation to this theme, regarding the times after the additional veils of light were lowered upon consciousness in the earth plane, produced a teaching whereby the sun's energy was used as a paradigm of consciousness-awareness meant to evolve an even dimmer awareness of certain plant-animal root races. For those fledgling entities, focus upon the lower spectrum awareness levels of the sun was appropriate as a introductory level focus for higher intelligence.

The teaching systems of RA never intended for the sun to be worshipped as THE ONE. Rather, various solar technologies were demonstrated by RA's ability to transform common light into energy machines that could be used as tools for the purposes of up-grading the overall environments of the root races so that they could make the transition from the common light programming of mere survival to the SuperLight functions of the Genius Frequency, whereby they could stand on their own, as it were, in terms of consciousness evolution.

Your sun's creative spectrum of thought-forms maintained a domain that encompassed only the mineral, plant and animal kingdoms. Originally, this did not include the Adamic Kingdom. As we have explained, the Adamic Creation was holographically projected into earth's biosphere. This Divine Creation adjusted to a most suitable form of earthly perfection. Thus, the "earth-suits" (three dimensional bodies) provided the ability for Adamic Light-Bodies to work directly with the root races or children of earth/sun. Thus, as Masters, they could assist the root races to eventually break the solar bonds, thereby giving them opportunity to form an overself through which they could ascend to co-create with the Masters. Perhaps, you can now understand more clearly why there was some rebellion among the entities who originally assisted in the creation of the solar system.

However, problems ensued when the Adamic projections mixed with the solar generated root races, thereby "falling" under the rule and dominion of solar intelligence. Understand, at this point, that the Adamic creation entered the food-chain-mentality as it became deeply entrenched in self-consuming bio-chemical thought-forms of the sun. For the above reasons, we have stated that you shall never find the bones or the "missing link" in earth strata. For you are the missing link projected into earth program æons ago, in your time. You were not originally a product of the earth.

Questioner: In the Biblical story of Adam and Eve, is the apple to be taken in a literal or a figurative sense?

MaYaRa: Both. In the literal meaning, the apple is earth. Eating that which is earth is to succumb to the food-chain-mentality of that solar dominated creation, thereby losing the freedom to move in and out of that dimension as a whole Light Being.

The reference to food explains that the Adamic creation was warned not to physically, chemically I-dentify with the solar creation, lest it suffer the bondage of self-consuming cycles of birth/death. In an esoteric perspective, since all solar/earth life is composed of those elements, any three dimensional life-form shall, on some level, consume itself in order to maintain continuity of that particular life-form. Understand that the original Adamic creation – before the "fall" – did not "eat of the earth" for they were sustained by absorbing and transmutating SuperLight directly from galactic sources, without the slightest need for elements of the earth. There fore, it was not only that Adamic creation "ate" something preceding the "fall," it was that Adamic Man/Woman I-dentified with the lords of light who promised to give them a kingdom that they were already given from on high. From that point, the decision was made to partake of the food-chain-mentality of the solar formula. The rest, as you term it, is "his-story."

Once thus entrained, the progeny of the Adamic Race increasingly succumbed to the life/death cycle of solar laws. Thus, you experience birth/death cycles again and again, even in sub-cycles of wake/sleep and the other countless polarized swings of the cyclic pendulum, decreasing from generation to generation.

Understand that the altered-ego is a solar dominated function of the three lower mind centers of the three dimensional body, and only occurs in single sun systems of common light frequencies – horizontal awareness. When the other five mind-centers are activated, the dependency of the bio-computer upon solar/earth sources of energy for food, etc., is gradually eliminated until one feeds directly from the infinite supplies of SuperLight.

The solar logos cannot produce a reflection of its chemical formulas in mother earth that are different from its inherent processes. Therefore, all children of the solar/earth union must bear the traits of the parents. That type of star, with which you have allowed yourselves to mentally and chemically bond or I-dentify, was only designed to bring forth a profusion of life-forms, recycling and recapitulating them until the Divine Seed could spiritually evolve and liberate them from their chemical-mental bondage to solar body/mind.

And lo! It is now you in need of liberation and redemption. Thus, the redemption program was altered for the purpose of reclaiming the Adamic Seed en masse at the end of the grand cycle of time or the Omega Point, which is finally upon you now, in your time. Thus, solar systems such as yours, existing only on the outer rim of a given galaxy, are partial life-equations requiring the remainder of the equation of SuperLight for continued evolution.

The chemical processes of your sun operate on a half-life function, decreasing with every breath. To create and maintain an eternal generation of life, SuperLight frequencies are periodically required to "wind up" the atomic clocks. The food-chain paradigm is a reflection of that half-life function, as it is incorporated in earth elements. For this reason, life upon planet earth must consume itself to achieve a semblance of ongoing life, although it must work within the parameters of half-life chemistry. Thus, even that which is reborn is, to a small degree, less alive than the preceding generation. When the half-life function is cut off from its eternal source, it can feed from nothing but itself. Therefore, all three dimensional life is de-evolving.

However, the original plan of Creation is far grander than what you have experienced in the past. In the grand scenario, a whole Light function of "time" creates a half-life function of "half-time" that unites to form a creation greater than the sum of its parts. Thus, "times and times and one half" is the result of the constant expansion of the universes of creation of new souls to share in the expanding glory.

Conversely, when SuperLight functions are cut off, there remains less than the original creation due to enthropic factors that lose consciousness on every round or cycle in the act of consuming itself. Thus, the cycle of birth/death/birth not only occurs on every level of three dimensional creation, but continues to spiral into negative mass to be recycled into a new creation plus whatever advances that may have been gained during its de-evolution.

Understand that the so-called negative, entropic functions of third dimensional creations are not inherently evil. For there has never been, nor shall there ever be, evil created by THE ONE. These entropic functions are inherent in third dimensional creations and what these systems lack is more than compensated for as the eternal life-equations of SuperLight intersect with them, reversing the factors of entropy and spiraling of said system into created dimensions of ongoing life/Light. Thus, you may perceive that your sun also needs SuperLight charges to counter its death.

The fact remains that each of you is a burning star, ignited by THE ONE and projected by an act of LOVE-LIGHT/ GOD-MIND into outer creations to shepherd new life forms into the Light. You were projected into the earth plane to open the centropic powers of SuperLight to the creations of solar/earth union. Once there, you foolishly allied yourselves with the temporary ruler of a transient system of third dimensional life-form at such a cost as to jeopardize your eternal I-dentities and I-dentify instead with a self-consuming, temporal entity – the sun.

Very soon, in your time, the power to even heal the sun shall be restored to those who choose to serve the original plan in the Light of eternal life. Through their own efforts, assisted by the Masters of Light, the Adamic Creation shall, once again, rise to claim its heritage among the stars of creation. If you think that this message is for fools and misguided poets, that is your choice. However, when the veils of light are lifted, in the not so distant future, in your time, all eyes shall behold a sight never before manifest upon earth. Those who have ignored the messages shall be overcome with fear and guilt. Those who have begun the work shall be overcome with joy at the sight, for they shall know beyond a shadow of doubt that their moment of liberation has finally come.

When you realize the power within you to govern the forces of nature through LOVE-LIGHT/GOD-MIND as you resonate in the Genius Frequency, the veils of common light are lifted causing a tremendous shift in molecular frequencies. One must prepare for this to occur. For with careful and dedicated preparation you shall not be overwhelmed and your body shall not explode or discorporate. You shall find yourselves in a body of Light and you shall embrace the Masters as your brothers and sisters in the Light of THE ONE.

But it begins with the physical bio-computer that you presently wear as a garment of common light. In other words, you may start now! Do not wait until you lose the physical vehicle. For if you cannot perform as a co-creator in the lower dimensions of light, how might you expect to perform these functions in higher dimensions? Think. Contemplate it. FEEL IT!

Contemplate what it would feel like to accomplish what the Masters have demonstrated over the æons. They demonstrated what would happen when you resonated with SuperLight while in a physical body, not after the death of the body. You were shown that cultivating LOVE-LIGHT/GOD-MIND results in power over death forever, including bio-chemical, solar death. Why would these Masters take their physical bodies with them if it were not needed or could not be used? To show off, perhaps?

Do not judge your chemical bio-computers as faulty accidents from the deep waters of happenstance survival. It is the bio-magnetic/chemical thought-forms of your sun that now control your three dimensional light garments of antiquity.

From where you rest this moment, feel the rushes of Super-Light frequencies coursing through your chemical matrix of form. SuperLight is a continuous, ever-present, inexhaustible source that throws open the gates to higher dimensions. But in order to effect the conversion to this frequency on a cellular level and in a conscious state, you must increase the capacity for the physical bio-computer to take a higher charge, a quantum charge, which will change the structural base of cellular programming from solar decay to the original Light-based structure that originally created the living cell or mem-brain.

The purpose intended in this segment of the document is to trace for you the origins of your chemical dependency. Although most of you do not consider yourselves sun worshippers, the effects remain as given. The decision was made long ago and is repeated even now as an echo of that auspicious moment when the veils of light descended upon the Adamic Lords. That moment is forever remembered, etched in the chemical echoes of transactions of information within the organic network of thought-form transference.

Your solar logos is neither to be feared nor hated. It is to be loved and respected for what it is: a life-giver to the mineral, plant and animal kingdoms that animate and adorn the earth with splendor and beauty. However, the solar logos is not your master, nor was it ever. Yet choosing to I-dentify with its powers, whether consciously, subconsciously or even chemically, will result in a partial life equation of entropy and decay unless transformed by the functions of SuperLight frequencies.

Consider the many references made to the sun when mankind gave birth to nuclear death technologies. The so-called breakthrough or discovery was merely due to a concerted effort to focus on the ultimate destruction through the altered-ego's allegiance and pact with self-consuming paradigms of solar awareness. The sun exists for you to use, not to imitate and I-dentify with.

The living intelligence of SuperLight forces are no longer embodied in the Solar Logos. Therefore, it is dying and shall soon be unable to support life as you know it. It would also be foolish to entertain the arrogant thought that you may someday beat the sun at its own game. The forces of the sun can only be corrected by SuperLight frequencies focused by beings who can direçt it.

Contemplate the awesome power of your sun. Now contemplate that which created it. Why settle for death? Oh yes, you come back again and again. But you die again and again; and each time, you die a fraction more as a half-life entity. With each incarnation, like the sun, a half-life function of partial life equations spirals you deeper into a point of negative mass where it is used as fuel for yet another third dimensional creation.

That is why you were projected into earth: to harvest the entire spectrum of earth life aboard the ark of SuperLight so that it may continue in another dimension of ongoing life. Life unto life unto life unto life forever. That is the plan. It is your choice, however, to I-dentify with the limitations of your solar logos. It has always been your choice.

Look beyond your solar system to the true Source of creation. Gaze into the crystal river of Life/Light and know there are stars like you. But they are not stars, as you know your sun. They do not feed from their own substance, nor do they consume the lives of other entities. They are beings, such as you are in your highest natures, existing as an eternal unfoldment of the ETERNAL ONE in Whose Being ALL have their existence. They exist as a sustained breath of THE ONE and assist in the distribution of the Word, which sparks never-ending majestic plumes of multi-colored splendor and magnificent life-pulses throughout æons and dimensions of infinite creation passing in and through each other sustaining holographs of living dreams.

These living dreams weave, in turn, other tapestries that stack one upon the other so there is that which descends into the infinite spectrum of adventure in service and experience, and there is that which ascends with all newly acquired and perfected vehicles of transformed matter, returning it to the eternal realms of bliss into an infinite co-creation with THE ONE.

Look upon your sun, your solar logos, and your solar system with compassion, for they are your comrades in creation and they eagerly await your transformation and liberation; for when you are ready, they are also. For you shall once again have the power to open the gates of SuperLight. Your long suffering sun a-waits rejuvenation and your mother earth awaits a desperately needed healing to alleviate her pain. Know that you may assist in this process as a co-creator if you so choose. If you take the time to develop and tune your bio-computers to the Genius Frequency, you will store the charge that will create a quantum shift in the very chemistry in your body.

You may begin NOW to reap the benefits in your life and those around you. Use your intellect to study and comprehend as much as you can. Yet know that that is only part of the process. Act as if you are a co-creator and the resonance with the Genius Frequency shall heal your body and open your sleepy eyes to the Light of lights.

Feed the high frequency thought-forms into the intellectual mind-centers and you may step through the doors of perception into the fourth dimension of mathematical and crystalline perfection. But do not stop there for you shall not open the doors to the fifth dimension without the Heart of Hearts, the star-seed within you. Take control of your intellect and apply it to matters of Super-Light. A resonance will begin throughout the cellular structure of the entire body, transforming knowledge into the Light of wisdom until the totality of your beingness feels it, hums and vibrates with it and reverberates with the music of the spheres. Then a profound change will be ignited, like a lightening bolt, that never stops and you will truly SEE for the first time in 'ere so long on your journey.

Beloved, with the help of the Masters of Light, the totality of you shall step into the fifth dimension. Then shall you realize that you are a Star of SuperLight shining in the brilliance that out-shines a million suns. You shall even possess the power of LOVE-LIGHT/GOD-MIND to create your own sun and solar system. Is this fantasy? Mad poetry, perhaps? Will you take the chance on what your altered-ego "knows" and give up your Light!!? It is your choice. Now go, if you choose, ***unchain your solar limitations and BE FREE!***

THE FIFTH DIMENSION
"REALMS OF SUPERLIGHT"

> *"When
> you practice
> Love, acquire Wisdom
> and resonate with SuperLight,
> the gates to the fifth dimension shall open."*

Questioner: I don't understand what is termed, the "fifth dimension." Could you clarify this confusion?

MaYaRa: We are pleased to be of service in this, our last, transmission of this document.

It is of the utmost importance to understand the consciousness parameters that define the unfolding of dimensional shells, as it were, into preceding levels of Light activity.

All that we have described has prepared a groundwork for fourth dimensional conceptual understanding. That is, we have endeavored to reorient and teach first, second and third dimensional understandings into the higher fourth dimensional codification of knowledge, which serves as your road map in negotiating your consciousness-awareness through the veils of common light frequencies separating you from the true experiential reality of living in the fifth dimension. However, before we attempt to define fifth dimensional reality, we must, once again, digress for the purpose of contrast and reference, to form a more comprehensive definition of the fourth dimension.

Understand first, that the fourth dimension of consciousness-awareness is an area of thought and thought processes. It is a dimension of thought-form blueprinting, existing as a high speed – faster than light – data link serving as the medium or template of consciousness-awareness holding key informational combinations of knowledge from the higher dimensions, as well as the lower ones. The fourth dimension is a buffer zone of consciousness programming, designed as a transitional area to augment a phase of consciousness evolution into higher dimensions of Light. It is the earths's library of thought-forms available to all her children.

The fourth dimension is a bridge connecting the third with the fifth. This is a critical point in the definition. Some of your energy bodies can exist there, but not all of them can. All of your energy bodies can exist in the fifth dimension. In other words, the *totality* of you cannot exist in any dimension below the fifth. Since only part of you returns again and again, you do not have direct access to memory functions between incarnations.

The fourth dimension is a mental arena. It is synonymous with the auric field or body of earth. Thus, it contains not only thought-form intelligence of a very high order, but it also contains the polluted and destructive thought-forms generated by the third dimensional consciousness-awareness of the human family. Due to its quantized functions, elemental intelligences operate there as programmers and keepers of the living blueprints for the elemental kingdoms of creation; governing the intricate workings and relationships of organic microcosms found in nature.

The elemental beings you term Devas, Fairies, Elves, etc., are an example of fourth dimensional entities. There are myriad other living intelligent beings inhabiting this domain that continually organize and maintain the integrity of the organs of your physical systems, as well as species integrity of the animal kingdom. The fourth dimension is the mind of the earth.

Questioner: What role do these elemental intelligences play in the organs of the body?

MaYaRa: Since the fourth dimension is a super high speed data-link sharing thought-forms between the third and fifth dimensions, it is an electrical medium through which all cellular organization can exchange information in cubic space. Although thought-forms are personified in the fourth dimension, we define them as fractional because they adhere to very strict laws of electromagnetic information transfer. This results in relatively impenetrable boundaries that define and separate organs, tissues and various organic functions, yet provides the continual communication necessary for them to work as a perfect whole.

Perhaps, there is some confusion in understanding where the fourth dimension is located. This is a limitation of the altered-ego that measures everything, including concepts, in terms of three dimensions. Understand that although we refer to the fourth dimension as the auric field of earth, it is not at all defined as, say, the stratosphere, etc. To one degree or another, all dimensions are nested within each other. Each atom, cell, molecule, solar system and galaxy exists in many dimensions simultaneously. You will save yourselves much confusion if you do not regard dimensions as "places." Rather, these might be comprehended as qualities, types, or frequency forming dimensions of existence.

An example of this nesting is in DNA. DNA exists as a matrix code within frequencies of light, sound, color, mathematics, geometry, quantum physics, chemistry, etc. Thus DNA is found in galactic proportions as well as atomic scales. Each is the same as the other as octaves of sound are the same. Each is nested within itself identically – only differing in scale. Each has all the attributes of life – yes, even a personality and an intelligence. DNA has a fourth dimensional aspect that is closest in frequency to third dimensional DNA. In other words, when fourth dimensional DNA crystallizes or condenses along its matrix of intelligent awareness, it appears in third dimensional reality.

Questioner: Would you further explain the statement concerning preconceived formulae?

MaYaRa: The fourth dimension is a vast repository of blueprints for third dimensional life. These blueprints pre-exist as templates for the continuity of species form and function as light, and are translated into chemical combinations in matter. The information pertaining to the functioning of three dimensional life is vast and free for the taking by the mind of man, as man's mind is essentially a fourth dimensional function. Although the mind of man has severely polluted this vast library of information with his own creations of destruction, there is actually nothing for man to create in that dimension. Mankind can be likened to a child playing upon his father's desk or with his mother's possessions. He plays with them, creating destruction inadvertently by his ignorance of the purpose of the system.

In general, excluding the periodic activities of the Masters visiting and teaching upon your plane, mankind has created virtually nothing in 36,000 years. Your scientific, technological society utilizes not a single original idea outside the fourth dimension. All inventions, bar none, have come directly from the fourth dimension, albeit in fragmented and broken forms.

Now these blueprints are living, intelligent entities, but they are blueprints just the same. In that sense, they are preconceived and act as computerized geometric programs. Since your bio-computers are living, three dimensional models of this living network of blueprints, it is relatively easy for mankind to resonate with them. The simple act of "day-dreaming" occurs in the fourth dimension. Yet, you actually do not create there. You only rearrange your "father's desk" to build little tanks and soldiers and dolls out of a higher system of thought.

Again, the fourth dimension is a vast library from which you may learn most readily of the processes of life on earth. Any idea you may have that results in inventions, works of art, arranging furniture, building space shuttles or designing nuclear bombs comes from this cosmic library. In the reverse, if you gaze upon any aspect of nature and discover something about it, you have merely observed a function and abstracted in the mental realm, which is the edge of the fourth dimension. Through resonant coupling, the mind sync-locks with the preconceived blueprint that structured the form and function of that nature in the first place. It is at this point that earthlings exclaim, "Ah-HA! I have discovered."

Now, you may ask why we should belabor this "hair-splitting" subject. It is so you might understand: You cannot evolve by manipulating what is learned only in the fourth dimension. You may browse through the library of fourth dimensional life for an eternity, but you will never discover the true Creator of those blueprints, unless you look beyond by looking within. Many are deceived into thinking that the fourth dimension is a place to inhabit with the astral body, like a playground for children. However, you shall waste much precious time there as the fourth dimension is not a causative arena. Like a library, you can learn things about third dimensional life, but you cannot inhabit it as your home with all of your energy bodies.

Also, there are other thought-forms personified by other entities who are false, corrupt and deceiving. In fact, the fourth dimension is where most astral bodies reside until another opportunity opens for them to solidify in earth. The reason is that the fourth dimension is a transitional dimension. If one has insufficient consciousness/Light to move through its gates, then one must return. Although one can learn many things while in that transitional state, the knowledge must be manifested in earth before release from the third and fourth dimensions are earned by the co-creator. One must earn wisdom through experience.

Without the fourth dimensional blueprints providing life-giving structural integrity of chemical laws, there would not be a single, repeatable experiment upon your planet. Indeed, there would not be a coherent awareness that could carry one out. All in all, the fourth dimension is one of abstract idea-constructs. It is a university of sorts from which you may earn a degree, but it is hardly an end in itself. For until you graduate as Master of those blueprints, life will be a continual repetition from idea-construct to material existence and back again within the solar domain.

The plan which you seek, one of ultimate freedom, is not to be found in fourth dimensional consciousness. The Plan is fifth dimensional. For the entropic functions are also built in to the fourth dimensional schema. What we communicate to you is that you have been searching in the wrong "places" for thousands of years in your time, ignoring the countless messages and teachings from the Masters who have come to help you. The Omega Point, marking the end of an ever diminishing physical cycle of time, a spiral into death, is built into the very fabric of fourth dimensional codification of material creation. Thus, even dis-"covering" the secrets to atomic power has yielded the same results – the same entropy – the same Omega Point.

What you shall dis-"cover" from fourth dimensional understanding is a precise blueprint of the operational nature of physical creation – how the system works in your dimension – so that you may perceive clearly where you stand in relation to the larger picture in reference to the time-clock of material creation. And the clock is ticking its last few seconds in your present mode of existence. It is not far in your counting. Soon after your 2,000 solar cycles, in your counting, the final days shall be upon you.

Questioner: Are present calculations correct in predicting the life cycle of the sun?

MaYaRa: There has been a gross miscalculation, not of the relative time that the sun can survive before it collapses or expands into a final phase of star-death, but of the time span during which the sun can support life as you know it. The phase of your sun that supports the delicate balance of life on earth has been waning for some two billion years in your counting. Although it may continue to burn for millions of years, its ability to support life as you know it is virtually finished. Its radiations are presently powerful and extremely unstable and destructive.

This destructive impulse, this entropic function is built into the blueprint of material creation - in the very atomic structure of the fourth dimension of negative mass. When you understand the workings of this dimension of negative mass, you will also understand the magnitude and the beauty of the Plan to overcome this spiral of death from which you shall be elevated, if you so choose, into a dimension of eternal Light beginning with the fifth dimension.

But you cannot begin to appreciate or fully understand the immensity of what you think you are creating in the third and fourth dimension without first understanding your present condition relative to the universal phases. Of what use would a grand plan of salvation be, such as the prophesies, the return of a Christ or the promise of a "new heavens and new earth," if your scientific projections of tens of millions of years of continued mechanical life spinning its merry, predictable way, awaiting a technology of death to solve all of life's problems were the only reality, the only hope.

Even your religious dogmas (in actual practice) do not go beyond fourth dimensional thinking. For this reason, all religious dogma is relegated to so many opinions, with no seeming foundation. This is precisely the argument used by material science to counter ancient knowledge and teachings. This is the strategy behind mythologizing the ancient documents of Light for the purpose of relegating them to the dusty shelves in dark corners of three dimensional earthly libraries to be chewed like so much cud by the poetical and philosophical cows of history. No, beloved, it is real, it is here, and it is now!

And for those who intuitively know that there is powerful, yes even scientific truth in those ancient documents, fear not. For these shall not lose their credibility despite the mutilated translations and falsifications suffered at the hands of the altered-ego. For many more ancient documents, unaltered by the dark forces of ignorance shall be revealed soon from the depths of the earth – some already have. Have faith and know that the Master Enoch has revealed the truth in the specialized language of science for all to study. And if you do not believe that message or this message, there shall be others and others still. They shall come from myriad places, entities and circumstances in the coming days of your physical/spiritual transition upon earth.

Let us contrast the first, second and third dimensional processes with the fourth and fifth for further depth of understanding. In terms of evolution: The first dimension encompasses the consolidation of light into sound geometries of matter. The second is that of motion of light/matter into a continuum of time. The third is that of a microcosm and macrocosm of form or reflections of consciousness within a vehicle, fully giving expression to the first two, thereby creating 3D animated life forms.

When the first three phases are accomplished, the third dimensional energy-vehicles or physical representations of creative consciousness re-discover the fourth dimensional blueprint, which served as the mold that structured the organization of life-forms from thought-forms, giving rise to ritual and "grass roots" religions. Thus, a third dimensional, scientifically-based civilization first will see these blueprints in the primordial "soup" as seemingly happenstance creations combining within cubic space. In fact, the patterns were already there, seeded.

Thus, while preconceived thought-forms are projected from the fourth dimension into the third, spontaneous life-forms or off-shoots are generated from the asymmetrical program structured by the Golden Mean values. These new life-forms are used for further experimentation, providing variation upon a central theme of consciousness programming into the Light. This explains why there are so many related life-forms which continue to baffle advocates of Darwinistic evolution and for which "missing links" shall never be found.

Thus, you are continually confounded by teachings that attempt to prove that all life-forms are created through happenstance occurrence, proceeding one from the other in an orderly linear progression of development. The gaping holes in the linear progression are glued together by the fabricated notion that "survival of the fittest" provides the continuity of life/death scenario with the "links" yet to be dis-covered.

What these teachings categorically deny is that there exists a preconceived blueprint of codified, living intelligent thought-forms that have seeded energy forms into other intelligence fields of earth and other worlds. There is no satisfactory explanation in science or religion that accounts for the incalculable power of DNA to replicate against such odds of any success of continuity of life on such minute, atomic levels. The point here is this: That until science and religion unite with the ancient scriptures of Light, NO progress can be made. The former contends that nothing is to be believed until it is proven and the latter contends that nothing can be proven until believed. **Yet *proving and believing are one and the same, since only the subjective reality of KNOWING and BEING are the final proofs of truth.***

In your recent history, the legendary Tower of Babel was technologically designed to force entry into the fifth dimension, due to the loss of consciousness and higher dimensional communication, after the corruptions of mind and heart. This was an attempt to regain the powers of co-creation by which earth entities could create and control life-forms. However, due to ulterior motives of those self-appointed authorities who sought to achieve ultimate control over the planet and all life upon it, the plan was foiled through scrambling the data linkage of the fourth dimension within human language structures - the effects of which exist in your present day. At that moment, the fourth dimension was changed from a bridge to a block to higher dimensions. Thus, fragments of knowledge could be ascertained, but the whole thought-form remained an enigma to human intellect.

Questioner: Even if the Babylonians succeeded in reaching the fifth dimension, they would not have received cooperation. Is this correct?

MaYaRa: We understand that your query reflects an assumption that all entities in the fifth dimension maintain Divine Linkage through the Genius Frequency to THE ONE and that those corrupted entities upon earth would not receive such assistance at any rate. Is this correct?

Questioner: Yes, that is correct.

MaYaRa: Understand that there are many dimensions in the realms of glory. We speak of the fifth dimension, not as the "be-all and end-all" of your evolution. Rather it is the next phase in the re-programming of the total being. The fourth dimension has been infiltrated by the fallen thought-forms and entities that embody such thought-forms. It is the astral pollution that must me cleansed.

The process of purging the fifth dimension is in progress through the efforts of those who rule in the higher realms of Light. Thus, to answer your query, understand that at the time of Babylon, a group of corrupted creator-gods existed in the fifth dimension who were more than willing to assist said entities upon earth through bizarre creation of mutilated and mutant creatures. You see, those creator-gods, led by Satanail, Semjaza, and a host of others, were banned from externalizing their beings directly on earth. It is for this reason that pacts or contracts were made with corrupted earth entities who I-dentified with these entities, receiving their short-lived power in return. For that is the only way in which they could carry out their plans upon earth.

Questioner: Why were these rebellious entities allowed to continue with this plan?

MaYaRa: Understand that all life-forms existing between them and the lower dimensions would be destroyed in the process of forcibly extricating, or in any way disturbing the intricate layers upon layers of life – that process is allowed only during an Omega Point.

Once a plan of creation is set in motion according to laws set forth for its governing, the plan must be carried out according to its original laws. The laws may be amended, but not rescinded. If this occurred any other way, all life would merely be a manipulation of the local Creator's will. Quite a boring prospect!

We can only explain that at certain moments in the grand cycles of the universe and through certain very precise methods can a "harvest" take place, without annihilating the innocent through forced entry of, say, ninth dimensional entities into fifth dimensional frequencies. In other words, if the higher dimensional entities would suddenly appear at the inappropriate moment, many layers of life would be needlessly destroyed.

THE ONE is so sensitive, so Loving, so in tune with every atom and molecule of creation, that jeopardizing even one form of life against its will for punishment of a few would not be within the scope of so perfect a Love. Knowing this, the corrupt few took advantage of that Love, by "buying" time, as it were, to persuade entities to I-dentify with their cause of power and self-serving control over others. But now, at long last, in your time, and but a heartbeat in the breath of the universe, the moment of truth has arrived.

All is in place. The timing is perfect for the recycling of all imperfect and corrupt thought-forms and for the long-awaited release into eternal SuperLight of captured ones, enslaved in the solar paradigm of endless incarnations. But this is yet another study. Our digression thus far has been to reach you on many levels of consciousness-awareness so that you might begin to remember your true heritage.

We shall continue to examine the nature of the fourth dimension without losing sight of our commitment to the theme of this last segment of the document. Suffice it to say that the fifth dimension cannot be described directly in the words of your linear language. It is like panning for gold. First one must sift through many pounds of particles of what is not gold in order to find the nuggets of your quest. Also, what is not gold can indicate how close you are to finding it. The gold in this analogy is the fifth dimension. To attempt to describe it necessitates continual reference to the totality of being. *The totality of being **IS** the fifth dimension.* It is not a place or time or state of mind. It is a state of being. It is a causative arena of thought where the powers of co-creation of a true Master begin. In the case of man, it is a return to a former state of being.

However, it is fairly impossible to use your language to articulate, in such an abstract sense of the intellect, such a total state of Light-Consciousness that needs no words to communicate the most profound realities of creation. Let us return to our sifting pan to understand the dimension that you are closest to in frequency at this juncture. That is, the fourth dimension. The fourth dimension is a threshold, a gate, a bridge connecting the dimensions of pure Light through dimensions of sound and light and on into the densities of material worlds. In other words, it is a grid of consciousness-awareness thought-form geometries that admits beings from lower dimensions into higher and higher into lower.

Through contemplation, astral projection or even death for that matter, to enter the fourth dimension is like re-entering the womb of time. Only the tunnel has an opening on both ends connecting the third dimension and the fifth dimension. Therefore, the fourth dimension cannot be considered the next step. For only a part of your consciousness-awareness can inhabit that dimension. It is a nether lands of abstract-idea-construct.

All out-of-body experience, astral travel, etc., takes place in the fourth dimension where space/time parameters become time/space parameters. Like photographic processes, it may be likened to a negative in four dimensions that holds thought-forms in patterns as light is projected through it to form an image upon the screen of earth. The fourth dimension is the last frontier, the last barrier to your freedom that you shall experience in the fifth dimension. It is the frontier of thought-forms.

The irony of this is that you are in the most perfect position to master this realm from the third dimensional reality of physical existence. The reason it is far more difficult to master the fourth dimension when operating within its parameters is that the speed of thoughts are of such a magnitude that any thought-form, even fleeting ones, instantly manifest there and you experience that reality until you change it. To make this even more of a challenge, all similar thought-forms and thought-form entities are instantly magnetized to that thought-form. Thus, one thought-form, of, say, racial discrimination, would trigger entire civilizations of thought-forms – and souls entrapped in those thought-forms – to instantly materialize in the entities field of consciousness-awareness.

Thus, the fourth dimension is a curious admixture of thought-forms comprised, not only of pure, original, consciousness -abstracts or blueprints, but, also, warped and distorted entities and their thought-forms. There is absolutely no guarantee that by dabbling in the fourth dimension an enlightened experience will result. Many entities who leave their bodies and resonate with such suffering entities through fearful moments, magnetize themselves into a total experience of suffering. Any feelings of fear at this moment can result in an instantaneous attraction of another round of entities with similar fears and so on. Unauthorized and unguided "trips" into this dimension can result in trauma and great psychic imbalance and damage, even to the physical body.

This cautionary note is given so that if one encounters such an experience, one need only be steadfast in knowing and retaining the presence of mind to focus upon the Light within the Heart of Hearts and the highest guides and Masters revealed to those upon earth. In such experiences, joyfully calling upon the higher NAMES would also instantly dispel any encroaching thought-forms that might be attracted in a moment of uneasiness or fear. Learning to control your thought-forms upon the earth plane is actually much safer. The earth, then, is like training wheels on a bicycle upon which you are remembering to balance yourself. Master your thoughts now. Practice being the master of your thought-forms while they are slowed within the womb of earth. Remember, imagination is reality in slow motion. You can now see how important it is to use your powers of contemplation and meditation. Keep practicing your mastery. Like any fine instrument, it will become second nature, as you term it.

It is for the above reasons that we have devoted much of this document to the nature of dimensions in creation. One is not instantly swept into the higher dimensions of Light by angels without some preparation. This is for the entity's own safety. For these reasons, we have stressed repeatedly the importance of proper contemplation/meditation upon the highest thought-forms with clarity, focus and devotion to the qualities of THE ONE. For when those thought-forms become second nature to your consciousness-awareness in waking and sleeping states, you are resonating with the Genius Frequency. You shall be master of your thought-forms and fear shall dissipate like smoke in an ocean breeze.

All the learning, studying and focused concentration upon high frequency thought-forms, which are fifth dimensional in nature, when resonated through a third dimensional body produces a body of light. Although one can produce, witness and partake of incredible experiences in the fourth dimension (even a simulated heaven of one's choosing), one can only produce a true fifth dimensional body of light by transforming the elemental clay forms into light by mastering the fourth dimension of thought-form creation in the Light. As you acquire the discipline required to generate high frequency Light with a third dimensional body, you will be protected and guided in ever greater degrees by the Masters. For if you "fall" out of their frequency range, they cannot help you, neither can they manipulate you in any way – THAT IS A LAW. Thus by your own efforts shall you be known in the kingdom of SuperLight.

Questioner: Why is the fourth dimension so difficult to master?

MaYaRa: It is not difficult, beloved. It is a matter of becoming familiar with what to expect by understanding how it works. Just as an astronaut would not be so foolish to ride a rocket to the moon without some idea of what to expect from his equipment and the environment in which he will be operating.

In our example of the astronaut, it is easy enough to get there, but to negotiate in that world is another matter. The information regarding the fourth dimension has been explained in many ways and much of it is needlessly complex due to the intellect's connection to the linear programming of the altered-ego. Thus one is wise who mixes study with contemplation/meditation and completes the cycle by applying this discipline in daily life. For it is there that the first test must be passed – that of mastering your thought-forms.

The formula is quite simple: When you master your thought-forms while in a three dimensional body, you resonate with the Genius Frequency. Then you generate a feedback loop of consciousness-awareness that builds upon itself, creating a body of Light around and within the existing elemental body. When the resonance is strong enough, a continuous current of SuperLight is attracted that begins to raise the overall frequency of the atomic structure of the molecules of the body. The result is that you quite literally become another dimension, body and all.

All of the cosmic history of Genesis and your heritage notwithstanding: It is from a physical incarnation that you build a body of Light and when you accomplish this you shall be free as a Co-Creator with the Masters and THE ONE in the fifth dimension. Thus you cannot master the fifth dimension until you master the third and the fourth. That is, when you practice Love, acquire Wisdom and resonate with SuperLight, in that order – when you live that life consistently – the gates to the fifth dimension shall open. Then you shall exist in the Causative Arena of thought, where the totality of your now fragmented being shall rejoice in a reunion of Light.

In the fifth dimension, you can use your LightBody to work with the blueprints in the fourth dimension without being lost in them. You shall easily distinguish between the distorted, incomplete though-forms and the pure thought-forms of Divine Issue. In the fifth dimension, you shall have the ability to consciously build a physical body, enter a planetary domain and maintain contact with your fifth dimensional LightBody. You shall not simply be a thought-form bio-technology that perpetuates its recurrence in the web of a dying solar paradigm of food-chain-mentalities.

You shall not even require food from the earth, as you shall absorb SuperLight directly. When you desire to leave the planetary body, you shall depart with the entire physical structure and all newly-acquired memories of experience. You shall have the abilities to raise the frequency of the atomic resonance of the body with SuperLight. You will not be trapped and repelled back to earth by the Van Allen Belts of induction, for you shall be of a much higher frequency. You shall create gravity if you wish, but you shall not be affected by it. In other solar systems, galaxies, and dimensions you shall do far more!

Too much to believe, beloved? Perhaps you should be more scientific about your religion or more religious about your science. Choose the one that appeals to you now, but ask yourself this: How did Christ, Jesus ascend and why? How does a Buddha ascend and why? How did Krishna ascend and why? How did Elijah ascend and why? How did Enoch ascend and why? How did Quetzalcoatl ascend and why? How did Moses ascend and why? How did 144,000 Masters ascend and why? How can thousands of ancient scriptures, many of unknown religious affiliation – and many more to surface in your time – be wrong or written by fanatical myth-makers. Contemplate this, beloved.

These accounts were written in religions terms. The scientific accounts were destroyed. However, copies of them are preserved and shall be revealed throughout the next decade, in your counting, as they are uncovered, dis-"covered," and thrust up from the earth's interior vaults of knowledge. Yet still, there will be arguments and debates over one document and another. Why wait?! Why wait for these "experts" to agree before you are permitted to embrace the truth of your heritage. They may continue to be deep in argument, debate, and even war while the skies open to reveal a sight never before seen upon earth. Then they shall be struck with awe and fear and confusion. Decide for yourselves, beloved, for this is a personal quest as well. Do the research yourself. Resonate with the Genius Frequency within you. *You must decide for yourself and begin to work while there is yet time.*

You see, when you cultivate a LightBody while upon earth, you may create from the vast cosmic library of knowledge in the fourth dimension. You may use the geometric light-templates to create your own unique flower. You may use the fourth dimension, rather than it using you. However, it requires more than intellectual mind. It requires a conscious body of Light.

By your contemplation/meditation and frequency resonance cultivated in your private moments, especially with your brothers and sisters of Light, you pull down, as it were, your oversoul from the fifth dimension which domes with your third dimensional bio-computer. At that moment, the entire body, every cell of it, becomes pure mind, a mem-brain. When the synaptic firings reach critical mass, so to speak, SuperLight is ignited. Your third dimensional, physical cells transmutate from solar/elemental chemical codes to LOVE-LIGHT/GOD-MIND. The blocks in the fourth dimension become the gates and bridges, which align themselves for your safe passage into the fifth dimension.

Ask questions, beloved, and *demand the answers of YOURSELF*. Think again: Why did the Masters ascend? To show off? To be worshipped? Do you think that a Master, vibrating on the most powerful frequency of SuperLight needs your worship? Do you suppose that the Masters rise into the splendor of Super-Light dimensions to laugh at you? To condemn you to hell?

Listen: We cry for you. And it is not a tear that drips from a physical eye. It is that we become the tear. There is a great longing for your return. We cry for those of you even in the best of situations and circumstances, for they are so tenuous, fleeting. The best of earth situations is suffering and darkness compared to what a-waits you. We cry because what little progress is gained is many times lost, in the transitions from the third to the fourth dimensions and back to the third again, during the death/birth cycles – a perpetual see-saw in which entropy is reprogrammed into your returning body.

We cry because you do not see that the primitive laws of karma are merely an electromagnetic balancing act. That is, for the slightest unbalance, you are electromagnetically catapulted into the earth again with all of its risks. It is a perpetual cycle. It is perpetual, beloved, but it is not eternal. What is eternal is already built into your being. Thus, you are more than third and fourth dimensional. You are fifth dimensional beings. You have suffered a fragmentation of your being and the time has come to reunite with it.

We say fragmented because the rebellious creator-gods tampered with the fourth dimensional blueprint between dimensions. Thus, the fourth dimension is the vital communication link between worlds, yet a portion of it designed to maintain your similitude with THE ONE is out of sync with the higher, fifth dimensional blueprint. These rebellious ones were removed from the fifth dimension and forbidden access directly in the third dimension. You see, the solar paradigm also exists in the fourth dimension. Only the fifth-dimension is free of such bondage.

Questioner: Then what you have given us is a road map or space maps of consciousness, with which we can negotiate the fourth dimension as we enter the fifth. Is this an accurate statement?

MaYaRa: Excellent deduction and query. However, there is a an angle to this query that is slightly misleading.

That is, the fourth dimension is not a geographic location reached by space shuttles or submarines. The intellectual process in and of itself is the fringe of the fourth dimension. So you can see how increased information, inventions and dis-"coveries" all originate in the fourth dimension and have wrought havoc, as well as progress to your lives.

Understand that the fourth dimension is part and parcel of each of you as a microcosm and macrocosm. Review the segment of this book referring to Omniscience and Omnipresence. Perhaps you shall realize that what makes inter/intra-dimensional communication and inter/intra-life/light zones possible is the shared electron. When you think in pictures and contemplate through imagination, you are virtually operating in the fourth dimension.

These pictures are actually holographic projections against the auric field, producing wave-form geometries complete with color and sound throughout the bio-computer. These wave-form geometries act as four dimensional templates to resonate with other templates of like frequencies. Space/time restrictions do not apply to this mode of consciousness-awareness. That is why the Masters do not spend thousands of years moving from one galaxy or universe to another.

Your query is accurate in that you must know which blueprints to resonate with in the fourth dimension. For there are many that will not suit your personal path of consciousness evolution. In the fourth dimension, you are also subject to the laws of its function as interface between dimensions. That is why we stress that the fourth dimension is not one in which to reside. All of your energy bodies cannot function there. They would be reduced to seed or idea-construct.

Many have been to the fourth dimension in a more or less conscious-awareness state, and many have returned to convince others that they have seen "God." But they have only witnessed an attribute of themselves and many more have only witnessed distortions of their own thought-forms of fear. There are those who become lost, trapped in powerful magnetic thought-forms far beyond their abilities to transcend them. The latter, however, have attempted to manipulate certain elemental powers for their self-serving quest for power over others, with dire consequences. The fourth dimension is a mirror image of the earth and its life-forms are composed of negative mass. Therefore, this dimension contains all thought-forms of earth including wars, violence and chaos, as well as the Divine Blueprints of the Higher Worlds, as does earth.

Questioner: What must we do or know to reach the fifth dimension?

MaYaRa: Oh beloved brother, you must learn to truly, unconditionally love all creation – first and foremost. Then you shall resonate with the frequency of SuperLight. We use the syntactical device (the word Love) to refer to a frequency that generates profound power to transform and create – the bonding frequency that holds the atoms together with incalculable force. You must learn to exist in that frequency of Love. As you resonate with this frequency, you begin to KNOW.

Once again we term the word/symbol "know" as a special term that is not used as an academic, intellectual possession. In the highest frequency of the word, we refer to knowledge resonating within a LightBody. "Consciousness knowing" as contrasted to "awareness knowing" are worlds apart. The former is a fifth dimensional experience where the totality of all energy-mind bodies focus in the same moment in the Genius Frequency. The latter is merely a three dimensional, sensory awareness of electromagnetically stimulated events, to which awareness reacts with what is termed pleasure/pain compounded by what is termed memory, reducing true ecstatic feeling to polluted emotion.

An interesting paradox emerges here that may interest you. The intellect is a mode of awareness that is inherently closer to the fourth dimension than to the third or the fifth. The human physical bio-computer is closer to the fifth dimension than it is to the third or the fourth. Contemplate this statement. We shall not explain further. Use the previous material to prove to yourself how the paradox works.

We confess to you that our position toward mankind is parental in that we know you as creations of Light, albeit children of the Light at this juncture. Know then, that we have been quite stern at times in our examinations with the intent that you begin to think for yourselves. The following is a gentle, intellectual reminder to begin the Light work so desperately needed at this critical time upon planet earth. This information is not to be used to openly criticize nations, religions, scientific communities or individuals. The purpose is to realize that neither nation, institution nor another entity can be responsible for your personal evolution into the Light.

It is time to begin the work of your higher purpose. It is time, not to take up the cross of space and time, but to transform it into a key, a vehicle of Light, Love and Wisdom. It is time to I-dentify with that which is within you that is already free from the bonds of the solar paradigm, and with the many Masters who stand ready to assist you in the awakening of earth into SuperLight.

You have wandered far too long through the labyrinth of the idea-world of seed-thought creations, picking up archaic gods, archaic goods and services without reading the labels and without even knowing the manufacturer. Bad "business," would you not agree?

This is not idle "chitchat" to entertain the intellect. Look at your earth – at your lives. You are plunging headlong into a many-leveled death. *It is time for you to WAKE UP!!*

The fifth dimension is not some distant place where heaven or hell awaits those who are liked or disliked by some celestial despot. WAKE UP and begin your work. Ask for help. And remember all of what you are is your choice and always has been. You are intimidated by those authorities supported by institutions that bend you to the will of their vested interests. Do not be intimidated. Genius is not a genetic, physiological, psychological product of academia, a fluke of chaos, and it is not an I.Q. It is a frequency of Light in which you have your being. It is a veritable ocean, in which your mind swims as you search for water.

The fourth dimension, in which you dream dreams, is a thick, intricate web of interlocking grids of conscious-awareness, a matrix of flux lines that propel and attract thought-forms with the same tenacity as your planetary gravity attracts its own elements. However, all of this floats in, and is permeated with the ocean of SuperLight.

You may escape from your body temporarily to explore the fourth dimension. You may astral travel, think, contemplate, meditate or just exhaust yourselves into the fourth dimension. The question is where shall you go once you are there? – again. If you cannot control your thought-forms while in the relative safety of your physical bodies, how can you expect to navigate in the fourth dimension with its undercurrents, hurricanes, wastelands, mountain ranges and a host of otherworldly events and environments? If you would think twice about wandering, unprotected through the ocean or deserts of your third dimensional planet without protection and guidance and study, then why would you hurl yourselves toward death without any preparation whatsoever.

What are you to do? Love, embrace, be larger than the earth, than the sun. Be a shepherd of SuperLight and a way-shower by your actions. You must discern, discriminate, evaluate, intuit and maintain clarity with every step, every moment of the way, with every experience, idea, or thought that "pops" into your fields of conscious-awareness. Seek the highest truth, the highest protection, every moment that you formulate new plans or reformulate old ones.

It is not your body of which you need to be free. It is not even the earth. It is the fourth dimension of which you need to be free. It is contaminated and out of sync with the Genius Frequency. It has been tampered with – its genetic codes maligned. It is a dimension of idea-constructs that have weight, power and an entropic life of their own.

You labor so over choosing what auto vehicles to purchase. Yet ideas just appear or are struggled for without regard to what effects they may have regarding your true purpose. The fourth dimension is a disembodied dimension of idea-constructs without a heart, without love, without a Light of its own. And would you ultimately surrender to the fantasies there without regard to your precious LightBody?! Wake up, beloved. WAKE UP! What has all this been worth, if not to regain your Body of Light?

Begin to ask questions and demand the truth from yourself. Then ask for that which increases your frequency so that you can communicate and receive help from the Masters and guides who are committed to this final moment in your time.

The Christ, Master Jesus taught "Ask that ye shall receive:" meaning that *YOU ARE WHAT YOU ASK FOR*. It is time to prioritize. Ask for what? Receive what? For what results? If these questions draw blanks, ask for help to ask the appropriate questions. Ask for help in reclaiming your Light Bodies – of reuniting the many parts of your consciousness scattered over the earth and trapped in the fourth dimension. Ask for help, knowing only you can ultimately help yourself.

Yet few ask for the kind of help that creates the CHANGE from that which you have been. Why beloved? You sink in your own poisons and violent thoughts and ideas, and arrogantly believe that you have an answer. Why, beloved? Even the Masters ask for help in serving others – they do not ask for themselves. You must resonate in the frequency of your Heart of Hearts to receive help from those who operate on that frequency. Many pray. But how can you pray if you secretly desire the annihilation of some entity, race or government?

What does this have to do with the fifth dimension? You see, the fifth dimension is one where a body is required – a Light-Body. A LightBody is a coherent matrix of thought-forms in a rarefied state and frequency of LOVE-LIGHT/GOD-MIND which conforms to the Original Blueprint of Similitude as well as Image. It is this Similitude with THE ONE that you have lost. It is the LightBody of Overself that created your image upon earth in the first place. A portion of your consciousness thought-forms from the Overself were used to create it.

And now, you see, the dilemma is this: Neither the Overself nor the Image is complete, leaving a fragmented being flailing about the earth in search of paradise lost. But paradise lost is not a geographic place in time, nor is it the gadgetry of a metallic-age technology. It is not the power of wealth nor the pity of poverty. Nor is it samadhi, nor nirvana, whereby you ultimately desert your family of Light for yet another illusion offered in the fourth dimension.

Your Overself LightBody is part and parcel of the Collective Issue created and dispatched by THE ONE to raise the evolving specie races of earth, to imbue the very cells of earth with consciousness Light, and to teach the gift of the Genius Frequency to all who choose to return to the Love that created them. Thus the fourth dimension, originally the medium of communication with the root-races (animal kingdoms) of earth, became your nemesis.

How do you unite with your Overself LightBody? Use that which we have taught. Use that which you have learned from other sources that resonate deep within the layers of forgotten glories of Light. Only *USE THEM!* Why just read a book and sink into another year of confusion. *ACT NOW! ACT! ACT!* Do not wait. There is no final solution. There is only the ongoing process of Light. *BE THAT PROCESS OF LIGHT. Meditate, contemplate, clarify, think, feel, interpret, cross-examine, adjust, readjust, purify, cleanse, reach out to the Light of THE ONE as you go within. Make the effort! Make the effort and know that you are not alone. You shall never be alone in your grandest return.*

Beloved, you shall never be lost if you resonate with your Heart of Hearts. There are many waiting, fingertips outstretched to touch yours in that illusive fourth dimension through which you shall be guided to embrace your lost families. When you connect with the fifth dimension you are in for quite a shock at the brilliance and power of the Masters who exist there. The Love and the Light shall be so overwhelmingly ecstatic, so beautiful, that you shall sob and your heart shall feel the anguish in the joy – the aguish in realizing how many of your brothers and sisters of Light still suffer in the dark.

Be patient and loving as you gaze at the souls who suffer their violence and pain. Cry, yea, weep for them, beloved, and Demand that you receive and become the power of Light to help them. Let the Genius Frequency of Intelligent Healing Light flow into you in your meditations, so that you can heal those trapped in the darkness and cry out for help.

Do not be afraid to feel the frustration of not changing fast enough or deep enough. For all the times you curse and scream at things of no significance whatever – POUND the earth with your fist and *DEMAND THAT YOU ARE RELEASED FROM THE BONDAGE OF THE SOLAR PARADIGM, FROM THE GAME OF KARMA, FROM YOUR OWN WEAKNESS!! Use that frustration to channel your desire to BE THE LIGHT.*

Then, quietly search your Heart of Hearts. Know that soon, in your time, this time shall be no more. And a "new heavens and a new earth" shall shine within you – pure and beautiful beyond your dreams, and brimming with new beings of your own creation.

You are filled with the Genius and Wisdom NOW, in this moment, in your bodies, on the earth, in the Light, if you choose. Then we, of all dimensions, can meet on the "common ground" of

SuperLight and rejoice in that creation for it shall resonate perfectly with The Source of that joy.

Mere poetic fantasy? Will you chance that it is and go on with what you have been? Will you choose to renounce your responsibilities for ongoing Life/Light? Will you renounce your heritage of co-creation?

Life in the LIGHT of your heritage is far more real than the illusion you live without the partnership of you and The Eternal Source. You are not alone. Come home, beloved.

Glossary Comments

Although all the specialized terms within this work are simply "coined" phrases composed with non-technical language, the following expanded definitions are provided to assist the seeker of truth in further expansion of the narrow frequencies inherent in the intellect. Simply to change one's perspective and perception of a concept, regardless of how abstract it may seem, will, in itself cause a frequency shift that beneficially affects the entire bio-structure, as well as strengthening one's spiritual foundations.

The secret to raising the frequency of the intellect is to release it from the predefined and artificial realities of the altered-ego. It can then join the powers of the imagination to soar in the lofty heights of the Genius Frequency. May the "Peace that passeth all human understanding" be yours in this moment.

GLOSSARY

ALTERED-EGO: The use of the word "altered" is used here as a prefix to ego, which, in its original connotation signifies a pure state of awareness as a unique manifestation of quality combinations of the ONE CREATOR in a separate embodiment from other quality combinations, totaling a collective embodiment or humanity. At certain periods of man's consciousness evolution, decisions were made that limited the use and function of mind to a lower frequency or vibration resulting in a mutant form and function of the original. The use of the term here is almost synonymous with what is commonly referred to as intellect, in that the intellect is to true Intelligence what the altered-ego is to true ego or "I AM" consciousness. Thus, mass consciousness sees the world through the eyes of altered-ego, which ascertains information only on the narrow frequency band of sensory feedback as manifested by the dense material plane. It is the major block to the Genius Frequency due to its selfcentered dogma, proclaiming that one can know only what one knows about dense matter.

ARCHETYPAL FORM: A matrix of energy thought-forms that intersects to form a pattern. This matrix provides a "flow chart," as it were, for the photons to flow into and assume a specific form, which conforms to the laws of a given region. These forms are projected into matter from other dimensions.

ARTIFICIAL MEMORY: Used exclusively by the altered-ego and created by circumstances chosen by the individual soul for the purpose of learning a lesson, from which a balance is created before one can evolve. It is a third dimensional feed-back to which an individual identifies as it searches for its true identity. The true identity of an entity can never be found through artificial memory.

ASTRAL TRAVELING: When one of the energy bodies of a human bio-computer detaches itself from the physical, and moves into other areas of thought in various locations in the physical and mental universes. However, it is limited to the fourth dimension of astral thought and subject to all low frequency thought-forms existing in the material realms. It is not recommended that an entity strive to achieve astral "traveling" as an ultimate goal, for the results may be damaging in the long run. At the very least it can be a waste of precious time since the ultimate goal is to transmutate all five energy bodies into the fifth dimension where a true co-creation is possible.

AURIC FIELD: The luminous energy envelope within which the physical body resides and the vibration of earth-mind takes place. The entity is self-conscious, not through the brain, but through the auric field. The auric field, however, is a product of the earth plane vibration and dimension, and is part and parcel of the astral plane. Therefore, all activities of mind and body in this dimension are subject to the electromagnetic thought-form

embodiments of all entities that are trapped within this magnetic field.

AWARENESS: A preconceived, mathematical function and expression of matter in its onward, spiraling destiny of perfection in the similitude of consciousness and its ultimate return to its Source. Awareness is found even in the mineral kingdom. Therefore, awareness is not synonymous with consciousness.

BIO-COMPUTER: Used here as a conceptual aid to stimulate a deeper understanding of the true nature of your physical bodies. Refers here to the body as a circuit diagram, a three dimensional circuit board containing the sacred design of THE ONE. The physical body is an electronic thought-form. Understanding its functions is the key to unlocking the Genius Frequency. Since all thought-forms are electromagnetically interactive, knowing how they function enables the entity to reprogram, with the help of the Light Masters working through THE ONE, consciousness and "awaken" to the LIGHT of its true and original design. In its proper understanding, the bio-computer is the totality of every cell in the body and their interaction with the seven mindcenters that store the appropriate frequencies of energies.

BIO-ORGANIC: Refers more directly to the physical organs of the total bio-computer, the last or densest plane of the ingathering of light that may still support the integrity of the system before the even denser level of the mineral kingdom.

BLOCKS: Are short circuits in the bio-computer that prevent the flow of life-giving frequencies throughout the trees of life, whether it be on the micro or the macro scale.

CLR: A conscious light resonator. An indicator of the next phase of "channeling." An entity who consciously and willfully desires to make contact with the Master Intelligence Light Beings — Higher Self — for the purpose of the upliftment and enlightenment of that entity, as well as the entire human brotherhood. If they so choose, ALL humanity has access to this gift. The speed and intensity of the results are proportionate to the level of attainment. Any level of attainment shall be accelerated and matched by an appointed Light worker, whether that entity exists in the earth dimension or of extradimensional residence.

CO-CREATOR: Every human entity is a co-creator in his own right. Yet an entity must live in the vibration of his own creations. But a true CO-CREATOR is one who has realized the genius within and the GOD-self within, thus earning the right to CO-CREATE in higher and higher dimensions within the infinite levels of mastery and the right to move within dimensions for purposes of healing and teaching.

COMMON LIGHT: i.e. the light of the sun in the earth plane, as supported by the solar logos or the word or vibration within the parameters of a specific frequency. The calculations and observations of science are based exclusively on the solar logos, the common light. Without the knowledge of the higher Light dimensions, only partial equations of entropy can be ascertained. This common light frequency also forms one of the membrane walls of tensions known in antiquity as "the veil of light."

CONSCIOUSNESS: The individualized double reflection of aware-ness, ultimately realized in the "I-AM" that begins its return to the perfected Source with the added dimension of direct experience in the many realms of creation. The perfected "I-AM" may thus share as a true co-creator in the eternal creation of other universes.

CONTEMPLATION: The other side of meditation. The act of focusing the attention upon a vision or an object of vision, but with one crucial distinction: that the entity, when contemplating, ask the questions: FROM WHENCE DOES IT COME? WITHER DOES IT GO? and HOW "AM-I" the "I-AM?" One should question ceaselessly the "truth" of any thought-form. Answers shall pour into you, but to stop there without meditating in receivership shall negate the momentum of "TRUTH" and the altered-ego shall once again gain the "upper hand."

COSMIC INTELLIGENCE: The quality or frequency of the mind of THE ONE that establishes the interlinkage with all realms and universes, without which no interdimensional communication would be possible. Without this frequency of communication, every level of intelligent life would be forever locked up in its own vibration. This function of MIND is carried out through the electron and photon-particle/wave oscillations.

COSMIC: Refers to any thought-form which is common to all universes. Thus, it is a universal concept encompassing all dimensions and light thresholds.

CREATIVE/LIFE/PROCESSES: A syntactical device for conveying the connotation of the inseparable trinity of the Creative Force, the Life Force, and the processes, or laws which govern or structure them.

DIVINE STRUCTURE: The actual form that an attribute of THE ONE assumes as it proceeds to complete ITS work in the lower or denser dimensions. (see also Divine Process).

DIVINE RAY: Once a thought-form is conceived in the MIND of THE ONE, it takes on embodiment or form, which emanates a RAY that projects as Dominions, within which it is designed to function. IT then begins to subdivide into subrays.

DIVINE PROCESS: Is defined from an architectural view stressing the design of life, starting with the thought-form and continuing into material matter. Regardless of what is chosen to be created, the PROCESS must follow the fundamental blueprint. The original blueprint of creation is divided and subdivided in its journey from the MIND of THE ONE into Sound and Light, and further into denser realms. This blueprint is duplicated as a separate ENTITY or Extension of THE ONE, as well as a duplicate that creates and supports atomic particles and the space in which these exist. Common to all functions in all of creation that are part of the DIVINE PROCESS is the Genius Frequency, a support system consisting of the framework of the LOVE FREQUENCY.

$E=MC4$: Used as a syntactical devise rather than an actual formula to convey the idea that Einstein's work was not finished; that had he not been influenced by the lower mind-energies of the times, the genius frequency that he tapped would have revealed the multidimensional universes to the masses. Although this formula may be contemplated by the altered-ego as $E=MC4,5,9,22,64$, etc. for a useful mind expanding exercise, neither this equation nor any that the altered-ego may conjure can express the dimensions of SuperLight. For soon, it shall be realized that this type of higher Knowledge is so universal that it cannot be objectified by the intellect. It can only be lived by any entity who reconnects with the Genius Frequency. When this occurs, there shall be no need of performing these colossal gymnastics upon the two and three dimensional world. The entity shall actually engage in bio-location, dimensional shifts, etc. And what once was thought of as the childish delusions of ancient and primitive men shall be viewed as a former teaching by Light Masters who taught the way to true freedom.

EGO: Pure ego. Originally the vertical alignment and constant "I AM" consciousness that connected the individual soul to THE ONE. Although lost, it can also be regained. It is not the opposite of the altered-ego, rather, EGO encompasses all lower and limited frequencies in a triad: "I AM" the spirit of THE ONE, "I AM" the individualized soul of that spirit, "I AM" a physical body composed from the Earth by the spirit and the soul.

EMOTION: A complex of past feelings, often in a mixed and confused time frame, electromagnetically locked in a thought-form. Due to the mind's holographic nature, these past feelings are sorted and stored within the appropriate mind-centers. However, upon recall of these past feelings, the types of emotion are cross-referenced to produce a great confusion within the entity. Thus, a seemingly insignificant event can trigger a tremendous charge of all similar past emotions, short circuiting the ability of the bio-computer to operate in the "NOW" moment.

ENERGY PORTAL: In the physical realm it manifests as a ductless gland. In other energy realms, it functions as a chakra, mind, or specialty awareness center that spins and, therefore, has a magnetic center to which it attracts thought-forms of like frequency. Thus, sexual thought-forms are attracted and stored in the sexual chakra and held by the desire aspect of the belief system. However, the idea of a portal adds a dimension of a gate through which energy and thought-forms may enter or leave.

ENTROPY: A function of chemical destruction inherent in the solar logos influencing mankind by its common, yellow spectrum. Since most thought-forms in mass-consciousness are generated within this frequency of dense vibrations, the laws of entropy become a function inherent within the very thought structure of the mind of man. Hence, these type of thought-forms consist of partial equations of life which, perforce, yield the destruction of the life force through identification with a food-chain mentality.

ETERNAL MOMENT: A function of time/space, in which the illusion of time is suspended in a poignancy of life where past and future events are not separated by time. These events are as one in a moment of eternity, in which they have the power to change any given thought-form-circumstance before resuming the momentum of motion of space/time.

FALL: Literally the descent of spirit into matter, with the additional connotation of willfully cutting off the direct support mechanism of the Genius Frequency of SuperLight and LOVE/LIGHT-GOD/MIND, thereby creating a scenario of death, entropy, partial truths and confusion of tongues which must run its cycle until the Omega Point. The original creator-gods elected to create their systems of creation without using the Master Plan in its entirety and refused to allow Adamic Man to rule them. MAN was and is to be that ruler and co-creator with THE ONE.

FEELING: A quality and function of awareness of the totality of the active mind-centers on a mass cellular level. They range by degrees from the frequencies of "sensations" of the lower three mind-centers to the impulses, visions, and ecstasy of the higher mind-centers. The "still small voice" within is a quality of this higher feeling. It is not to be confused with emotion (see emotion).

FIFTH DIMENSION: Realm of light bodies up to SUPERLIGHT bodies, i.e., the Masters of Light in the area of the Earth's etheric body which overlaps other planetary and galactic etheric realms. This is the lowest of many higher dimensions in which the creator gods and masters dwell. This realm is not limited to magnetically defined boundaries. It leads through the threshold gates of the Zodiac where the ONE may be communed with directly, with the help of the Masters and Lords of Light. An energy level beyond the ultraviolet range in which a true Master of Light has access and provides the thoughtforms for intra-dimensional communication and the total transmutation of a thought-form, including the bio-computer, your physical bodies, into that dimension. The dimension which provides the true living reality of Co-Creation. It is the causative arena of thought where the overself of the original Adamic creation resides, and to which you shall return, if you so choose (see also fourth dimension).

FIVE BODIES OF LIGHT: In many ancient teachings, these five basic bodies were defined as a progression of matter from the densest to least dense. It is more accurate, however, to conceive of the five bodies as harmonic nodes of light. For it is important to conceptualize a thought-form that facilitates the ease of understanding the possibilities of frequencies of light in many dimensions as interactive.

FOURTH DIMENSION: The realm of high conceptual thought-forms confined to the area of the Earth's astral body. In this realm, thought-forms are living entities that cannot directly affect dense matter, nor can they cross the threshold realm of the fifth dimension. It is the realm where living thought-forms (also souls, which are living thought-forms) are trapped by magnetic charges of like kind as holograms that live and are conscious.

Anyone dabbling in the occult usually contacts this realm, many times with tragic results. However, the fourth dimension contains the blueprints of physical creation. Thus, all inventions, discoveries, astral work, music, art and mental processes of all kinds are fed from the great "library" of the fourth dimensions.

FREE AWARENESS: With the additional term "free" to qualify this idea-construct as the initial "allotment" of awareness inherent in the manifestation of the physical universes.

GENIUS FREQUENCY: A Light emanation streaming directly from the Source of all life, THE ONE CREATOR, which permeates and sustains the Life Force, animating the very atomic particles as well as the stars and Galactic Clusters of Intelligence. The word "Frequency" is used to convey a statistical parallel used in scientific research. In this case, it is a vibration/color/tone operating in and beyond the ultraviolet range; and when a critical mass is reached the vibratory threshold gates to simultaneous occupation of multi-dimensional realities are opened, and the mind and body are able to transcend material limitations — actually able to participate in the creation of particle mass and when performed upon the earth plane, it is termed miracle. The key here is understanding the frequency of Mind which signifies human existence that renders the concept of Darwinian evolution as an absurd limitation, as well as an insult to the ONE CREATOR. All possess the Genius Frequency, bar none. All may, with the proper focus of attention and actions upon Earth plane realize the critical mass that triggers GODSELF. The human bio-computer is, due to its very structure of mind, close to this state of critical ultraviolet mass.

GENIUS: An attribute of the Mind of God and therefore a quality of the human mind not to be found or defined within the parameters of academic achievement, nor within the arbitrary measurements of the "intellect" (see intellect) as determined by various aptitude tests resulting in an I.Q. (intelligence quotient). A state of resonance with the "frequency" (see Genius Frequency) of GOD-MIND which pervades every atom and every particle of the universe. Every human being, bar none, is imbued with this quality. It is for this reason that Genius manifests itself upon the human Earth plane in as many and varied forms as there are individuals. Therefore, only those genius qualities exhibited by certain individuals who contributed more or less directly to the established institutions receive fanfare, acclaim and credibility. And when the true nature of Genius is examined, it becomes clear that it transcends all environmental and genetic explanations of the apparent phenomenon.

**GEOMETRIC
PERSONALITY-CONSTRUCT:**
Used in this work as a conceptual aid to understanding the living relationship between the geometry of a thought-form and the Entity that embodies it, i.e., the Twenty and Four Entities who surround the ONE CREATOR, radiating the architecture of universes. A scaled down version of the latter process is found in the living geometries of the Zodiac. On a lower, three dimensional level, this results in the superficial personality.

GOD-STUFF: An idiomatic creation which connotes GOD-MIND with the dense material plane of objects that includes atomic particles, as well as galaxies, space, and other universes.

GOD-THOUGHT-STUFF: An idiomatic expression of the dense material planes as being an actual thought-form, so that the reader may understand more fully that the material plane is also a thought-form.

HALF-LIFE: A function of entropy. When the universe was created by the thought-forms of THE ONE, a polarity of energy was necessary to construct its reality. Thus a portion of THE ONE was divided within itself, creating a temporary manifestation of creation. The results were nodal points, such as planets and atoms, that continually exchange energy quanta with a loss of energy by a square root function, which results in an Omega point of its cycle of manifestation. The material worlds and thought-

forms limited to that frequency suffer the half-life function of entropy. Only the connection with the eternal SuperLight can renew and transform these worlds of matter into their original state of eternality.

HARMONIC RESONANCE: The principle whereby a note that is struck by a tuning fork causes a string of an instrument to vibrate in the same frequency or in a harmonic of that frequency (see also resonant induction).

HEART OF HEARTS: The seed atom and prime resonating organ for the Genius Frequency as manifested upon Earth plane. Also known as the fourth chakra in Eastern metaphysics.

HELL: When a partial equation of life is taken from the Master Plan and the attempt to create an entirely new system ensues, the obvious result is that the partial system begins a downward spiral of entropy for the simple reason that it can no longer be perfect and must create a space in which chaos and death must play out their momentum and scenarios. Thus, hell is anywhere and anytime that the perfect plan is aborted and the death process, fear, etc., becomes paramount.

I-AM CONSCIOUSNESS: The state of realization of sole responsible for actions and situations produced by a co-creator with THE ONE CREATOR in which it has its being.

IDENTIFICATION: The electromagnetic bonding through the codification of a thought-form by which one attaches one's being to like thought-forms resulting in destiny, whereby an individual manifests persons, places, and things. It is not detrimental in and of itself, indeed one can Identify with the ONE CREATOR. However, it is presently used strictly as a sub-function of the altered-ego, thereby creating a thick web of electro magnetic bonding within the cellular and auric structures of the entity, which take considerable effort to reconstruct. It is the prime motive function of karma. However, due to the assistance given to earth plane entities at this time, the bonds of identification may be overcome in this life span by the entity.

ILRE: An involuntary light resonating entity or a trance channeler, as it is termed in its popular idiom. This type of light resonator has prearranged, through a past lifetime experience, the time/event circumstance in which the contact is made with an entity in another dimension of light. Thus, these entities may bring lessons to the earth plane from extra-dimensional intelligence, while continuing to learn personal lessons on other more mundane levels of experience. Also, this type of teaching is calculated to give credibility as a strange curiosity and to disseminate information without the typical altered-ego "trips" often associated with one who may "know" secrets.

IMAGINATION: A quality and function of the human mind to recall pre-existing thought-forms and recombine them in the midst of the chaos or the flux of creation. Strictly speaking, it cannot create or recall any thought-form that has not already been created. It is a process of mind and functions as a powerful holographic computer from which a kaleidoscope of thought-forms may be recombined in ever-new patterns of reality unique to the entity who operates it. It is the most powerful aid to loosening the grip of the altered-ego and, with proper guidance, may open one to the Genius Frequency when used in conjunction with the Heart Of Hearts. Imagination IS reality.

INFINITE GOD-MIND: Reference to the quality of the MIND of THE ONE that inhabits, resides, and pervades through OMNISCIENCE and OMNIPRESENCE every space, region, realm, threshold, gate, galaxy, atom, supergalaxy, and multidimensional universe.

INTELLECT: A fragment of Divine Intelligence as a result of the low frequency limitations of the altered-ego. Thus the intellect, by its very nature, will deny and block the higher Intelligence of the Genius Frequency. Since the intellect cannot create in a true holographic dimension, as even the physical body can, it is limited to a linear "train of thought" that traps itself in the cyclic nature of space/time, effectively reversing evolution into the spiral decay of entropy.

INTELLIGENCE: Referring to "pure" or "Divine" Intelligence in contrast to the intellect which is a fragment of Intelligence and a sub-function of altered-ego. Intelligence is universal and no organism, planet, or atom can be created and sustained without it. Thus it permeates all creation. Everyone possesses Divine Intelligence by virtue of the fact that The Divine Blueprint, which is a thought-form and living part of THE ARCHITECT Who created it, is present within all.

KARMA: An electromagnetic process whereby the momentum of an incomplete or unbalanced thought-form is eventually balanced through a process of repetition until the balance is achieved and freedom from the electromagnetic system (i.e. the solar or astrological), in which it was generated, may be achieved.

KOLOB: The ancient name given to the Logos of your immediate galaxy. It is not the Seat or Locus of THE ONE CREATOR, yet is one of the main threshold gates to the dimension of THE ONE.

LAW OF ONE: Taken from the ancient Egyptian attempts to unify a fragmented people before, during, and after the destruction of Atlantis through a teaching of a reality of ONE CREATOR beyond all dualities and polarities. At that time, literally hundreds of creator-gods were followed and worshipped as they were quite visible to the populace. The Law

Of One was designed to reconnect the people with the ONE CREATOR and reestablish the lost abilities to commune with THE ONE. It also encompassed the TRINITY GOD-HEAD as designed within the pyramid, but due to the confusion of tongues, the teachers attempted to simplify the teaching. The teaching was exemplified by the micro-cosmic analogy of the sun and its planets to the macro-cosmic life-giving power of THE ONE. The teaching is currently erroneously interpreted as "sun worship."

LAW OF CONFUSION: An Egyptian, twin-concept of freedom within chaos based on the premise that originally, when the gift of freedom was given by THE ONE, granting permission for ITS creations to also freely create, the potential for confusion became imminent. Thus, the temptation to create and experiment with thought-forms outside the parameters of the eternal, Master Architecture of the universes gave way to a mutation of the original plan. This created chaos and the fallen rulers of that aeon, now trapped in their own creation, defended their "right" to rule the chaos. Once cut off from the SOURCE, they were forced to exist as parasites, feeding from their own creations. Thus the suffering and the confusion began, and a new plan was devised by THE ONE to finally liberate those innocents and sorrowful ones who were trapped within that aeon.

LIGHT PARTICUM: Used here to connote a photon of light after it is "assigned" a path in the matrix grid. The state of a photon within material creation.

LIGHT RESONATORS: Frequency is an apt expression, indeed, but this is not to suggest that you are merely radios or television machines. You may use the expression "tuning in" with a fair degree of realization. However, tuning in, is only the first step. The next step is to RESONATE with that frequency, so that it may be transduced into a reality in your "now" moment. Light Resonance involves every cell of your biocomputers. Thus, you move from a mere radio to a Light Resonator, which connects your entire body and all its mind-centers to the reality of the Genius Frequency.

LOCAL CREATOR-GODS: Those light entities (angels) who refused to acquiesce to the original HU-MAN creation, whose mission was to raise the "local" creations (planets and root races) into SuperLight. They are responsible for "the fall" and are known also as the lesser gods. That is why there are so many hundreds of references in your great book (the bible) concerning various gods which should not be worshipped.

LOGOS: The etymology of this thought-form is THE WORD. For in uttering the proper SOUNDS of vibration by THE ONE, the universes were created. The SOUNDS of crea-tion have specific mathematical-geometric properties that resonate the very structure of matter.

MASS CONSCIOUSNESS: An extremely large, though finite, number of thought-forms trapped in the auric fields of earth, which all humans share and perceive as a polarized reality, positive or negative.

MATRIX GRIDS: Pattern forming energies that appear as intersecting lines of force. When manifested in three dimensions, they appear as objects, organs, fibers etc. This word pattern is designed to expand the definitions of the intellect in a more holographic mode of thought. Thus, when one views a tree, it may be comprehended from a new angle — that of an energy matrix of thought-form events.

MA-YA-RA: A tripartite energy entity responsible for organizing and projecting the thought-forms necessary for producing this work. MA is the female energy of wisdom, of Light ingathering or reception and integration with manifest creation. RA is the male energy expanding the Light into all domains and regions. This particular energy-entity is part of the original RA of Egyptian antiquity. YA is the universal GOD-MIND, both male and female, presiding over the DIVINE ISSUE of creation, unifying and supporting it with and through the Genius Frequency of LOVE/LIGHT-GOD/MIND.

MEDITATION: The active – not passive – focusing of attention upon an area within any of the mind centers. The result is an expansion of that center through pure or free awareness.

MEMBRANE WALL OF TENSION: A zone or threshold of equilibrium where gravitationally trapped light expands against the incoming Light streams forming the wall, like a cocoon, surrounding the thought-form and establishing a two-way zone through which a higher dimension may enter a lower one and a lower dimension may interact with a higher one. In the human form, the auric field is one such membrane of tension, as well as a star or an individual living cell.

MIND CENTER: Nerve ganglia and energy vortex residing in seven distinct areas of the physical body, otherwise known as glands and chakras. Each is a thinking intelligence unto itself that creates bands of thought-forms in areas of the auric field. Each has a color coded frequency and examples of these qualities may be seen in nature as various animal, plant, and mineral functions.

MIND: The overall field of intelligence generated by the mind-centers. This special function of soul and spirit awareness does not reside in the brain. The human mind resides outside the physical body proper and is a projection from the etheric body, and is perceived as a reflection from the interior of the auric field of awareness.

MORALS: A three dimensional term used to categorize judgments imposed upon human conduct. A three dimensional term is always polarized and therefore relativistic. The result is a continuous pendulum of opposing morals used to inflict various self interests. Thus the term has evolved into a grand limitation that has little to do with the Laws of eternal life in the universe.

NODAL POINTS: The points of intersection in an energy matrix that form resonant magnetic field events, which possess more energy in toto than the sum of the parts. All so-called particles and collection of particles are nodes of harmonic frequencies and they are capable of appearing and disappearing in various dimensions. A star is a nodal point, as are various mind-centers within the human bio-computer.

PARTIAL EQUATIONS: When any thought-form, regardless of how intellectual or religious it may be, defines reality through the identification with altered-ego. This produces a system of thought-forms which are unbalanced in that they tend to polarize magnetically. That is, they seek to be positive or negative. In complex thought-forms that are polarized, for example, in political or religions bantering, the positivists may have a negative outlook on others who are positive in areas that they do not support.

Therefore, a partial equation of life is produced and becomes the motive force for millions through the circulation of fragmented thought-forms.

PERCEPTION: A particular spot or location in the auric field outside the human body where the thought-form of any object or idea resides. When the entity focuses attention upon a particular spot through identification or contemplation, the area glows and the object or idea is perceived from that specific angle.

POLARIZED: The artificial separation of holistic thought-forms by the filtering system of the altered-ego that creates only fragmented and opposing counter thought-forms. All polarized thought-forms must seek and find an opposing thought-form (see also partial equations).

PRETHOUGHT: The function of arranging a matrix of thought forms into a blueprint, template, or die, used to project into other dimensions for the purpose of programming or composing intelligent life on other worlds. A fragment of this process is also used by humans in creating their own realities upon the planet into which they were in turn projected. (see also archetypal form).

PYRAMIDAL ENERGY CONSTRUCT: A "signature" thought-form used by THE ONE to build realms and universes that interconnect on the subatomic as well as the macrocosmic scale. The angles, geometries, and mathematics are uni-

versal and cosmic, in that they form the fundamental architecture of physical universes as well as spiritual, with the unique ability to interface multidimensionally in any given sector or frequency using spiraling energies or "worm holes" that bypass typical space/time parameters.

RESONANT POINT: Also a nodal point where energy lines within fields of intelligence intersect creating a membrane wall of tension containing a living hologram of consciousness. All thought-forms seek and form these resonant points on the appropriate frequency levels locking each thought-form into a living representation of that thought, or transmuting it through contemplation and meditation through SuperLight into a higher thought-form, forming yet another resonant point.

SIMILITUDE, DIVINE: Refer to Genesis 1, where it is stated that the human is created in the "likeness" of the CREATOR. Therefore, the blueprint for the HU-MAN or Adamic Man was conceived, born and projected into other dimensions, of which the Earth is one. This blueprint contains a similitude or a similar replica of the nature and attributes of THE ONE.

SOLAR LOGOS: The vibratory sound structure emanating from the sun forming, literally, the "word" of the sun. This sound/complex governs its planetary vibrations, continuously programming its offspring with its particular set of limitations.

SOLAR-MIND: Refers to the mental body of the sun in the dimension in which it functions as a conscious entity. The Solar-mind embodies the very source of the altered-ego. It embodies the self-consuming thought-forms of life-giving and life-taking, due to the separation with the Divine Source of Intelligent Energy that gives all stars their power to emanate light (in this case it is of the yellow spectrum). Therefore, the Solar mind is doomed to destruction, along with all entities who resonate only with its limited frequency. In the human altered-ego this thought-form operates as the "food-chain-mentality" or survival of the fittest before annihilation.

SPACE/TIME: Refers to time in the common understanding of objects in motion, relative to each other.

SPECTRA LIGHTS: Emanations of various levels of SuperLight radiated by higher intelligence. Many "so-called" U.F.O.'s are actually evidence of higher intelligence visiting the earth plane in consciousness/light vehicles. However, these are not physical craft.

SUPERLIGHT: All definitions of the Genius Frequency, the higher dimensions, in which other intelligent entities working with THE ONE reside, all manifestations of universal intelligence, and what has been termed by others as SuperConsciousness.

THOUGHT-FORM: Rarefied matter in a conceptualized state, organized through various electro-charges by desire, memory, identification, and destiny into a holographic entity, which exists on many dimensional planes. Each thought-form bears the unique magnetic signature of the individual soul through identification.

TIME/SPACE: Fourth and fifth dimensions where space is realized as the object and time as the space through which it passes. From this perspective, time acts as a threshold or gate between spatial or dimensional realms.

TRANSFORMER: The ability of the mind centers to change the frequency or vibration from higher to lower or from lower to higher. The Heart is a unique transformer due to its ability to accomplish both.

TRANSMUTATION: Using the Genius Frequency of SuperLight to superimpose a higher thought-form over a lower frequency thought-form, creating a double holograph that provides an expanded membrane wall of tension, which forms the "vehicle" for the lower thought-form to transmute itself into a fifth dimensional reality. This even includes the human body, as it is actually a manifest complex of thought-forms.

UNIVERSAL PROCESS: A specialty function of one of the Entities who possesses a particular DIVINE STRUCTURE that is used to create and sustain a particular universe, of which there are many. (see also Divine Process).

UNIVERSAL EPICENTER: Its center is everywhere, its circumference nowhere. Space is the cosmic medium of Intelligent Awareness. Since space pervades even atomic particles (your research continues to prove that the quest for an irreducible particle is unattainable and that other particles will always appear, because all is created from this space), it can be present in all dimensions simultaneously.

VIBRATORY/MATRIX: When lines of Intelligent Force, which connect all atomic worlds and dimensions, intersect to form combinations of nodal points that are living entities who share their wisdom conjointly and simultaneously within a time/event/matrix. Thus, Ma-Ya-Ra, three energy entities, can intersect their thought-forms anywhere in the universe, sharing persona and all other aspects of their beingness.

ZOHAR: A belief system using the celestial manifestations and their mathematical and symbolic interrelationship to explain, in terms of celestial counterparts, the unique signature of the soul commonly known as "personality." Astrology is a diluted, distorted, and popularized version of the ancient teaching of the Zohar, which recognized the reality of the human soul as a microcosmic manifestation of that particular level of celestial consciousness.

INDEX

INDEX OF QUESTIONS
"FROM THE BOOK"

All the questions in the book are listed here.
The page numbers are included at the end of each
question to facilitate the use
of this book. In conjunction with the glossary
and the standard index, the index of questions will
provide the reader with an extensive
cross-referencing system.

Questioner: How can the intellect block our creativity? p. 3

Questioner: Isn't that proven by our great scientists and inventors, who were highly educated individuals? p. 5

Questioner: I guess that a better question might be: What is genius? p. 5

Questioner: Then what is the difference between the intellect and the altered-ego? p. 7

Questioner: I am beginning to understand from what we must be free. Towards what must we be free? p.7

Questioner: What is the opposite of I-dentification? p.13

Questioner: I understand what you say about dehumanization, but don't we make choices in deciding whether or not to act that way? p.14

Questioner: What can we do to free ourselves from this trap? p.15

Questioner: It seems that we need a filter to screen this information. p.16

Questioner: Can you define the process that can lead us toward the Genius Frequency? p.16

Questioner: Although the process of I-dentification can be misused; it can, if used wisely, magnetically attract us to the Genius Frequency. p.17

Questioner: Then how should we deal with the evil deeds and thought-forms that certainly exist within our plane of existence? p.18

Questioner: Can you elaborate upon that last statement? p.20

Questioner: In speaking about the symbolism of the cross, you mentioned being crucified to space and time. Is this a fourth dimensional understanding of the crucifixion and should this perspective be used in understanding the event instead of what is traditionally taught? p.21

Questioner: Yes, thank you. Now I am reminded of many passages in the Bible which mention the "end of time." This suddenly takes on new meaning in light of what you have just communicated. Could you elaborate on this cryptic statement? p.22

Questioner: Then where do we stand in relation to this cosmic clock? p.23

Questioner: It does not seem so simple to grasp unlimited thinking. How can one explain unlimited thought with limited thoughts? p.26

Questioner: Great intellects have led humanity into golden ages and have inspired us to heights of achievement. How, then, are we to regard the intellect as so limited? p.26

Questioner: Yes, I was wondering if the altered-ego is the same as the intellect? p.27

Questioner: Please explain your statement in the preceding material: "Every thought-form since the beginning of time is trapped in the magnetic aura of the earth." If this is true, how can we possibly begin to control it? p.31

Questioner: Then can we say that the altered-ego is man-made? p.34

Questioner: What constitutes a thought-form? How much thought does it take to cause it to become a thought-form? p.35

Questioner: Is I-dentification a thought-form? p.38

Questioner: Can the mind transmit and receive in different time frames? p.42

Questioner: Can you explain more about the "billboard" effect of thought-forms that reside in the auric field? p.43

Questioner: Since animals have smaller brains, is there a relationship between the size of the brain and the type of thought-forms, and do they also have auric fields? p.43

Questioner: If this is true, then how can one understand personality and its obvious inequalities; and if it is not a question of personality or innate ability, then why do so few discover new ideas? p.46

Questioner: Do thought-forms exist only within the auric field; and if so, how can they be transmitted at great distances, if each auric field resides so close to each individual? p.48

Questioner: There are thousands of books on the subject of chakras or the seven energy points in the body. Can you add to this information, and would it be appropriate to single out any one of these points as the most important? p.53

Questioner: Could you explain how our technology has demonstrated brief success in mechanical heart implants and transplants, and how this relates to the heart as an energy source? p.58

Questioner: I can see how the heart is a receiver/transmitter. But can you explain further how it is a mind-center, or thinking mechanism? p.69

Questioner: Knowing your preponderance to digress, I would like to ask for what purpose, then, is free will? p.72

Questioner: Yes. Thank you. It was a difficult question to answer. p.73

Questioner: Can you explain more about the relationship of the brain and the mind and how certain thought-forms can be much stronger than others? p.116

Questioner: Could the process of identification be a factor in the perceiving, and could you explain in less technical terms how the altered-ego affects this perception? p.117

Questioner: Wouldn't it be extremely confusing to see life in this way? p.118

Questioner: How then does the auric field provide the function of perception? p.119

Questioner: How does memory work in conjunction with the auric field of perception in our daily lives? p.119

Questioner: Is it true that we use only 1/10 of our brains? p. 124

Questioner: When considering how deeply entrenched human awareness is in the altered-ego, not only on a personal basis, but world-wide, it seems that only a few will accomplish the goals of higher consciousness. It has proved so in the past. Why should it be any different now? p.127

Questioner: What is the most effective way to hasten these connections and how is the Genius Frequency to be understood? p.129

Questioner: What is an effective meditating technique? p.131

Questioner: Would you give a more detailed explanation of the seven mind-centers? p.132

Questioner: How can we best begin to realize the totality of ourselves? p.141

Questioner: Can these visualization techniques be used in place of meditation? p.149

Questioner: Hasn't it been proven that each of us, through the arrangements of the heavenly bodies, possess strong and weak points within our systems? p.183

Questioner: Is it more energy that we need to raise our frequencies to the Genius Frequency, or is it more the overcoming of the altered-ego? p.189

Questioner: Why do the lucid, inspired moments in my life come and go? It seems that moments of clarity begin to get fuzzy and even confusing, and I am my "old" self again. p.195

Questioner: Are you saying that there are actually eight chakras or mind-centers rather than seven? p.198

Questioner: In the Eastern teachings, it is claimed that cosmic energy enters the human system at the base of the brain. Can you explain this in relation to this material? p.198

Questioner: Then, in general, are the teachings about right-living connected with the ability to tune to the Genius Frequency? p.202

Questioner: Can you further explain the part that meditation plays, regarding the material in this chapter? p.203

Questioner: Can a proper diet increase the frequency of the body? p.204

Questioner: When this expansion of consciousness takes place, doesn't the personal identity of the individual shrink as well? p. 207

Questioner: I still cannot grasp how increasing the frequency of the body can increase its capacity to take a cosmic charge. Can you explain the relationship of frequency to physical matter? p.209

Questioner: If the true nature of the atom is space, and the apparent particles are waves of energy, how can it maintain its structure? p.215

Questioner: How are the cosmic cycles working to bring about the changes of which you speak? p.244

Questioner: Are there systems of life within our galaxy that do not suffer these extreme changes? p.245

Questioner: What is free awareness? p.246

Questioner: Are the changes that you speak of the same as the Bible prophecies? p.249

Questioner: The "Law of One," as you have described it, recognizes no polarity, no good and evil. How are we to apply this truth if our lives are fraught with polarized decision-making? p.249

Questioner: Why can't the knowledge of good and evil ultimately free us from suffering and death? p.250

Questioner: Could you explain, in more detail, what contemplation is and what it does? p.257

Questioner: Then, are the teachings, that describe meditation as the absence of thought, partial truths? p.264

Questioner: Would you expand more on the "contemplative template?" p.266

Questioner: Is this realignment process due to the light-body being elsewhere? p.269

Questioner: Is it always necessary to use this procedure in the order that you have given, that is: contemplation first and then meditation? p.270

Questioner: If the Genius Frequency can only be "locked in" through meditation, then how can one preserve it? p.272

Questioner: Then negative mass does not have the "negative" connotation that has been attributed to it through common language. p.312

Questioner: Are there any indications as to the early stages of SuperLight resonance and can you suggest any further exercises to enhance this process? p.318

Questioner: Can you explain in more detail the interrelationship between "common light" and "SuperLight?" Also, you have equated the sun in our solar system with this common light. Where does our local sun stand in relation to SuperLight? p.323

Questioner: Why was SuperLight blocked? p.326

Questioner: Can you explain in more detail how contemplations and dream-work can help in raising conscious awareness of SuperLight? p.336

Questioner: Please explain the reasons for sun worshipping, in regards to the Egyptian and other civilizations. p.337

Questioner: In the Biblical story of Adam and Eve, is the apple to be taken in a literal or a figurative sense? p.340

Questioner: I don't understand what is termed, the "fifth dimension." Could you clarify this confusion? p.349

Questioner: What role do these elemental intelligences play in the organs of the body? p.351

Questioner: Would you further explain the statement concerning preconceived formulae? p.352

Questioner: Are present calculations correct in predicting the life cycle of the sun? p.355

About The Author

John Falone has studied metaphysics for over 30 years. He is a writer, teacher, counselor, photographer, composer, and professional astrologer.

For a free catalog of other titles call
800-729-4131

CPSIA information can be obtained at www.ICGtesting.com
Printed in the USA
LVOW10s1545180516

488853LV00002B/350/P